CONFLAGRATION

CONFLAGRATION

HOW THE TRANSCENDENTALISTS SPARKED THE AMERICAN STRUGGLE FOR RACIAL, GENDER, AND SOCIAL JUSTICE

JOHN A. BUEHRENS

BEACON PRESS
BOSTON

BEACON PRESS
Boston, Massachusetts
www.beacon.org

Beacon Press books
are published under the auspices of
the Unitarian Universalist Association of Congregations.

23 22 21 20   8 7 6 5 4 3 2 1

This book is printed on acid-free paper that meets the uncoated paper
ANSI/NISO specifications for permanence as revised in 1992.

Text design and composition by Kim Arney

Library of Congress Cataloging-in-Publication Data
Names: Buehrens, John A., author.
Title: Conflagration : how the transcendentalists sparked the American
struggle for racial, gender, and social justice / John A. Buehrens.
Description: Boston : Beacon Press, 2020. | Includes bibliographical
references and index.
Identifiers: LCCN 2019020651 (print) | ISBN 9780807024041 (hardcover : alk. paper)
Subjects: LCSH: Transcendentalism (New England)—History. |
Transcendentalism (New England)—Influence. | Social justice—United
States—History. | Transcendentalists (New England)
Classification: LCC B905 .B68 2020 (print) | LCC B905 (ebook) |
DDC 141/.30973—dc23
LC record available at https://lccn.loc.gov/2019020651
LC ebook record available at https://lccn.loc.gov/2019980766

There is properly no history,
only biography.

RALPH WALDO EMERSON

CONTENTS

LEADING DRAMATIS PERSONAE

Charles Follen and Eliza Lee Cabot Follen
William Ellery Channing
Elizabeth Palmer Peabody
Ralph Waldo Emerson
Frederic Henry Hedge
Lydia Maria Francis Child
George and Sophia Dana Ripley
James Freeman Clarke and Anna Huidekoper Clarke
Horace Mann and Mary Peabody Mann
Nathaniel Hawthorne and Sophia Peabody Hawthorne
Sarah Margaret Fuller and Giovanni Ossoli
Theodore Parker and Lydia Cabot Parker
Caroline Wells Healey Dall
Lewis Hayden
Henry David Thoreau
John Albion Andrew
Thomas Wentworth Higginson and Mary Channing Higginson
George Luther Stearns
Franklin B. Sanborn
Samuel Gridley Howe and Julia Ward Howe
Henry Whitney Bellows
Thomas Starr King
William James Potter
Emily Dickinson
Frederick Douglass
John Muir

Grandchildren of the Revolution

MANY OF US FIRST MEET the Transcendentalists in literature classes in high school or college. This gives us the impression that we should think of them primarily as writers. We read some Emerson: a few poems and essays, probably including "Self-Reliance." Thoreau's *Walden*, about going to the woods to live more deliberately, is now the most read American book written before the Civil War. We then come to see Transcendentalists as centered in rural Concord, asserting their individualism against the demands of society. Perhaps it does not help that our meeting with them often comes in our own adolescence, when the drive to self-differentiation, individuation, and idealism is natural.

History provides another perspective, focused less on their writings than on their lives and deeds. Many Transcendentalists and their followers were also fervent activists, sparking the intellectual, spiritual, moral, and political struggle in America for racial, gender, social, and environmental justice that continues to this day. They also were far more religious and urban than most people realize. This is because history also has a tendency to erase many lives and the places associated with them. Here we will lift up less well-known Transcendentalists who were courageous in challenging tradition and injustice. Rather than being pushed around by history, they were great souls who instead tried to shape it—toward a more just, hopeful future.

The Transcendentalists truly *did* change American history. Many were grandchildren of leaders in the first American Revolution. Emerson's grandfather, from the Old Manse in Concord, watched it all begin at the

Old North Bridge. Theodore Parker's grandfather, Captain John Parker, led the Minutemen on the town common in Lexington that same morning of April 19, 1775. Both Emerson and Parker were peace-loving ministers. Yet like most Transcendentalists, they gradually came to realize that ending slavery in America was a moral imperative that would require the conflagration, strife, and sacrifice of a second American Revolution. They refused to obey the Fugitive Slave Act. Parker even backed that most radical, violent white abolitionist, John Brown.

Frederick Douglass, by then America's most articulate and famed fugitive slave, foresaw that Brown's plan to start a slave insurrection would fail. Yet he agreed with Parker's call for a second American revolution. In a speech he gave in May 1857, in response to the Dred Scott decision, he quoted verses that he had written earlier that year:

> *The fire thus kindled, may be revived again;*
> *The flames are extinguished, but the embers remain;*
> *One terrible blast may produce an ignition,*
> *Which shall wrap the whole South in wild conflagration.*[1]

Emerson and Thoreau helped to make Brown the Christlike martyr whose death might make even civil war redemptive—if it resulted in ending slavery. When that war came, some Transcendentalists surprised even themselves by organizing the greatest humanitarian relief effort in American history to that date. They sometimes presented themselves as coming to their convictions out of their own immediate inspiration. Yet to understand them properly, we would do well to begin the story of the Transcendentalists with their wisest, most courageous teachers and mentors.

Karl (Charles) Follen and William Ellery Channing were among the most important. The former was a German-born radical and émigré turned Unitarian minister and abolitionist. He taught at Harvard from 1825 to 1835, bringing to his teaching of future Unitarian ministers a direct connection to the transcendental ethics and German idealism then stirring among them. When Harvard fired him for being an abolitionist, Channing mentored him into the ministry and made him his personal representative in antislavery circles. When he died in January 1840, in "the Conflagration of the Steamer Lexington," on Long Island Sound, that tragedy became in retrospect almost a prophetic sign for the nation as a whole: a ship laden with slave-picked cotton, steaming ahead, no one steering, toward the conflagration of civil war. Follen's death profoundly influenced the last years of the one spiritual mentor whom all Transcendentalists gladly acknowledged: Dr. Channing, the spiritual founder of American Unitarianism and of liberal theology. Even Emerson referred to Dr. Channing as "our bishop."

To a degree often overlooked, Transcendentalism was a movement almost entirely within the congregational churches of the Boston area that had become Unitarian. It was a spiritual and moral renewal movement among ministers and laypeople in those churches. It is also almost impossible for many readers in our secular culture to realize how influential churches were in mid-nineteenth-century America, especially in Boston, the epicenter of its dominant religious culture, although historian Sidney E. Mead once wisely called us "The Nation with the Soul of a Church."[2]

The Transcendentalist movement called forth efforts to make liberal religion more genuinely democratic and more effective in bringing about the many reforms needed to make society more democratic as well. Channing was not only a mentor to Follen, and to almost all the Transcendentalist ministers, but also to lay reformers such as Dorothea Dix, in her crusade for decent care of the mentally ill, and Horace Mann, in his work to promote high-quality, tax-supported public education for all. Perhaps Channing's closest spiritual disciple (at least in her own mind) was Elizabeth Palmer Peabody. She considered him the true founder of Transcendentalism in New England (whether he did or not), since it was he who had introduced her to the writings of Samuel Taylor Coleridge, to the word "transcendental," and to a distinction between mere empirical understanding and more transcendent, intuitive reason.

Many today regard rural Concord as the geographic center of the Transcendentalist movement. Again, history suggests otherwise. Prosperous Concord has been able to preserve many places associated with Emerson, Thoreau, Alcott, and Hawthorne. Their graves lie along Authors Ridge in Sleepy Hollow Cemetery. The Emerson House, the Old Manse, the

Alcotts' Orchard House, and Hawthorne's last home, The Wayside, all receive visitors. Walden Pond is a popular state park. In Boston, by contrast, many homes, churches, public halls, and places associated with the social activism of the Transcendentalists simply disappeared as the city grew. Only a few sites still remain—among the homes, perhaps only Channing's townhouse on Beacon Hill, at 83 Mount Vernon Street, and across the common, at 13 West Street, the shell of what was once the home and bookstore of Elizabeth Peabody.

If Transcendentalism had a geographic center, it was surely there. To 13 West Street, the literati and reformers came not only to peruse, buy, or borrow avant garde literature from Europe, but also to meet, converse, argue, and organize. In the Peabody parlor, Margaret Fuller held many of her famous "Conversations for Women" that sparked the American struggle for gender equity. Other discussions Peabody supported had to do with applying what she called "the social principle" in religion to economic inequality and the many urban social problems it brought. George and Sophia Ripley left Boston in April 1841 for a Transcendentalist experiment in egalitarian living at West Roxbury's Brook Farm. That very month, another Transcendentalist minister, James Freeman Clarke, supported by the Peabody and Channing families, came there to organize a more egalitarian and activist urban church: Boston's Church of the Disciples.

Clarke, close to Fuller from their young adulthood, exemplifies the Transcendentalist commitment to the practice of spiritual friendship— often transcending differences in gender, class, opinion, and—particularly radical for the time—even race. That ideal stemmed from the conviction that only by helping others realize their moral, spiritual, and creative potential can one fulfill one's own; and that only through mutual concern can just communities begin to emerge. Perhaps one of the most neglected of the original Transcendentalists, Clarke appears in this narrative at many of its dramatic events to reconnect with others now better known. As Channing's spiritual heir as pastor to Boston's liberals, Clarke often officiated when they married and consoled them when there was a death. He presided, for example, also at 13 West Street, when Sophia Peabody married Nathaniel Hawthorne, and when Mary Peabody became Mrs. Horace Mann—and then left for a lengthy honeymoon in Europe with the reformer Dr. Samuel Gridley Howe and his new young wife, Julia Ward Howe. He later led the funerals for men as different as Hawthorne, Emerson, Howe, and others.

As a minister, Clarke also supported women in troubled marriages, including his congregant Caroline Healey Dall—a now almost forgotten feminist who wrote twenty-two books and cofounded the American Social Science Association. She and her minister husband never legally divorced. He merely lived in Calcutta for most of their marriage. Julia Ward Howe was another member of Clarke's congregation. If anything, Julia's marriage was even more challenging. Her domineering husband, eighteen years her senior, forbade her to write for print or to speak in public. She was with Clarke as she delivered her first public speech. He then encouraged her to write "better words" to "John Brown's Body"—the "Battle Hymn" that made her famous. She went on to found the first Women's Ministerial Association in America—without ever being ordained, all because Clarke felt that both women and men of character, whether lay or ordained, were all ministers.

Clarke met John Brown while paying a pastoral call on his neighbor Charles Sumner, then recovering from a beating on the floor of the US Senate for his speech against the expansion and sexual exploitation of slavery. Other white abolitionist lawyers in his flock included Ellis Gray Loring, who had befriended both Frederick Douglass and the first black lawyer in Boston, Robert Morris; and John Albion Andrew, who helped Lewis Hayden become Boston's leading black abolitionist. Clarke's steadfast friendship with his more radical Transcendentalist colleague, Theodore Parker, cost him the support of some key congregants, all Unitarian Christians. Yet without it, Parker might never have found a Boston audience for his eloquence. He coined phrases now associated with others who echoed them: "government of the people, by the people, and for the people," adapted by Lincoln from Parker; or "the moral arc of the universe is long, but it bends toward justice," taken up by Dr. Martin Luther King Jr.

During his seven-year apprenticeship as the Unitarian minister in Louisville, Kentucky, Clarke edited the first Transcendentalist journal, the *Western Messenger*. In it, he published the first essays by his friend Margaret

Fuller, encouraging her to be a writer. She encouraged him to become a true religious leader. He then returned to Boston to challenge the complacency of Unitarians in their home territory. She became a pioneer among women in journalism. Editing the *Dial*, Fuller not only demanded gender justice in an essay, "The Great Lawsuit: Man vs. Men, Woman vs Women," but also in a book based on it, *Woman in the Nineteenth Century* (1845). She went on to write for Horace Greeley's *New York Tribune*, not only on arts and letters, but also doing investigative journalism, looking into the realities of asylums, hospitals, orphanages, and penitentiaries affecting the lives of women and children. She then went to Europe, and became the first American female foreign correspondent, covering the 1848 revolutions.

In Rome, during its rebellion against Pope Pius IX, she met a young Italian revolutionary, Giovanni Ossoli, eleven years her junior. She had a child with him. When the 1849 Roman Republic failed, she, their son, and the baby's father fled to Florence while seeking a way to America. There Elizabeth Barrett Browning renewed her acquaintance with Fuller. Her sympathy for her, like that of many, grew when Fuller, the baby, and Ossoli perished in a shipwreck off New York's Fire Island. Clarke had recently buried his own firstborn son and nearly died himself, but joined Emerson and Dr. Channing's nephew, his close friend the Reverend William Henry Channing, in editing *The Memoirs of Margaret Fuller Ossoli*. The aim was both to preserve her literary legacy and her advocacy of women's rights, and to defend her honor as a married woman. She never received the letter inviting her to preside over the first truly national women's rights convention, held in Worcester, Massachusetts, just months after her death.

When the question arises, "Who is to be called a Transcendentalist?" I take a broad view. The original "Transcendental club" was quite small. It met for only four years, 1836 to 1840. Designed as a study group for younger Unitarian ministers, it gradually expanded, over thirty meetings, to include some thirty individuals, ordained and lay, male and female. The average attendance was eleven. Follen came only once; Channing, likewise. The latter surely would have refused the name "Transcendentalist"—as he tried to refuse all such labels—yet he clearly preached the human "capacity for transcendence, its ability to yield to the new, to push in thought, imagination, and moral harmony beyond its current limits."[3] This small ministerial group also had many disciples—not only in Clarke's Church of the Disciples, where I will often refer to members as Disciples, but also among readers and activists, later often described or self-identified as Transcendentalists. They saw self-transcendence both as evident in an evolving natural world, and as a moral/spiritual imperative for humans trapped in unjust social structures.

Often their spiritual friendships transcended differences not only in gender, background, and social location, but also in theology and ideology. Clarke, for example, remained a Unitarian Christian, while maintaining a loyal friendship with Parker, whom many considered an "infidel." Parker found an "Absolute Religion" at the core of all faith traditions, asking only that we love God (or the ground of our shared existence) and our neighbors as ourselves, and helped to inspire Clarke to use a period of recuperation from a serious illness to study non-Christian traditions. Clarke taught the first American academic courses on "ethnic religions" at the theological school founded by his wife's father and brother, in Meadville, Pennsylvania. Later in life, he taught the first courses in comparative religion at Harvard, and published a two-volume study, *Ten Great Religions*, that went through twenty-two editions. With their openness to religious pluralism, the Transcendentalists then helped to pave the way for greater interfaith dialogue and cooperation in matters of justice.

Despite their devotion to *Nature* (the title of Emerson's first book), the Transcendentalists fought the materialistic philosophy of their teachers, including the empiricist assumption that all knowing comes to us via the five physical senses. Their alternative view stressed intuition and the inner life. It derived from German idealism. Kant argued that there are categories of ideas that precede and transcend the data simply derived from the five senses, and that form the inner basis of spiritual and ethical life. Transcendentalists not only practiced self-culture and self-development, but had also absorbed Kant's "categorical imperative" in their ethical thought. This required seeing and treating others—including children, the poor, women, and the enslaved—not as mere objects, but as subjects, as moral agents whose spiritual and moral potential was to be given opportunity and encouraged. These spiritual convictions gave rise to a literary and cultural "American Renaissance." Their ethical stance gave rise to nothing less than the start of a second American revolution—demanding an end to slavery, greater equality for women, and greater social opportunity for all.

One cannot understand the origins of the women's rights movement in America without pondering the unequal unions that constituted "Marriage in the 19th Century," as Fuller might have put it. Here we will see that even many of the Transcendentalists felt the pain of difficult marriages in an era of gender injustice. Nor can we fully understand the hard debates among abolitionists over ends and means in that cause without exploring their personal and domestic lives, not to mention the many analogies to separation or divorce in antislavery politics. Some abolitionists followed William Lloyd Garrison in favoring disunion: the North seceding from the South. This, as Douglass and others soon came to see, would have allowed the slave states simply to go on with their "peculiar institution." Douglass regarded the US Constitution as tainted with sin, like most human institutions, but also as capable of amendment. As religious idealists, some Transcendentalists began as pacifists—committed to "Christian non-resistance," in the language of the time—but gradually became more resistant and militant following the Fugitive Slave Act of 1850 and the fight to stop the extension of slavery into Kansas. Ultimately, they chose the painful purgation and conflagration of civil war rather than allow slavery in America to continue. The "Battle Hymn" constitutes a fervent prayer for that war to be redemptive.

Some have blamed both slavery *and* the abolitionists for the conflagration of civil war. That has been a standard racist line. Many surely had a burning desire for justice within. Human and imperfect, they could not fully see what lay ahead. If they had, they might have balked. Some did. Seen from the distance of a century and a half, they also clearly wore many blinders, raised in a society more patriarchal, racist, and repressive than the one we inherit from them. If we wish those who will follow us to be merciful in judging what we have done and left undone, perhaps we should begin by approaching these forebears with some equal compassion. After all, in transcending the norms of their own time, they now challenge us to do even more. Many enjoyed privilege. So do most of us, in the richest nation on the planet. The question is always, "What do we *do* with that privilege?" Their spiritual method included deep, honest self-reflection—shown in their journals and letters—and a commitment to justice, wholeness and the creative pursuit of beloved community—the kingdom (or commonwealth) of God here on earth.

Far from being mere individualists, they also demonstrated what a later theologian called "the power of organization and the organization of power."[4] By the time of the Civil War, Transcendentalism had reached even the West Coast, in the person of Thomas Starr King, whom Parker had called "the best preacher in Boston." As secretary of the American Unitarian Association, Clarke had worked with his friend Henry Whitney Bellows to send Starr King to the mission field of gold-rich California. A prodigious fundraiser and advocate for the Union cause, Starr King helped Bellows develop the greatest humanitarian effort to that point in American history—the US Sanitary Commission, a precursor to the Red Cross. Building on that organizational success, Bellows, Clarke, and others then tried to unite all Unitarians as the core of a new "Liberal Church of America." That effort succeeded only in part, however. After Parker's death in 1860, differences between Unitarian Christians and the more radical Transcendentalists of the new Free Religious Association only deepened. The women's rights movement also suffered division over giving the vote to freed black men before white women received it.

Differentiation, however, is in the very nature of evolution. The Transcendentalists were also among the first religious Americans to give a positive reception to Darwin's *On the Origin of Species*, partly because it rejected racialism and gave scientific support to a unitary theory of human origins and kinship.

Today we are suffering through a recession in commitment to science, to human rights, and to global unity. There have been previous such periods. One took place following the Civil War. A Gilded Age of wealth inequality collided with a populist rebellion deflected into racism and xenophobia. Americans pillaged nature and the environment of Earth as though both were infinite rather than finite. The spark that the Transcendentalists lit became dim after the second American revolution. Yet it survived. It reemerged in the Progressive Era. This account cannot trace all the lines of continuity and succession.

Yet our present crisis of global climate change does recall Thoreau's close observation of the seasons, his notes on the quickening pace of deforestation, and his prophetic insight that "in wildness is the preservation of the world." That phrase, taken up by John Muir, crossed the North American continent to become the motto of the Sierra Club. He may have also pioneered the (often male) individualistic stance of being "spiritual but not religious," but Margaret Fuller may have been wiser.

Fuller demanded that men in power remove all "arbitrary barriers," while also seeing the necessity of women aiding one another. She had the insight that "there is no wholly masculine man, no purely feminine woman," adding that "a woman may be in love with a woman, and a man with a man. It is pleasant to be sure of it, because it is undoubtedly the same love that we shall feel when we are angels."[5] Even Emerson, whose male aloofness often frustrated her, once wrote to his journal, "The finest people marry the two sexes in their own person. Hermaphrodite is then the symbol of the finished soul."[6] While Thoreau was keeping house for himself at Walden, young Julia Ward Howe was writing a novel that she never dared to publish, *The Hermaphodite*.[7] It reflected a realization that just as her husband felt she was invading his sphere by writing or speaking in public, he too felt trapped in cultural expectations of "manliness." She once told him that it was too bad that his close friend Charles Sumner had not been born a woman; then *they* could have married.

Contemporary concerns for "intersectionality" and a more unitary demand for justice may seem new. They are not. We can find them in our Transcendentalist forebears, and when we return to the sources, we may find a deeper meaning. In a review of "Emerson's Essays, by a Disciple," one Sarah Helen Whitman wrote this:

In nature all lines blend and converge toward a common centre. The moment we attempt to distinguish and define, to draw lines and affix boundaries, we are perplexed and baffled by her fluidity and sameness. In the crystal we already detect a paradigm of vegetable forms, in the vegetable an approach to sentient instinct, while sensation and volition present strange and subtle analogies with electricity . . . for mind itself, in so far as we are acquainted with its mode of being, is but a subtle force vibrating to the impulses of other forces external to itself.[8]

Like the poems of Emily Dickinson, such long-forgotten texts by Transcendentalists and their disciples are now far more accessible than ever before. New anthologies, reprints, and online archives abound. In recent decades, scholars have also brought forth a number of insightful overall reassessments of various Transcendentalists, not to mention new, well-researched biographies drawing upon their journals, letters, and other archival material.

This work, as something of a group biography, is greatly indebted to such scholarship. Only in a few places does it contribute new archival research. Rather, its purpose is to connect stories of individual Transcendentalists and their disciples through the dramatic events and deep spiritual friendships that shaped their lives and enduring legacy. The main characters are often male, because they then had access to greater roles on the public stage than were available to women in the same era, but the female genealogy and generativity of Transcendentalism find more emphasis than has often been the case.[9] Exceptional instances of spiritual friendship transcending race also emerge.

May this narrative help each of its readers to find some story, some forebear, some suggestion as to how to become more self-transcendent in these difficult times—and to make a difference for those who will follow us.

PART ONE

Fire

And the LORD went before them by day in a pillar of cloud,
to lead them the way;
and by night in a pillar of fire, to give them light;
that they might go by day and by night.

EXODUS 13:21

And there appeared unto them
cloven tongues as of fire,
and it sat upon each of them.

ACTS 2:3

Awful Conflagration of the Steam Boat LEXINGTON In Long Island Sound on Monday Eve Jan 13th 1840, by which melancholy occurrence, OVER 100 PERSONS PERISHED

Exposition

In which an abolitionist minister
dies at sea amid burning bales of cotton.

IN RETROSPECT, THE TRAGEDY SEEMS SYMBOLIC. In 1840, the nation itself was like a ship—steaming ahead, out of control, laden with slave-picked cotton, and with fears fueled by the "incendiary" demands of a growing number of abolitionists, moving toward the conflagration of civil war. At the time, however, few could foresee that terrible future—not even the prophetic visionaries among the Transcendentalists. One of them, the Unitarian minister Charles Follen, died that January night as the *Lexington* burned. He was an active abolitionist and had already found himself feared and rejected for supporting the cause of ending slavery.

Images of the nation itself as aflame were not new. In Boston, William Lloyd Garrison had employed them in the manifesto with which he began his abolitionist newspaper, the *Liberator*, on January 1, 1831. "Assenting to the 'self-evident truth' maintained in the American Declaration of Independence 'that all men are created equal, and endowed by their Creator with certain inalienable [*sic*] rights—among which are life, liberty, and the pursuit of happiness,'" he said that he had spoken too moderately at the Park Street Church on July 4, 1829, in calling merely for gradual emancipation. Now he demanded that the public repent, as he had, and support the "immediate enfranchisement of our slave population." He harshly condemned the churches for not doing so.

> I am aware, that many object to the severity of my language; but is there not cause for severity? I will be as harsh as truth, and as uncompromising as justice. On this subject, I do not wish to think, or speak, or write, with

moderation. No! no! Tell a man whose house is on fire, to give a moderate alarm; tell him to moderately rescue his wife from the hand of the ravisher; tell the mother to gradually extricate her babe from the fire into which it has fallen;—but urge me not to use moderation in a cause like the present. I am in earnest—I will not equivocate—I will not excuse—I will not retreat a single inch—AND I WILL BE HEARD. The apathy of the people is enough to make every statue leap from its pedestal, and to hasten the resurrection of the dead.[1]

Not every abolitionist found Garrison's rhetoric helpful to the cause, Follen among them. Yet at great risk to his own career, he had joined Garrison's Anti-Slavery Society and spoken out publicly on its behalf.

When he boarded the *Lexington* at its East River pier just before 4 p.m. on that January Monday, he surely must have noticed that a hundred fifty bales of Southern cotton had been loaded onto the deck, bound for the textile mills of New England. His mind, however, was on other matters. He had been in New York giving some lectures. Friends there wanted to help him earn some money. He was between pastorates. His wife, Eliza, and their nine-year-old son, Charlie, had come along. She had taken ill in New York. Still too weak to travel, she had wanted Charles to take their son with him. At the last minute, however, he decided to have the boy stay behind with his mother.[2] Follen had a sermon to finish—for the dedication on Wednesday of the new meetinghouse in East Lexington, ten miles outside Boston. He was to be the minister there. The octagonal design was his idea, meant to be less hierarchical in distance from the pulpit and all on a single level. During the groundbreaking, he had delivered a brief but eloquent prayer. He asked that "this church never be desecrated by intolerance, or bigotry, or party spirit; more especially its doors might never be closed against any one, who would plead in it the cause of oppressed humanity; within its walls all unjust and cruel distinctions might cease, and all men meet as brothers."[3]

When Eliza became ill, he had written to the lay leaders of the East Lexington congregation, asking them to delay the dedication for a week. They replied that plans were too firmly in place. So he had stayed with his wife as long as he could, then chose the steamboat as the fastest, most convenient way to go from New York to Boston. Stagecoaches on the post roads were slow and often rough; the railroads, still incomplete. The *Lexington* went down Long Island Sound by night to the railhead at Stonington, Connecticut. Arriving at dawn, it then connected with a train going to Providence and Boston. It was also quite affordable. The owner, Cornelius Vanderbilt, was famous for undercutting the prices of all competitors until he had established a virtual monopoly on a new route.[4] The fare for deck passage was only fifty cents. Given the freezing January weather, however, and the deck cargo, all 104 passengers boarding that night paid a full one dollar each for indoor transport in the "saloon," which even included a supper: a choice of either flounder with wine sauce or mutton with tomatoes.[5]

The *Lexington*'s captain normally was the owner's brother, Jacob Vanderbilt. That day, however, Captain Jake, like Eliza Follen, was feeling ill. He had found and hired an experienced substitute, Captain George Child, but had not fully briefed his replacement about the steamship's issues. With its furnace recently converted from wood to hotter-burning coal, there had been instances of the steamer's smokestack overheating. Just a few months before, the crew had seen the wooden casing around the stack begin to smolder. They had quickly repaired the scorched area, however. There was no hint that there had ever been a fire, so no one told the loading crew not to put the cotton bales tight against the stack casing.[6]

As the steamer headed up the East River, past the narrows at Hell Gate and into Long Island Sound, the wind was sharp. The air, below freezing. The whitecaps were already forming crystals of ice.

The captain ordered full steam. The crew stayed indoors, helping the food servers during supper. About 7:30 p.m., as the meal ended, someone saw the stack casing already on fire. The first mate, then on watch, sent for the captain, trying not to alarm the passengers. The crew formed a bucket brigade. They also tried a small, hand-pumped "fire engine." It was already too late. The cotton bales were fueling the blaze. They could neither reach nor signal the engine room to slow or to stop the vessel. They tried to deploy the three lifeboats aboard. The first, at the bow, launched successfully but hit the turning paddlewheel. All occupants fell into the Sound and were lost. The two aft lifeboats, rigged improperly, went down stern first and promptly sank.

One can only imagine the panic among the passengers and crew. The pilot tried to steer the ship to shore, hoping to beach it, but fire had burned the ropes from the wheelhouse to the rudder. The *Lexington* steamed on down the Sound, out of control, burning. The center of the main deck soon collapsed. The fire then spread to the whole superstructure. As the engine stopped, crew and passengers shoved baggage containers, cotton bales, and planks into the sea to use as rafts. By midnight, most had jumped into the frigid waters. Many succumbed to hypothermia by the time the *Lexington* sank, around 3 a.m. Of 143 persons aboard, only four survived. The sloop *Merchant* picked up three around dawn. One washed ashore later, clinging to a bale of cotton. New York papers spread news of the *Lexington* quickly.

Just three days before, Henry Wadsworth Longfellow had published in New York a new poem called "The Wreck of the Hesperus."[7] Perhaps because of that, or because he and Follen, both Unitarians, had taught languages at Harvard, rumors arose that Longfellow had been aboard; then, that he canceled at the last minute to stay behind to talk to his publisher about a new book to include "The Wreck." Neither was true. Three days later, the city's largest newspaper, the *Sun*, carried a colored print, "Awful Conflagration of the Steam Boat LEXINGTON." The lithographer was young Nathaniel Currier, twenty-six. One of his previous depictions of a fire may have been the first colored print ever in an American newspaper.[8] This one, however, made his career. The *Sun* offered him a contract to provide a colored insert every week, and Currier gave up ordinary printing to do only mass-produced colored prints. The conflagration also helped popularize a poem that begins, "The boy stood on the burning deck/ whence all but he had fled," and that ends, "but the noblest thing that perished there/ was that young and faithful heart."[9] Young Charlie Follen had not died on a burning deck, but his father truly had—or in the freezing water, amid burning cotton—at the age of only forty-four.

To start the epic story of the Transcendentalists with Follen's death is to begin *in medias res*. It opens early in the very year that the original Transcendentalist circle ceased meeting and leads us into the story of how that group first emerged among Boston Unitarians and embraced German idealism. Their story can also help us see how the activist, antislavery stance of the Transcendentalists was related to other urgent issues of their time: church reform, equality for women, resistance to growing economic inequality, more universal access to education, and deeper respect for other races, religions, and cultures—all issues that remain with us today. The death of Follen is a mere footnote in most treatments of the Transcendentalists. Yet its impact on his contemporaries was real and deep. To understand why, we must become better acquainted with the abolitionist who died that night.

Charles Follen
(1796–1840)

CHAPTER I

Conviction

In which a German-born scholar flees to America,
carrying the torch of his native land's idealism to Harvard,
and comes to hold "incendiary" ideas on the subject of American slavery.

CHARLES FOLLEN SEEMED calm and scholarly on the surface, but within him burned a steady flame of conviction. He had a far more radical youth in his native Germany than his American friends ever fully understood. He was born in 1796, during Napoleon's Rhine Campaign invasion. His father, a judge in the small university city of Giessen, in the German principality of Hesse-Darmstadt, took the family out of the line of fire to his native village. There he had his second son baptized as Karl Theodor Christian Friedrich Follen. Along with his older brother, Augustus, he came of age during the conservative period after the defeat of Napoleon at Waterloo in 1815. Young student radicals such as the Follen brothers, calling for both *freiheit*, freedom, and for German national unity, challenged the princelings and reactionary regimes in divided Germany.

Karl excelled as a student in his father's field of law, even joining the legal faculty of the more liberal University of Jena as a young *privatdozent*, but also voiced a principled justification for resisting tyranny, if necessary, with force or violence. He was active in the *Burschenshaften*, clandestine networks of young radicals. His poem "The Great Song" became popular at their meetings, as they sang, "Take out the knife of freedom!" When Follen was still only twenty-three, his friend Karl Ludwig Sand actually used a knife to kill a prominent reactionary, the diplomat and dramatist August von Kotzebue, who had ridiculed young idealists. While Sand was in prison, and before his execution, police found that Follen had loaned him the money to make the trip on which he committed his crime. There was nothing to prove that Follen had known of Sand's intent, yet he was marked as guilty of what today we would call "condoning terrorism."[1]

Follen sought sanctuary in Switzerland. Friends there suggested that he go first to Paris to meet the intellectual leaders of European republicanism—not only the social thinkers Victor Cousin and Benjamin Constant but also the aging Marquis de Lafayette, the hero of revolutions in both America and France. When the assassination there of another conservative, the Duc de Berry, made even Paris unsafe, Follen next took refuge in the Swiss canton of Grisons, a historic haven for radicals and heretics. There he taught Latin and history until local Calvinists accused him of denying the divinity of Christ, the doctrine of original sin, and the total depravity of humankind. They were probably correct about Follen's theology. He then fled to Basel, another historic center of tolerance, where liberal German exiles had revived the university. One was Wilhelm de Wette, a biblical scholar and theologian. He reconciled religion with reason by interpreting parts of scripture as more poetry than history. Teaching philosophy and law in Basel, Follen became close to de Wette's German stepson, Karl Beck, another young radical.

With demands for their extradition growing, the two young scholars decided to leave Europe and go to America. Lafayette was planning to return there himself for the fiftieth anniversary of the American Revolution. He provided them with letters of introduction, suggesting that they try the relatively liberal university in Cambridge, Massachusetts. Especially helpful to the young Germans were two young American scholars just returned from their own studies in Germany. George Bancroft, the future historian and son of a leading Unitarian minister, was incorporating progressive German educational methods in his innovative Round Hill School, at Northampton in western Massachusetts. He hired Beck to teach Latin, while Follen introduced gymnastics. Late in 1825, George Ticknor, Harvard's first professor of modern languages, asked Follen to teach German and French there. Beck then followed, becoming Harvard's professor of Latin.

At Harvard, Follen was a popular teacher. The English writers Coleridge and Carlyle had created great new interest in German thought and litera-

ture. So had the 1813 book by Madame de Stael, *De l'Allemagne*. Young
New Englanders who had studied in Germany found scholarship there on
philosophy and religion to be both advanced and liberating. On both sides
of the Atlantic, younger minds in the English-speaking world felt that empirical philosophy, from Locke to Hume, had reached a dead end. When
the idealist Bishop Berkeley dared assert that "to be is to be perceived,"
Dr. Samuel Johnson tried to refute him, recounted Boswell, by simply kick-
ing a rock, as though matter alone were real. Yet if that is the case, can mere
material experience account for our moral and spiritual ideals? Immanuel
Kant and the German idealists who followed him said that even before we
take in any sensory information, transcendent categories of thought, already within us, help us to make meaning of it all: bad/good, now/then,
fleeting/eternal. These categories are both practical (ethical) and spiritual (metaphysical). Empiricism has limits in both areas. Follen was not
only a German and an idealist but also one of the younger members of the
Harvard faculty. He further endeared himself to students by introducing
German gymnastics—indoors in University Hall during the winter but in
warmer weather also outside, on the Delta, a triangular lawn just north of
Harvard Yard. Soon he also opened, in downtown Boston, the first public
gym in America.

While trying to master the English language, one of the first books
Follen read was an American novel, *Redwood* (1824), by Catherine Maria
Sedgwick. The daughter of a prominent politician and jurist in western
Massachusetts, Sedgwick had met Follen as he was helping Beck at Round
Hill. When she visited Cambridge and Boston the next year, she looked him
up and then introduced him to her good friend and fellow Unitarian, Eliza
Lee Cabot. He then invited the young women to his Boston gym to see his
young men go through their exercises. Sedgwick and Cabot were amused
to see a caricature of Follen posted prominently—and impressed that he
had both the humility and the self-confidence to join in laughing at it.

Charles, as he now called himself, was nine years younger than Eliza.
Although her family was one of most prominent in Boston, she was only
one of thirteen children of the late Samuel Cabot, comfortable but not
rich. Eliza then lived with two other unmarried sisters, devoting herself

to religion and good works. She initially saw the young German scholar as something of a protégé but one worthy of meeting other Boston intellectuals also trying to apply ideals to the real world. In late 1826 she asked him to come with her to a weeknight meeting at the home of her minister, William Ellery Channing, the spiritual leader of Boston's Unitarians. She taught in the Sunday school of his Federal Street Church, and these evenings in his Beacon Hill townhouse had begun as teachers' meetings. Yet since the teachers—Eliza Cabot, George Ticknor, Elizabeth Peabody, Jonathan Phillips, and others—were themselves intellectuals and critical thinkers about biblical interpretation, and could bring guests, Channing's parlor was often crowded with people eager for conversation on how to understand, teach, and embody real Christian ideals.

That night, the theme was "The Death of Christ." Elizabeth Peabody was present, taking notes as usual. She described that evening years later in her *Reminiscences of Dr. Channing*. After others spoke, Dr. Channing asked their German visitor what people in his country had to say on the subject. Follen replied that when he was a boy, cultivated German society was largely atheistic, ignorant of the New Testament. Once, he had sat for a university exam. The task was to write a brief essay on what could worthily motivate a person to be willing to lay down one's own life. His mind was so blank, he said, that he had to seek help from the Infinite Mind. His ideas ran over history, natural and human. Animals protect their young but do not willingly give up life. He pondered human acts of self-sacrifice—for family, friends, country, most often, for rather partial or selfish ends. Too often, these were acts of self-devotion for one's own glory. He then began to ponder the death of Jesus, as one death that had no motive other than one of infinite love—for all God's *other* children on earth, to bridge the chasm between the finite and the infinite.

"When he ceased to speak," as Peabody later recalled, "there was profound silence in the room." It was by far the most remarkable thing that anyone had said all evening. Channing himself did not speak but simply arose, and then the guests with him. As Follen prepared to leave, Channing held out his hand to him saying, "Sir, we must know each other better."[2] Peabody felt that she had just seen form a great, enduring spiritual friendship. Ever observant, she also felt that at later meetings, the two dialogued with one another too much to the detriment of others. Eliza Cabot, on the other hand, simply fell in love. Her memory was that Follen's "frank and fearless expression of his opinions encouraged others to speak freely; while his unaffected respect for the views of others, and the place of a learner, which his modesty always led him to take for himself, made him the model for all." After another such evening, she turned to Follen and asked him, "Why do you not become a preacher?" He replied that he felt not "sufficiently fitted, though it would be my highest ambition." He also asked if she truly thought that he, born a foreigner, could ever preach well enough in English. She told him that his spoken English was, if anything, better than her own. She then made him promise to consult with Channing, who soon agreed to mentor him in preparation for the Unitarian ministry.[3]

The two met frequently. Later, the older man wrote him, "There are few with whom I feel myself so strongly united, and the years are fast flying in which I can enjoy such friendships on earth."[4] As a candidate for the ministry, Follen began preaching in Unitarian churches in and around Boston. In addition to his language classes, he taught ethics and church history in the Harvard Divinity School, and influenced a new student Philanthropic Society. Treated warily by conservative faculty there, he was less a firebrand than a lamp of enlightenment. Yet there is reason to believe that Follen's thinking began to influence Channing, and not just vice versa. While Follen lectured about Kant, de Wette, Schleiermacher, Schiller, and others, he not only influenced students for the Unitarian ministry who were to be among the first Transcendentalists but may also have helped to shift his mentor's thinking. Channing's most proto-Transcendentalist sermon, "Likeness to God," given in 1828, follows his friendship with Follen. His increasingly firm antislavery stance also follows his request that Follen represent him in abolitionist circles.

Despite their differences in age and background, Eliza and Charles married in September 1828. Follen was thirty-two. He had been engaged in Europe, but his fiancée had declined to come to America. Eliza had just turned forty-one and her marriage had the blessing of her family. Channing, much to Eliza's distress, did not officiate; he was still summering in Newport, Rhode Island. He had advised Follen to ask Professor Henry Ware Jr. of the Divinity School to preside at the wedding. This was a good example of Channing's sound political sense. He did not think it advisable for the young German to appear only as *his* personal protégé for the Unitarian ministry. Eliza found their union was so happy that she later published a book about it, *Sketches of Married Life* (1838).[5] Unlike many men of his time, Charles treated his wife as a true spiritual equal and encouraged her as a writer, a poet, and an activist. In 1831, after giving birth to their only child, Eliza wrote a poem—meant to be a hymn—called "Remember the Slave." It begins:

> *Mother! Whene'er around your child/ You clasp your arms in love,*
> *And when, with grateful joy, you raise/ Your eyes to God above,*
> *Think of the negro mother, when/ Her child is torn away,*
> *Sold as a little slave,—O, then/ For that poor mother pray!*[6]

Later stanzas called on fathers, sisters, brothers, and, finally, all good Christians to begin to use their moral imagination, to deepen their empathy, and to then join the antislavery cause.

That same year, driving back in his carriage from a preaching engagement in a hard rainstorm, Follen stopped to give a ride to an anonymous, elderly black man. They discussed David Walker, the black abolitionist who had recently died. Shortly before his death, as a fugitive in Boston, Walker had published *An Appeal to the Coloured Citizens of the World* (1829). It was a call for black unity, self-help, and justified violence in the struggle for freedom. Walker then died mysteriously.[7] Some whites blamed Walker for Nat Turner's Rebellion, in August 1831, in the Tidewater region of Virginia. It was an insurrection in which more blacks than whites had died, but the fears of those opposing abolition often projected white violence onto the slave population. Reading the *Appeal*, Follen heard notes of what he had said as a student in "the Great Song." Then he met with William Lloyd Garrison, who had known of Walker's *Appeal* before issuing his own demand for an immediate end to slavery.

Raised in Calvinism, Garrison saw slavery as white America's original sin. However right that diagnosis, his early ideas of repentance remained Calvinistic: repent *now*—to escape hellfire.[8] God's grace will then follow— *if* God has predestined you (or us) for salvation. His rhetoric was harsh not only toward slaveholding and its direct perpetrators but also toward all bystanders—churches, merchants, and politicians. Yet he did not recommend participating in national politics even by voting. Channing and Follen worried over this approach on many levels: theological, rhetorical, practical, and political. Individuals might repent immediately but an entire nation? Not likely. Moreover, if the enslaved were suddenly freed, with no transitional assistance, what would become of them?

When Channing grew up in Newport, the slave trade was still active there. His own nanny was, or had been, enslaved. After college, he worked as a tutor on a plantation in Tidewater Virginia. In the winter of 1831, he went to the Virgin Islands for a rest cure for his chronic tuberculosis. There he came to see white racism as another chronic illness, not one easily abolished simply by will or fiat. He saw what the British were trying to do about it in their Caribbean island colonies. That year, Britain had passed an Act for the Abolition of Slavery. It did two things that Garrison could not accept, perhaps with reason.

First, it compensated slave owners for relinquishing their "property." Second, emancipation was gradual, with up to six years of "apprenticeship," during which time owners were to continue to provide food and shelter for former slaves as they transitioned to competing for market wages. Garrisonian abolitionists demanded emancipation *now*, without compensation. Rather than be accused of fomenting violent slave rebellions, these white abolitionists also declared themselves firmly committed to nonviolence, and to ending slavery by moral persuasion. This did not always go down well with black abolitionists, who must have muttered, "Easy for you to say!" Still, most subscribers to the *Liberator* were free blacks, not whites. Garrison drew them with rhetoric that condemned every white Northerner who did not support immediate abolition. Despite animadversions about his language and strategy, some white abolitionists joined the Anti-Slavery Society in hope of making its tactics and rhetoric more effective. These

Lydia Maria Francis Child
(1802–1880)

included attorneys such as Ellis Gray Loring, Samuel Sewall, and David Lee Child. The last was married to a woman who wrote a stronger argument for the abolition of slavery than even Garrison had been able to set forth.

Garrison called this woman, Lydia Maria Child, "the first woman in the Republic," having read her book *An Appeal in Favor of That Class of Americans Called Africans* (1833). It laid out, in eight well-organized chapters, over 230 pages, the many reasons to consider black slaves as Americans, to end chattel slavery, and to refute its defenders on ethical, humanitarian, theological, economic, and statistical grounds. It was a challenge for the privileged to become activists for antislavery. Born Lydia Maria Francis, she was the younger sister of Convers Francis, the Unitarian minister in Watertown, who in 1836 presided over the first meeting of the Transcendentalist circle. She sent a copy of her book to Dr. Channing. Although his health was failing, he then walked several miles from his townhouse on Beacon Hill to Child's modest cottage on Roxbury Neck, simply to thank her for the book. He sat with her for several hours, saying that he now worried only over *how* best to break his own silence about slavery.

This was typical of Channing, to consider not only ends but also means. Even before, he had written to a sometime congregant, Daniel Webster, that the North ought to say to the South,

We consider slavery as your calamity, not your crime, and we will share with you the burden of putting an end to it. We will consent that the public lands [in the West] shall be appropriated to this object; or that the general government shall be clothed with the power to apply a portion of revenue to it . . .

We must first let the Southern States see that we are their *friends* in this affair; that we sympathize with them, and from principles of patriotism & philanthropy, are willing to share the toil and expense of abolishing slavery, or I feel our interference will avail nothing.[9]

As a Unitarian who had rejected Calvinism, Channing not only hated the hellfire and brimstone tone of Garrison's demand for immediate repentance over slavery. He also felt that such a change of heart was far more likely to occur if Southerners felt they had friends in the North prepared to help them with the challenges of emancipation.

Charles and Eliza Follen also read Child's *Appeal* in mid-1833, perhaps using Channing's copy. They were renting a small cottage near the Channing summer home in Newport, Rhode Island, so that Charles could continue to prepare for the ministry under the guidance of her revered pastor. One night, after they had both finished the book, Charles told Eliza that he now felt called to join the Anti-Slavery Society. Yet he still hesitated. Such a step, he warned her, would almost surely result in losing any chance of a permanent post at Harvard. He also worried if he would then ever be able to earn a living for her and their child. He did not want to make her, due to his decision, suffer any privation. Eliza replied that he had already given up his native country, and more, for the cause of freedom, and that he should "not think that we are not worthy and able to make the slight sacrifices, which we may be called upon to make in this cause."[10] Channing echoed this. Feeling too ill and too old to persuade the younger Garrisonians to be more practical and persuasive, he asked Follen to serve as his voice in antislavery circles.[11]

He surely did not mean for it to do so, but Channing's blessing of Follen's abolitionism may have cost his friend his Harvard professorship. The five-year subsidy supporting it, raised by Eliza's family and friends, was to end in 1835. Follen had also clashed with Harvard president Josiah Quincy over a system meant to suppress student insubordination by adding behavioral points to grading. Quincy himself was no apologist for slavery. In 1811, as a young congressman, he had opposed the admission of Louisiana to the Union as a slave state. He had declared that "if this bill passes, the bonds of this Union are virtually dissolved; that the States that compose it are free from their moral obligations; and that, as it will be the right of all, so it will be the duty of some, to prepare . . . for a separation, amicably if they can, violently if they must."[12]

Yet by 1835, Quincy had tired of defending the radical immigrant abolitionist on his faculty. That year, chairing the arrangements committee for the first New England Anti-Slavery Convention, Charles Follen had helped to draft an "Address to the People of the United States." "Every Fourth of July," it argued, "is to us a day of exultation for what we have done, and a day of humiliation for what we have left undone." Demanding the immediate abolition of slavery, challenging all its legal justifications, the address then said that those trying to perpetuate slavery in the United States only increased "the danger of a servile or civil war . . . every day."[13]

That August, Theodore Lyman, Quincy's successor as mayor of Boston, presided at a public meeting at Faneuil Hall. Called by business leaders, it denounced Garrison, the *Liberator*, and all abolitionist activity.[14] To gain support for it, a conservative Boston newspaper editorialized, "*These dangerous [abolitionists] must be met.* THEY AGITATE A QUESTION THAT MUST NOT BE TAMPERED WITH. *They are plotting the destruction of our Government.*"[15]

President Quincy then made no further effort to raise funds to continue Follen's professorship. He could stay as a language instructor but at only one-third of his previous salary. Instead, Follen quietly resigned. There were newer German immigrants who could teach the language, and who needed the work. By then, he had also begun preaching to the Unitarians in the village of East Lexington. They could afford only a weekly fee for a minister to supply the pulpit with preaching, but not a salary for a full-time pastor. He and Eliza, with help from her family, had built a house in Cambridge, just north of the Common, then at 11 Waterhouse Street— surrounded today by Follen Street. There they entertained a well-known houseguest from England, a fellow Unitarian and abolitionist.

Harriet Martineau was the older sister of England's leading young Unitarian minister-theologian, James Martineau. She had come to America as a pioneering female journalist and sociologist. Like her French contemporary Alexis de Tocqueville, she wanted to see what he later called *Democracy in America*. Both wondered whether American pretensions to democratic equality, especially after the 1828 election of frontier populist Andrew Jackson, had any deeper reality. Harriet was tall, forceful, hard of hearing—often holding a large ear trumpet—and sometimes loud. Her book *Society in America* came out the same year as de Tocqueville's, but in trying to be objective, she insulted some who had entertained her, so that her book was soon forgotten here, while the more suave and eloquent Frenchman was remembered.[16] Thankfully, she also penned a more gracious, personal account, *Retrospect of Western Travel*. In it, she recalled two episodes from her stay with the Follens. The first involved an abolitionist meeting in downtown Boston.

Conservative Boston business leaders with ties to the cotton trade in 1835 felt that British abolitionists were conspiring to enrage the South, destroy the Union, and then return more of North America to English rule. They had received warnings that an eloquent English advocate for abolition, George Thompson, intended to address the Boston Female Anti-Slavery Society at their annual meeting in October. The *Boston Commercial Gazette* then printed handbills saying,

> $100 has been raised by a number of patriotic citizens to reward the individual who shall first lay violent hands on Thompson, so that he may be brought to the tar kettle before dark. Friends of the Union, be vigilant![17]

Thompson then wisely decided to stay away from Boston. Garrison agreed to speak in his stead. The Boston Female Anti-Slavery Society was to meet in a modest hall adjacent to the messy little third-floor office where he ran the Anti-Slavery Society, printed the *Liberator*, and often ate and slept. An ominous group of white men, made up of well-dressed leaders followed by paid ruffians, gathered outside, jeering at the white women who entered and roughly jostling two courageous black female abolitionists. During the opening scripture reading and prayer, the mob grew so loud that the woman presiding suggested to Garrison that it might be best if he left. He went to his office. Mayor Lyman then arrived with constables, saying, "Ladies, do you wish to see a scene of bloodshed and confusion? If you do not, go home!" They protested but then voted to march out in dignity. This infuriated the male mob. Hearing that Garrison had replaced Thompson, they began to search for him. Garrison had left his office, crossed an alleyway, and taken refuge in an attic. Found there, he was tied with a rope, stripped of his clothes, and dragged to the Common—some wanting tar and feathers, others a hanging. Lyman and the police intervened again, taking him into protective custody, mostly to prevent a martyrdom. Let it be noted that first urban riot in Boston over the issue of slavery was, in 1835, led by pro-slavery, anti-abolitionist forces.

This lawless riot and near lynching was morally shocking to many proper Bostonians. Chief among them was Wendell Phillips, then twenty-four, a son of one of Boston's wealthiest families—orthodox Calvinists who had endowed academies at both Phillips Exeter and Phillips Andover. He was then a young lawyer, trained at Harvard in effective rhetoric.[18] Converted to the antislavery cause, Phillips soon became one of its most influential and eloquent advocates. The Massachusetts legislature, however, reacted to the riot by taking up petitions from Southern legislatures asking them to regulate abolitionist activity as injurious to the US Constitution. Follen, then on the Anti-Slavery Society board of managers, spoke at the legislative hearing in opposition. As a naturalized citizen, he focused on American rights of free association and free speech, and against mobs and lynch law. He did so calmly and, as always, rather eloquently.[19]

So when Eliza Follen invited Harriet Martineau to come with her to the delayed annual meeting of the Boston Female Anti-Slavery Society, she knew the risks, as did Charles, who escorted them. When asked to address the meeting, Martineau, thinking of her hopes to meet and talk with people of all opinions in America, was rather hesitant. "I foresaw," as she later put it, "that almost every house in Boston, except those of the abolitionists, would be shut against me; that my relation to the country would be completely changed, as I should suddenly be trans-formed from being a guest and an observer to being considered a missionary or a spy." She decided to speak only briefly, calling slavery "inconsistent with the law of God," and saying that she was in agreement with the Anti-Slavery Society's principles.[20] That was enough. Reports went out. Many Americans did indeed deny her further entrée into their homes. She had hoped to travel more in the South, but newspapers there now declared her persona non grata. Instead, the Follens asked their fellow abolitionists, Louisa and Ellis Gray Loring, to begin arrangements for Martineau to visit "the West," the Great Lakes to Kentucky and Tennessee. There were former New Englanders and other antislavery supporters in that part of America.

Between Christmas and the New Year, Martineau was again staying with the Follens. Puritan New England took little account of "popish" Christmas but did celebrate the New Year. Nostalgic for some of the Christmas customs of his native Germany, Charles decided to recreate some of his memories for the benefit of Miss Martineau and his then five-year-old son, Charlie. The Follens invited some of their son's playmates and their families to a New Year's Day party; Eliza greeted them in the front parlor. Meanwhile, in a back parlor separated by sliding doors, Charles had taken a small spruce tree that he had cut, set it up in a tub, and decorated it—with small dolls, gilded eggshells, and paper cornucopias with candied fruit. The tricky part was placing and then lighting small wax candles in their holders on branches where they could not cause, well, another conflagration. Once he had lit all the little candles—with a bucket of water standing by—Follen flung open the sliding doors to the room where Charlie and the other guests were waiting.[21] They looked up, amazed. As Martineau then wrote:

> It really looked beautiful; the room seemed in a blaze, and the ornaments were so well hung on that no accident happened, except that one doll's petticoat caught fire. There was a sponge tied to the end of a stick to put out any supernumerary blaze, and no harm ensued. I mounted the steps behind the tree to see the effect of opening the doors. It was delightful. The children poured in, but in a moment every voice was hushed. Their faces were upturned to the blaze, all eyes wide open, all lips parted, all steps arrested.[22]

Martineau's narrative, reprinted in a popular women's magazine, then in a penny pamphlet, provided the first vivid description in English of the lovely German custom of the Christmas tree. Old and New England were then still a single cultural zone. The practice soon caught on, first in America but soon also in England, where Queen Victoria's 1839 engagement and later marriage to the German Prince Albert made popular and fashionable all things German.

In the summer of 1836, the Follens accompanied Martineau to Niagara and on a trip to the Great Lakes—one that may have inspired Margaret Fuller to take a similar expedition seven years later. In Chicago, Charles preached for the New England Unitarians living there, inspiring them to organize a new church. He also visited some fellow Germans who had formed a pietistic community in Economy, Pennsylvania, south of Pittsburgh. The leader, George Rapp, said that the community had succeeded only because it had entirely separated itself from "the world." Follen replied that in the Gospels, Jesus never stood entirely apart from the worldly but had rather embraced them. Rapp then ended the visit abruptly. In Philadelphia, he again preached for the Unitarians and spoke against slavery in the presence of a wealthy slave owner but without causing direct offense. Then, in New York, they bade farewell to Harriet as she boarded a ship to return to England.

During that summer, as the Follens traveled and Channing was at his summer home in Newport, four younger Unitarian ministers—George Ripley, Frederic Henry Hedge, Ralph Waldo Emerson, and George Putnam—made plans for what became the Transcendentalist circle. They all considered both colleagues as "like-minded" men whom they wished to include.[23] Follen had shown just how much he had in common with them in a multipart essay, "Religion and the Church." In it, he argued that the church was often the enemy of religious freedom, trying to control rather than nurture the spiritual instincts. All religions, he declared, even the most elemental, are valid in their own cultural context, in that they express "the tendency of the human mind to the infinite" and the yearning of the soul for some form of self-transcendence.

After leaving Harvard, Follen had worked as a well-paid tutor to some Unitarian boys whose wealthy father had died. When he realized that their mother had quite different ideas about their education than his own, he quietly resigned. The Unitarians of East Lexington, to whom he had preached in a community hall, were raising the funds to build an octagonal meetinghouse for which he had provided the architectural concept. Follen was ordained at Channing's Federal Street Church. Eventually, Emerson, glad to preach old sermons for pay but not to be a pastor, took the role of "stated supply" preacher in East Lexington. In October 1836, just as the Transcendentalist circle was forming, Follen became acting pastor of the First Congregational Church (Unitarian) in New York City—later known as the Unitarian Church of All Souls. Channing had helped his sister and her husband organize that group back in 1819, when he went through New York on his way to and from Baltimore, where he gave his most famous sermon, "Unitarian Christianity," advocating the use of reason, as a spiritual gift, in the interpretation of scripture.[24]

Since he was a relative novice in the ministry, Follen agreed to go to New York on a trial basis. The church leaders wanted to wait before deciding whether to make him their permanent pastor. That decision would depend not on the hundreds of congregants who, like young Nat Currier, regularly attended Follen's preaching, and who generally approved of his ministry, but rather on the much smaller, wealthier group of pew owners who constituted the "Congregational Society." Follen was completely open about his abolitionism from the very start, saying in his first sermon that antislavery had a claim upon a minister's conscience and duties. On Thanksgiving Day, however, when he said in passing that gratitude for one's own freedom should inspire efforts to end slavery, two of the most conservative pew owners got up and left in anger while he was still preaching. When the society next met, on March 19, 1837, there was a vote on the question, "Shall Rev. Dr. Follen be invited to remain with us?" Yeas, twenty-seven, nays, sixteen. A second vote was on the question, "For how long a time?" The result: for one year, twenty-eight; for two years, six.[25]

← →

Follen felt crushed. His first inclination was leave immediately. Perhaps to return to Germany. But that would be unfair to his wife and child. Friends said that the first vote was understood by some as meaning, "remain as *acting* pastor," so that some who wanted him as *permanent* minister had voted nay. They said he had only three real detractors. He then agreed to stay on for the year offered. That April he went to preach to the Unitarians of Washington, DC, from where he wrote back to Dr. Channing:

> And how, you ask, is it that I, the incendiary, and my equally incendiary partner [Eliza], are here in the midst of this slave-holding community[?] I came here at the urgent request . . . of the Committee of the Unitarian Society . . . and have succeeded in drawing a good number to the church . . . I am obliged to be silent on abolition, but I preach, with all my might, on the dignity and rights of human nature, on the great texts, *Honor all men*, and *All ye are brethren*, and pray for the oppressed . . . I have never been so strongly impressed with the intrinsic anti-slavery tendency of Unitarianism, as taking its stand on the absolute worth and eternal destiny of human nature.[26]

Given how he died, his description of himself as "incendiary" seems both ironic and poignant. Yet he understood that many people truly feared that abolition might bring racial or civil war. The East Lexington Unitarians had almost finished the meetinghouse he had designed for them and wanted him as their pastor. The salary would be small, but he and Eliza would be near her family and friends. So he accepted.

After the fire aboard the *Lexington*, and with her husband missing and presumed dead, Eliza insisted that the building dedication go ahead without him. In shock, she felt that by refusing to delay the building dedication, the Lexington church leaders had *caused* his death. Knowing that no one in Boston grieved her husband's death more than the man who had helped to prepare him for the ministry, she went to Channing for spiritual support. He suggested that, given her own gifts as a writer, she might begin to gather Follen's papers and then publish *The Works of Charles Follen*,

with a Memoir of His Life, as her personal memorial to him. More immediately, the question of where and when to hold a public memorial service
for Charles Follen would trouble not only the two of them but also have
a dramatic impact on his mentor, ending Channing's own long preaching
ministry at Federal Street.

Statue of William Ellery Channing
(1780–1842)

CHAPTER II

Inclusion

In which a revered advocate of inclusion
suffers grief and resigns in place.

THE BRONZE STATUE OF WILLIAM ELLERY CHANNING standing at the corner of Arlington and Tremont streets in Boston makes him appear eight feet tall. In fact, although regarded by many in his own time as a spiritual and moral giant, Dr. Channing was physically a rather small and frail man. Standing a little over five feet and five inches in height, he at times weighed less than a hundred pounds. Portraits show him with deep-set eyes and sunken cheeks. He had tuberculosis, the pandemic disease of the time. Yet when he preached, his faith in God and in humanity here on earth was inspirational. He transformed lives that in turn transformed history. Flanking his statue, one inscription reads, "He preached with spiritual power and led a great advance toward Christian ideals." The other, "He breathed into theology a humane spirit, and proclaimed anew the divinity of man." That latter assertion is surely at least "proto-Transcendentalist."

His friend Elizabeth Peabody once declared, "In the history of the so-called Transcendental movement of New England I know of no name older than Dr. Channing's."[1] When she first met Channing, she was a convinced Unitarian (perhaps more than he was) but confounded by trying to prove spiritual truths using dubious material miracles. Channing, a mentor to nearly all the original Transcendentalists, introduced her to Coleridge and thence to the word "transcendental." Yet he would almost surely have shunned the label. His approach to religion was inclusive: he tried to avoid all ideological terminology, trying to transcend sectarianism. He even resisted calling himself a Unitarian, although he found the doctrine of the Trinity a problem at many levels: as unscriptural, contrary to reason, and historically imposed upon the church in order to subject it to the state. He felt that the Protestant emphasis on salvation by faith had degenerated into salvation by mere formulaic belief, forgetting that faith without works is dead. He sometimes called himself a *catholic*, meaning inclusive, Christian. Yet he became the spiritual leader of the Unitarians by arguing that it was better to try to follow the one God of all reality in the path of love and justice laid out by Jesus, than to stand in fear of the wrathful, all-sovereign deity of Puritan Calvinism.[2]

He also declined to call himself an abolitionist, although he stood strongly opposed to slavery, feeling that Garrison and others using that label were often too angry and self-righteous. He felt that a demand for immediate abolition not only displayed impatience with divine providence but could be "inconsistent with the well-being of the slave and the order of the state."[3] Recent African American historians of the antislavery movement have defended Channing's stature as a staunch, persuasive white ally.[4] He did not pretend to know the mind of God in relation to any individual or nation, but he did not regard white America as God's chosen people nor support its supposed manifest destiny to rule the continent. He therefore strongly opposed the annexation of Texas, since it would expand slavery. If the nation, and the church, still needed further reforming, he thought, it had to begin within each individual. He balanced the Reformation emphasis on human sinfulness and repentance with an even more ancient biblical doctrine: that deep within every soul there also lies an *imago dei*—the image and power of God, waiting for recognition, nurture, and creative opportunities for use in the world in the service of others.[5]

Channing was at home, evidently in the same room where he had first heard Follen speak about the death of Christ, when another friend brought him the tragic news about the *Lexington* and the death of his friend and protégé. Normally he was a self-controlled, even stoical, Christian. Once, asked how he had been able to conduct a funeral service for a member of his own family without ever losing his composure, he had quietly responded, "My tears do not lie so near my eyes." On hearing this news, however, he covered his face with both hands. He wept, as Jesus did over the death of his friend Lazarus. Recovering, he then murmured, "It is well," and then thanked the friend who had brought him the report so that he could now take his leave.[6]

Channing was then approaching sixty but already feeling his own death as near. Because of his illness, during the previous year he had been able to preach only six times. By then he had been pastor at Federal Street for thirty-seven years. When he first ordained there in 1803, at the age of twenty-three, he had been more promising than prominent. Joseph Stevens Buckminster was the spiritual and intellectual leader of Boston's liberals. Scholarly, eloquent, even younger than Channing, he was among the first New England ministers to study in Germany, and to bring back the German historical-critical method of interpreting the Bible. As pastor of Boston's fashionable Brattle Street Church, and as the first Dexter Lecturer on Biblical Criticism at Harvard, he defended the liberals when Calvinists attacked them as Unitarian heretics.[7] When Buckminster died in 1812—of epilepsy, at only twenty-eight—those same liberals found in Channing their new young leader, not only because of his respect for the use of critical reason in religion but more because of his inclusive style, emphasizing not dogma but rather "practical religion."

Channing also came from a distinguished family; he was named for his maternal grandfather, William Ellery, who signed the Declaration of Independence for Rhode Island in 1776. His father, who became attorney general there, helped persuade his state finally to approve the federal constitution, the last of the original thirteen to do so, in 1790. His father then also became the US attorney. Three years later, he was suddenly dead, at the age of forty-two, leaving behind five sons and four daughters. The future minister was thirteen. He was living with his uncle, Reverend Henry Channing of New London, Connecticut, preparing for Harvard. His boyhood pastor, Ezra Stiles, a Calvinist who later became president of Yale, had taught submission to the will of God. Yet young William Ellery sensed early on the contradictions in Calvinist culture, with its combined beliefs in predestination, repentance, and the value of education. So did his uncle Henry. One anecdote from his childhood stands out.

His politician father had taken him along to a local revival meeting. The preaching was full of terrifying images of the wrath of God, of hellfire and brimstone. The boy was frightened, wondering what his father would say about what they all should now do to escape destruction. Getting back in their carriage to ride home, his father only remarked, "Sound doctrine, that! Leaves no rag of self-righteousness to wrap the sinner in." Then he began to whistle as they rode. Over a good dinner, he said nothing more about avoiding the vividly described wrath to come. The son began to sense a gap between the doctrines people profess and what they actually do.[8]

At age fourteen, he went to college. Not to Yale, however, where orthodox Calvinism prevailed, but rather to more liberal Harvard, where a greater emphasis on human free will had taken hold and where an older brother, Francis, had preceded him. Not that he approved of too much liberality. It was the era of the French Revolution, and reverence for the past and for its wisdom seemed under challenge everywhere. He became a critical but compassionate thinker, as hard on those cutting off heads in Paris in the name of the goddess Reason, as he was on Calvinist revivalists nearer to home. When he was chosen as commencement speaker for the Class of 1798, the faculty forbade him to speak on events in France or on religious controversies. This only made him a stronger supporter of free speech and inquiry. In order to help his family's finite resources stretch to provide an education for two younger brothers and dowries for his four sisters, he took work as a tutor on a Virginia plantation belonging to the Randolph family, who summered in Newport.

He liked his employers. They were generous, unlike penny-pinching New Englanders, and he heard them deploring slavery and wondering how to end it. He had a school of twelve rambunctious white boys. He saw how white children of privilege could scorn opportunities to learn, while black servants and their children had no right to literacy nor to opportunities for spiritual, intellectual, and moral growth. He probably saw, or suspected, sexual exploitation of the enslaved. In any case, as a young male of Puritan heritage, with his conscience and hormones tormenting him, he became an ascetic, eating little, studying late, sleeping on the floor, asking God to give him purity and to make him worthy of being a future minister. He may have also permanently ruined his health.[9] After two years in the South, he returned home to begin to prepare for the ministry at Harvard.

Like his uncle, he honored John Calvin as a church reformer and as a Christian humanist. Both found great wisdom in a tradition that began by asking, "What is the chief end of man?" and replied, "Man's chief end is to glorify God, and to enjoy him forever."[10] Yet later Calvin*ism*, at least in its New England version, had developed a spirit that almost defeated that great end. Moreover, while the Reformation had begun as a protest, questioning tradition and authority, relying on Martin Luther's *sola scriptura, sola fide, sola gratia*, later Calvinists had adopted a fivefold formula: Total depravity; Unconditional election; Limited atonement; Irresistible grace; the Perseverance of the chosen saints. This mnemonic acronym, TULIP, summarized how Dutch Calvinists at the Synod of Dort in 1618–1619 condemned Jacobus Arminius's idea of free will. His disciples, known as Arminians, dared to believe that God, as both good and just, allowed humans enough freedom to become good and just themselves—by the grace mediated through his anointed son, Jesus, the transcendent model for living a life of altruism and discipleship, via *imitatio Christi*. With the gradual coming of Enlightenment rationalism in the mid-eighteenth century, some of the educated clergy in New England began to incline toward this Arminian position. Some went so far as to see no need to profess faith in the seemingly irrational mystery of God as a Trinity, three persons in one God.[11] They also found the image of God offered in Calvinism to be angry, irrational, difficult to love, and all too likely to inspire similar behavior in his worshippers. Some, including Channing, came to believe that Jesus was the better model, the human incarnation of the preexistent logos, the eternal word of God, but still subordinate to God as the loving father and creator.

This critique of the Trinity made Channing an "Arian" in his Christology. That is, he took a position close to that of Arius of Alexandria (256–336 CE), whose ideas were condemned at the Council of Nicaea in 325. The Emperor Constantine then made creedal belief in the Trinity mandatory for all Christians. During the Reformation, as biblical humanists like Erasmus researched the original texts of the Gospels, they found that the few instances of Trinitarian formulas were later additions. Some then began to take an even more radical view of Jesus—as entirely human. They saw him as anointed to a divine mission, however: an inclusive mission to obtain disciples meant to bring about that ideal state known as the kingdom, or commonwealth, of God on earth. This "humanitarian" view was also termed "Socinian," after the Italian-Polish radical Faustus Socinus (1539–1604). The influential English Unitarian minister-scientist Joseph Priestley (1733–1804) also took this view in his *History of the Corruptions of Christianity* (1782).[12]

If all of this sounds too theological and abstract to be relevant, a woman as practical and down-to-earth as Elizabeth Palmer Peabody would strenuously object. She had come to a humanitarian view of Jesus rather early in life. It made her a lifelong humanitarian herself, and like Charles Follen, both a disciple of Dr. Channing and an influence on his later thinking, perhaps far more than is often recognized. Peabody saw herself and other Transcendentalists not as disciples of Emerson but of Channing. She was surely right in this: Channing taught them all. He was a key figure in the evolution of religious thinking in postrevolutionary New England.[13] Like herself, he represented a link between that generation of New England religionists who had rejected predestination, embraced free will, and admitted to being Unitarians, and the younger Transcendentalists, with their emphasis on the capacity of individuals to transcend themselves and implement the reforms demanded by what Peabody called "the social principle" in religion.

Growing up in Salem, she had first heard Channing preach there when she was nine, taken by a mother who knew his reputation for being able to reach even young listeners. Elizabeth, a relentless reader and restless thinker, saw in him the sort of man whose guidance she yearned for. Her own father, Dr. Nathaniel Peabody, was, to put it kindly, rather distant and disappointing as a father figure. Although trained as a physician, he had never succeeded in properly supporting his family. Her mother (and namesake) had met him when both were young teachers. The elder Elizabeth, attempting to make ends meet, often kept a school in their home. She also raised her daughters to be able to teach as well. When the younger Elizabeth moved to Boston to start a school there, Channing helped her. He found her to be an intelligent young congregant committed to unfolding the moral and spiritual awareness of children in line with what he had come to call "self-culture." When that initial school did not prosper, Elizabeth and her sister Mary imitated Channing by going away to tutor the children of wealthy families, not in Virginia but in central Maine. Elizabeth kept up her correspondence with Channing even then. She observed, and decried, for example, the divisiveness of revivalism. She described one revivalist as separating those present in two groups at the end of his sermon: those who had "obtained a hope" of salvation on one side, and those still unmoved on the other, saying that this is how it would be on Judgment Day. That meeting broke up when one of the supposed unsaved said that the preacher had just substituted his own judgment for that of God.[14] Finding herself then, like Follen, unable to work for parents whose values she did not share, Elizabeth returned to Boston and, with Mary, made a second attempt at a school. This time they had active help both from Eliza Lee Cabot (later Follen) and from Dr. Channing. He not only promoted the Peabody sisters as educators but also entrusted his own daughter Mary, then eight, to Elizabeth's tutelage. She was to be Mary's teacher for the next seven years. Peabody spent many evenings in the Channing home, reading aloud, conversing, and acting as something between a governess and the minister's unpaid secretary. She often walked with him as he mused on a sermon, to help him to clarify his thoughts. On Sundays, she took shorthand notes on what he had said, transcribing and preparing texts for publication.

Channing told Peabody that no one had influenced his own theology so much as had Coleridge, with his distinction between mere sense-driven understanding and transcendent moral reason. The more he discussed such things with spiritual friends like her, and Follen, the more he struck Transcendentalist notes. In "Likeness to God" (1828), he said that it belongs to our "higher or spiritual nature [and] has its foundation in the original and essential capacities of the mind." Inscribed on the back of his monument is a longer passage from the same sermon:

> I do and I must reverence human nature. I bless it for its kind affections.
> I honor it for its achievements in science and art, and still more for its

examples of heroic and saintly virtue. These are marks of a divine origin and the pledges of a celestial inheritance, and I thank God that my own lot is bound up with that of the human race.[15]

Peabody may have been the first American to use the term "transcendental" in an essay. Starting in 1826, she wrote six essays on "The Spirit of the Hebrew Bible," and on how to interpret that part of the Bible with which the Puritans had so deeply identified. Three of these finally appeared in 1834 in the leading Unitarian journal, the *Christian Examiner*. The fourth related her method of interpretation to the transcendental, rather than the empirical. That one was never published. Harvard's professor of biblical studies, Andrews Norton, was one of the editors of the *Examiner*. A staunch empiricist, he had objected to it, and the series ended abruptly.[16] This would not be Norton's final blast against such "new views" in religion.

Like Peabody, Channing was never simply a sunny, naive optimist about human nature. He realized the full reality of human sin, and a need for continual repentance, including his own. Yet he preached the goodness of God, and the capacity of human beings to try to approach such "disinterested benevolence," despite how far short of God's glory, or of the model set by Christ, human beings often fall. The aftermath to the tragic death of Charles Follen reminded him of that. It provoked a spiritual trial deeper than just another instance of loss and grief. It caused him to question whether he had ever had any effect at all in converting those under his pastoral care to more Christlike thinking and living.

Several days after the news of the *Lexington* first reached him, Channing received another visit from a friend. His colleague in Unitarian ministry, Samuel Joseph May, had come on behalf of the Anti-Slavery Society to discuss a public memorial service for Follen. Some six years previously, in late 1834, May had also paid Channing a visit. Channing had returned to Boston after a summer of rest in Newport to a city deeply divided by race, religion, ethnicity, and social class. A working-class Protestant mob, threatened by low-wage Irish immigrants and influenced by centuries of Puritan anti-Catholic rhetoric, had burned an Ursuline convent in nearby Charlestown. Almost alone among the city's Protestant ministers, Channing spoke out against this outrage, earning the enduring gratitude of Boston's Roman Catholic leaders. Then why, May asked during their conversation, was he still silent about slavery? After Lydia Maria Child's *Appeal*, he had promised to speak out. He had not done so. Why? Channing replied, "Brother May, I must acknowledge the justice of your reproof. I have been silent too long."[17]

He spent the next summer writing a small book called *Slavery*, laying out his position. Condemning slavery in uncompromising terms, Channing also rejected the label "abolitionist" as tainted with both harsh rhetoric and unrealistic, immediate solutions. As with all moderate utterances amid deep political polarizations, he pleased no one. The *Liberator* at first said that he would draw people to the cause whom they could not reach. Garrison in his columns then grew increasingly dismissive, however. He called the book "utterly destitute of any redeeming reforming power" and, in so far as Channing had criticized his methods, "calumnious, contradictory, and unsound," unworthy of being "appropriated by any genuine abolitionist."[18] Another antislavery publication saw him as the epitome of all those clergy who deplore the sin of slavery but then oppose "active measures" to end it. Conservatives were even more scathing. Denunciations from the South were entirely predictable. More hurtful were critics close to home. Massachusetts Attorney General James Austin, a Unitarian himself, accused Channing in print of appealing to prurient interests by alluding to sexual exploitation of the enslaved, and of fomenting a "doctrine of INSURRECTION."[19] Former President John Quincy Adams, another Unitarian, now in the House of Representatives, admired Channing's courage but described his book as "an inflammatory, if not an incendiary publication."[20] Some of Channing's oldest friends in the church that he had pastored for over thirty years began to stay away from his sermons. Some even began to avoid him on the street. Through all this, he kept both spiritual friendship and pulpit fellowship with "Brother May."

Rather than subject him to any further conflict with his congregants, May now told him, the Anti-Slavery Society, with Eliza's support, wished to sponsor the memorial service for Charles Follen. He himself would prepare and deliver the eulogy. Yet surely the appropriate place for such a service was the Federal Street meetinghouse, where Follen had been ordained,

and with Channing presiding. All of that agreed, Channing ended by saying that he would, of course, have to ask the trustees of his society for
permission for this use of their meetinghouse. Initially, they too agreed.
Then, under pressure from anti-abolitionist members who had objected to
any announcements at services of abolitionist meetings, they met without
Channing present and voted, unanimously, to deny the use of the Federal
Street Church for the Follen service sponsored by the Anti-Slavery Society.

Channing was simply stunned. His own nephew later put it this way:

> It was not only the insult to the memory of a beloved friend that grieved
> him, though this could not but shock his quick and delicate feelings; still
> less was it the disregard, under such touching circumstances, of his well-
> known wishes, that wounded him most deeply; but this manifestation
> of a want of high sentiment in the congregation to which, for so many
> years, he had officiated as pastor, made him question the usefulness of
> his whole ministry. To what end had he poured out his soul, if such con-
> duct was a practical embodiment of the principles and precepts which he
> had so earnestly inculcated?[21]

What should he now do in response to this betrayal of all that he had
tried to teach them?

For some time, Channing had felt that what kept some of his people
from fully applying the Christian law of love to all their social relations
was simply love of money. He decided that he himself would no longer
accept any money from them. That would then liberate him, as a "public
teacher of religion and morality," from dependence on the trustees. With
his infirmities, he had already reduced his own salary. More duties and compensation could now go to his junior colleague, Ezra Stiles Gannett. More
conservative in his social views, Gannett had disappointed Channing by
not supporting his stance on slavery, but rather favoring colonization—
sending African Americans back to Africa. Let the trustees now give *him*
their money. He would not give up the role of being their chief pastor,
however—the shepherd of their souls—unless they asked for his resignation. He would also preach one last sermon, about the death of his friend.

Channing gave his "Discourse Occasioned by the Death of Dr. Follen," on January 25, 1840.[22]

This sermon deserves far more attention than it has received among his writings, since it concerns the problem of evil and the reality of suffering, yet ends in an exhortation to persist in good works, believing still in a benevolent God. Its text comes from I Peter 4:19: "Wherefore, let them that suffer according to the will of God commit the keeping of their souls to him in well-doing, as unto a faithful Creator." Staring straight at the very Federal Street conservatives who had so hurt him, he began by saying that "faith in virtue" is sometimes "shaken by the turpitude of those to whom it has given its trust." Yet there are "still deeper pains, those of the conscience, especially when it wakes from a long sleep, when it is startled by new revelation of slighted duties, of irreparable wrongs to man, of base unfaithfulness to God." With unaccustomed irony, he then offered this trenchant insight: "The most skeptical men, the most insensible to God's goodness, the most prone to murmur, may be found among those who are laden above all others with the goods of life, whose cup overflows with prosperity, and who by an abuse of prosperity have become selfish, exacting, and all alive to inconveniences and privations. These are the cold-hearted and doubting."[23] On the other hand, "the profoundest sense of God's goodness, which it has been my privilege to witness, I have seen in the countenance, and heard from the lips of the suffering." He then imagined his dear friend Follen, aboard the "flame-encircled boat . . . and as he rises to my mind, I see no terror on his countenance. I see him with collected mind and quick eye looking round him for means of escape, using every energy of a fearless spirit, thoughtful too of others . . . [and] desisting from no efforts of love and prudence till the power of effort failed." While sermons should chiefly be about Christ, he ended, he had dared to speak of Follen only because "God is honored and man edified by notices of such of our race as have signally manifested the spirit of the Divinity in their lives, and have left a bright path to guide others to a better world."[24]

The public memorial service for Follen was finally held at Boston's Marlboro Chapel on Good Friday, April 17, "the anniversary of the crucifixion of Jesus, whom he loved and served as the perfect example of self-sacrifice," as Samuel May put it in his eulogy.[25] Channing took part, giving a prayer. He waited to write to his church trustees, declining to take any of their silver, so that he could do so calmly, yet before the annual meeting of the congregation. Rather than resign as pastor, he left the question of his spiritual leadership to them. He said simply that if *they* should want a "dissolution of the [pastoral] relation," then he would "wish it to be immediate."[26] He clearly still felt his responsibility to care for their sin-sick souls, but he was no longer sure that his ministry with them was either effective or wanted. The trustees, of course, did not dare to dismiss the revered Channing as their pastor and had no choice but to accede to his wish that he no longer consider his public ministry as being on their behalf, nor receive any salary.

His family and close friends were aghast at his treatment, Elizabeth Peabody perhaps chief among them. Just as Follen had been his personal link to the Anti-Slavery Society, she had become one of his principal conduits to those of his disciples who had been meeting periodically now for three and a half years. Their meetings began out of shared dissatisfaction with the moral, spiritual, and intellectual atmosphere within the Unitarian churches generally. They had varied intellectual, literary, and reformist interests, and had been discussing them in what they called "the Symposeum" or the "Like-Minded." We know them as the "Transcendentalist circle."[27] They had invited Channing from the very start to join them. He attended at least once, when his health allowed it, and kept in touch with their discussions through others, especially Peabody.

Not that he always agreed with all them. When Emerson, their most public voice, spoke in 1838 to the Divinity School graduates in his famous address, he had offended the faculty. Andrews Norton blasted his ideas as simply "The Latest Form of Infidelity." Channing and Peabody both felt otherwise. Emerson was right, they felt, when he said, "The evils of the church that now is are manifest." He was also right in saying, "The remedy to their deformity is, first, soul, and second, soul, and evermore, soul." Especially in pointing to Jesus Christ as the highest exemplar of divine living, saying that "[he] belonged to the true race of prophets. He saw with open eye the mystery of the soul. Drawn by its severe harmony, ravished by its beauty, he lived in it, and had his being there. Alone in all history, he estimated the greatness of man. One man was true to what is in you and me." Peabody pointed out that Channing himself had said much the same thing fully ten years earlier, in his sermon, "Likeness to God," especially in a passage that a young friend, William Batchelder Greene, suggested to her as having summed up the whole Transcendental movement: "The divine attributes are first developed in ourselves, and thence transferred to our Creator. The idea of God, sublime and awful as it is, is the idea of our own spiritual nature, purified and enlarged to infinity. In ourselves are the elements of the Divinity. God does not sustain a figurative resemblance to man; it is the resemblance of a parent to a child, the likeness of kindred natures." Channing still believed that, then added this caveat:

> But the development of the divine attributes in ourselves is the realization not of what is peculiar to any individual, but what is common to all men, and manifested in the utmost purity by Jesus Christ, the Son of God, who is the unfallen ideal man. The danger that besets our Transcendentalists is that they sometimes mistake their individualities for the Transcendent. What is common to men and revealed by Jesus transcends every single individuality, and is the spiritual object and food of all individuals.

Peabody then asked, "Don't you think Mr. Emerson recognizes this?" Channing replied, "Yes . . . But some of his . . . followers *do not*, and fall into a kind of *ego-theism*, of which a true understanding of Jesus Christ is the only cure, as I more and more believe."[28]

Was Channing a Transcendentalist? Even Emerson thought so. Peabody remembered him as saying, when Channing was quite ill, "In our wantonness we often flout Dr. Channing, and say he is getting old; but as soon as he is ill we remember that he is our Bishop, and we have not done with him yet."[29] Others of his many Transcendentalist disciples might well have agreed. Yet Channing worried over all his spiritual heirs. He worried that many conservative Unitarians seemed to think that merely in dispensing with the Trinity, the work of using the spiritual gift of reason for the further reform of the church or of their own souls was now complete. Much to his distress, they had become just another self-congratulatory sect, sure of their moral superiority because of holding a better, more rational doctrine. "No!" he almost wanted to shout, during his last years, despite his limited lung capacity. "Shun sectarianism as a spirit from hell."[30] Right religion is not about right belief. It is about right feeling and action, sustained by good character. Even his most radical disciples felt that. He worried over them also. Yet it was why they had gathered in the first place.

Frederic Henry Hedge
(1805–1890)

CHAPTER III

Mutual Inspiration

In which a group of young, like-minded, Unitarian ministers
united in dissatisfaction with their alma mater
and with the intellectual, spiritual, and moral state
of the churches and of society,
form a discussion circle,
open to Pentecostal inspiration.

THANKS TO INCLUSIVE LEADERS LIKE CHANNING, Unitarians had taken over Harvard and many of the established churches and institutions around Boston and in eastern New England. What brought the original members of the Transcendentalist circle together was a fiery dissatisfaction with the complacency of this new Unitarian establishment. They also felt that they could detect its philosophical source: in a materialistic theory of knowledge, in which the mind is a blank slate, receiving all that it knows in the form of sensory data. This treats the soul as passive, not active. It hardly conforms to the biblical image of Christ's disciples gathered at Pentecost, their souls and their minds touched with holy fire, allowing them to speak to and to understand even people quite different from themselves.

The spark that ignited the Transcendentalist circle came from Frederic Henry Hedge, the intellectually gifted minister who was so central to the circle that Emerson sometimes referred to it as "Hedge's Club." From the first, meetings often took place when he could travel from his new pastorate in Bangor, Maine, to the Boston area. He not only first suggested the group but also served as its resident expert on the German sources of the philosophical idealism that was at the core of their being "like-minded." With the exception of Follen, largely absent during his time in New York, only "Germanicus" Hedge had actually read Kant in the original German and could draw distinctions between his ideas and those of disciples such as Schelling, Fichte, and Schleiermacher—or of English interpreters such as Carlyle and Coleridge. Moreover, he came to this role almost by inheritance. His own father, Levi Hedge, was professor of logic, metaphysics, and natural philosophy at Harvard from 1810 to 1830, before suffering from a paralyzing stroke. His approach followed Locke's empiricism and the Scottish "Common Sense" school of philosophy, both assuming that all that we know comes in only through our five senses. His son, after studies in Germany, broke decisively with his father's method in philosophy.

Young Henry Hedge, as his friends always called him, was such an intellectual prodigy that he passed the Harvard entrance exam at the age of twelve. His father wisely judged the boy not yet entirely ready for college, yet with intellectual gifts that deserved encouragement. Henry's tutor, eighteen-year-old George Bancroft, had decided to go to Germany for his own studies and was asked by Levi to take Henry along and to place him in a German gymnasium. Despite good intentions, Henry did not adjust to teenage life in another culture without some drama. His first school peers treated him as either a barbarian or a twit. Levi's Harvard colleague Edward Everett, then also in Germany, had to intervene to arrange for another school. Three schools and four years later, however, a rather poised young man of seventeen returned and entered the junior class at Harvard.[1]

Back in Cambridge, he became friends with another local teenage intellectual, Margaret Fuller, and encouraged her interest in learning German. Graduating with the Class of 1825 as class poet and valedictorian, he turned down a chance to assist Follen in teaching the language. Instead, at his father's urging, he entered the Divinity School. There he became a lifelong friend of Ralph Waldo Emerson. After graduating in 1829, Hedge was ordained as pastor of the Unitarian church in West Cambridge (now Arlington), marrying Margaret's friend Lucy Pierce, whose father was the Unitarian minister in nearby Brookline. Thomas Carlyle later described Hedge as "one of the sturdiest little fellows I have come across for many a day. A face like a rock, a voice like a howitzer, only his honest gray eyes assure you a little."[2]

Hedge initiated the Transcendentalist circle in 1836 out of several levels of dissatisfaction with the status quo. One was with Harvard, where his father had taught but which compared poorly with his own education in Germany. A second was with the churches surrounding it, including his own, in West Cambridge. He found people contentious over all the wrong things: not over ideas; but over status and material matters. The third was intellectual. He had written an article for the Unitarian *Christian Examiner*, "Coleridge's Literary Character." He passed over the fact that Coleridge had briefly been a Unitarian minister and then, after going to Germany, had left the denomination, finding its premises too fixed in empiricism rather than in higher and more intuitive reason. Instead, he regretted that Coleridge had never offered a full interpretation of the Copernican revolution that he felt Kant had wrought in philosophy by transcending materialism. He admitted that not all are "born to be philosophers, or are capable of being philosophers, or poets, or musicians," unless we "raise ourselves at once to a transcendental point of view." Then he declared that "as in astronomy the motions of the heavenly bodies seem confused to the geocentric observer, and are intelligible only when referred to their heliocentric place, so there is only one point from which we can clearly understand and decide upon the speculations of Kant and his followers; that point is the interior consciousness, distinguished from the common consciousness, by its being an active and not a passive state."[3]

This article truly ignited something in Hedge's friend Emerson. In a letter to his brother Edward, Waldo pronounced it "a living, leaping logos."[4] He soon began to read more Coleridge himself and to study German, seeking reading suggestions from Hedge. Emerson's biographer Robert Richardson suggests that this moment marks the real emergence of Transcendentalism, and of "minds on fire," in America.[5] The two Divinity School friends shared another connection. Emerson's widowed mother had rented the Cambridge home of Levi Hedge, running a boardinghouse there to care for the paralyzed professor while supporting herself and Waldo's siblings, one of whom was developmentally disabled. There were then no pensions, social security, nor provisions for the disabled. The two sons joined in seeing most Boston Unitarians as holding a philosophy more materialistic than spiritual, more selfish than ethical or intuitive.

Another young minister who wrote for the *Examiner* agreed with them on the need for a radical change in philosophy. George Ripley, the first host of the Transcendentalist circle, provided the most frustrated tinder. A farm boy by birth, he was then serving a downtown Boston church heavily impacted by social and economic inequality. The ninth child of a Calvinist farmer in the Connecticut River Valley, he had a background less privileged than that of Hedge or Emerson, the sons of a professor and of a prominent minister.[6] His father had gradually prospered, however, becoming a storekeeper in the nearby town of Greenfield. As he did so, his theology also shifted from a belief in predestination to one more oriented to crediting free will. He then sent his son to prepare for college at Harvard under the tutelage of two older Ripley cousins, father and son, both of whom were Unitarian clergy.[7]

True to the piety of his mother, George was a traditional Trinitarian in his college years, at least until he studied with Andrews Norton, professor of biblical literature and author of *A Statement of Reasons for Not Believing the Doctrine of Trinitarians*. Norton held such intellectual authority among liberals that some called him "the Unitarian Pope." He found Ripley one of his best students. Given the antagonism that later developed between them, it is notable that when Ripley, at age twenty-four, became the minister of a newly organized Unitarian congregation in downtown Boston, Norton gladly took part in his ordination.

Located close to the waterfront, the Purchase Street Church had members who were more middle class than prosperous or intellectual. They had built a rather squat, unattractive meetinghouse. Their new minister seemed well meaning, intelligent, and presentable, with his spectacles and a curly head of hair. He brought with him the kindness and social prestige of a lovely young wife, Sophia Willard Dana Ripley, born to a distinguished Cambridge family.

George was never, by anyone's standards, including his own, an effective or rousing preacher. Often his sermons read more like essays. In that format, however, he could truly express himself. He supplemented his salary by writing often (and anonymously) for the *Christian Examiner*. It paid him a dollar for each page printed. In 1831, Ripley reviewed for the *Examiner* the inaugural lecture given by Follen as Harvard's professor of German language and literature.[8] Both tried to deny that German idealism led to skepticism or to atheism, and Ripley implied that empiricism was much more likely to lead that way. Professor Norton must have made his displeasure clear, as Sophia was soon referring to him in her letters as "*the wicked Mr. Norton.*"[9] The idea that German influences might lead to skepticism was not entirely wrong, however.

The story of Emerson's older brother, William, constitutes a case in point. Designated from birth for ministry and named after both a father and a grandfather who had been the sixth and seventh generations of a Brahmin dynasty of preachers going back to the founding of New England, William was predestined to be the ordained member of the eighth generation. When he was ten, and Waldo only eight, their father suddenly died. He was then pastor of Boston's First Church. His widow, Ruth Haskins Emerson, left the parsonage to take in boarders in a rented house. The trustees gave her a small amount toward the education of her sons, but the two eldest had to share a single winter coat when they attended Boston's Latin School. William studied diligently and, after graduating from Harvard, worked as a teacher before going to Gottingen, Germany, in 1824 to prepare for ministry by learning the new historical-critical approach to the Bible. After one year, he returned, saying that he had learned how to criticize the Bible but now felt no call to preach it or to be ordained. He even told their step-grandfather, Ezra Ripley, that he now believed that Jesus had never meant for the Last Supper to become any sort of "perpetual memorial."

When William balked at being ordained, choosing law instead, their father's unmarried sister, Mary Moody Emerson, seized on Waldo as the spiritually sensitive son to continue the tradition. Aunt Mary's lively piety and individualistic faith, deeply rooted in New Light Calvinism, reflected a life of voracious reading and searching after "metaphysics and illuminati," as another Emerson brother, Charles, phrased it.

Emerson, while preaching in New Hampshire, had met the beautiful, fragile young Ellen Tucker. It did not hurt that she also came from a wealthy family. Young ministers in New England, educated well but never paid well, were well advised to seek spouses with "pecuniary means," as some then put it. Channing, for example, had married his first cousin, Ruth Gibbs—the wealthiest young woman in Rhode Island. This is not to imply authentic love was not involved. Both loves were genuine. Nine months after they first met, Emerson married Tucker. He was then junior colleague to the Reverend Henry Ware Jr. at the Second Church in Boston. When Ware left to teach at Harvard, young Emerson became the pastor. Like so many in that era, both he and Ellen had tuberculosis. Hers was far worse. Sixteen months later, Charles Emerson described her end in a letter to Aunt Mary:

> Ellen is still with us, though her spirit seems winged for its flights. She suffered a great deal of distress last night, but today (with the exception of perhaps two or three times a half-hour) she has been in less pain— sometimes torpid under the influence of her opiates, but at others se- rene and fully conscious. She spoke this afternoon very sweetly of her readiness to die—that she told you she should not probably live through the winter—tho' she did not know that she would have been called so soon—she saw no reason why her friends should be distressed, [since] it was better she should go first, and prepare the way—She asked Waldo, if he had strength, to read her a few verses of Scripture—and he read a portion of the XIVth chapter of John—Waldo is bowed down under the affliction, yet he says t'is like seeing an angel go to heaven.[10]

As she died, Ellen prayed and said that she had not turned angry at the world or at God. Her last words were "I have not forgot the peace and joy." We cannot truly understand Emerson nor the Transcendentalists without remembering this scene. While it is true that some months later Emerson went to Ellen's coffin and opened it—which seems macabre—for him, the point was that her body had truly perished, as merely matter, yet her spirit had clearly remained with him.

Waldo received an inheritance from Ellen's estate. It would be easy to say that he used it to leave the ministry. In fact, his inner process was more complicated. He said that he was resigning his pastorate over scruples about conducting the communion service. He explained himself in an essay based on William's reasoning and that of Quakers. One emotional factor may have been that the Puritan form of communion was a gloomy memorial, not a eucharistic thanksgiving. Offering to stay if he did not have to preside at "the Lord's Supper," his people kept the traditional service and allowed him to leave.

The real problem was that the pastoral side of ministry had never been easy for Emerson, and that it is never easy for a grieving minister to deal well with the grief of others. At Second Church, he had attended at the deathbed of a Revolutionary War veteran. The traditional role of a pastor was to read from scripture, pray, and comfort family members. The old soldier lingered. The young minister, who had lost his own father at only nine, noted that the bedchamber held a collection of colored glass bottles and began to wonder aloud about their meaning to the man. The old soldier then finally lifted his head and snapped, "Young man, if you don't know your business, you had better go home."[11]

Emerson now needed time and space to go home to himself, to work out in his own thinking and feeling the relationship between matter and spirit, thought and nature, death and life. He sailed for Europe via the Mediterranean, landing in Malta and proceeding north through Italy. In Rome, he bought a print of Raphael's *Transfiguration*, symbolizing the ongoing tie between body and spirit. His goal was Britain, to meet the writers whose ideas on spirit and nature he most admired: Coleridge, Wordsworth, and Thomas Carlyle. He had to reach the last by hiring a driver to take him to Carlyle's house in the north of Scotland. On the way, in the Jardin des Plantes in Paris, he had a revelation: nature is but a symbol and vocabulary of what is eternal and spiritually most real.

He knew that Swedish mystic Emmanuel Swedenborg and his Harvard disciple, Sampson Reed, had seen something similar but had ended up as new sectarians. He wanted to be more inclusive.

When he returned home, Emerson tried to reinvent his ministry as one free from the pastorate, doing guest preaching and lecturing, and hoping to be an independent scholar, poet, and writer. He was now studying German, reading the works of Goethe. He had also begun writing, alone, in Concord's Old Manse—where his grandfather had seen the Revolution begin at the North Bridge—his first and most revolutionary book, *Nature*. While out lecturing in Plymouth, however, he encountered Lydia Jackson, who became his second wife. By 1835, they were married and living in Concord in a large house on the Lexington Turnpike. He even added rooms intended for his brother Charles and his fiancée, Elizabeth Hoar, when they too married. The original plan for his book comprised two parts: "Nature," and "Spirit," for the objective and subjective poles of experience.[12] Then Charles died, much as Ellen had. Bereft once again, he reduced "Spirit" to two chapters, closing a book now simply called *Nature*.

As he worked over the summer of 1836 to finish it, Emerson was not the only young Unitarian minister feeling spiritually alone. Hedge was another. For that, Emerson was, in part, to blame. Preaching as a guest at the Independent Congregational Church in Bangor, Maine, and impressed by the intelligence of its members, he encouraged Hedge to take the ministry there.

Hedge accepted the call to serve a burgeoning church replete with community leaders. Bangor was quite a prosperous boomtown, then known as "the Lumber Capital of the World." One visitor counted some thirty lawyers, five judges, and a former governor. They were also diverse in both background and theology—Unitarians, Orthodox Congregationalists, Methodists, and others—united chiefly by what Channing had earlier called "practical religion," meaning the pursuit of good works in a growing city. They were not any easy flock to shepherd, however. They were more materialistic than spiritual, and there were no other liberal clergy in or near Bangor with whom Hedge could commune. He had spent a lonely winter there, the snowiest, coldest in anyone's memory, while his wife, Lucy, stayed in Boston, too ill and overwhelmed with two small children to join him.

When spring came, Hedge visited his wife and children and his aging, disabled father as soon as possible. During the visit, he saw that the *Christian Examiner* had published a long article by Ripley, "Schleiermacher as Theologian," praising the German thinker's metaphysics, intuition and spiritual-emotional basis for religion. It described how the author of *Speeches on Religion to Its Cultured Despisers* (1799) had shifted the basis of liberal Christian apologetics away from rationalistic arguments about biblical texts to locate its ground in shared feelings of ultimate dependency.[13] Hedge feared that it would draw the ire of Andrews Norton and other Unitarian conservatives. That May, the annual meeting of Unitarian ministers in the Berry Street vestry of Channing's Federal Street Church only confirmed his apprehensions. He felt "stunned by the lamentable want of courage shown by the members in their discussion of subjects [theological and moral] and the utter neglect of truth for expedients." Ripley was there and had a similar reaction. George Putnam, the Unitarian minister in Roxbury, must have agreed. The three decided that articulating and defending their ideas merited a new clergy study group, and that Emerson was a likely ally. Hedge then wrote to him:

> I have a project to communicate to you, in which I trust to have your sympathy & cooperation, for, if I remember right, you once proposed something of the same sort . . . The plan is namely this, to have a meeting, annual or oftener if possible, of certain likeminded persons of our acquaintance for the free discussion of theological & moral subjects. By likeminded persons I mean not such as agree in opinion, but such as agree in spirit,—men who earnestly seek the truth & who, with perfect toleration of other men's freedom & in the avowal of their own opinions, however abhorent [*sic*] from the general faith, unite in perfect toleration of other men's freedom & and other men's opinions.[14]

Hedge proposed that the four of them meet at the upcoming Harvard bicentennial celebration, held on Thursday, September 8, 1836. Thirteen hundred Harvard alumni gathered in the Yard, plus two hundred undergraduates. Many processed, led by an eighty-six-year-old member of the class of 1774, to a service in the Unitarian church of Cambridge. There they heard the first singing of "Fair Harvard," composed for the occasion by alumnus Samuel Gilman, the Unitarian minister in Charleston, South Carolina.[15] President Josiah Quincy then gave a two-hour discourse about

Harvard history. It was almost entirely an exercise in self-congratulatory retrospection. Hedge, Emerson, Ripley, and Putnam soon fled to nearby Willard's Hotel. They ranged in age from twenty-nine to thirty-four. They may have had things to say to one another about the inadequacy of Harvard and its curriculum; about its disciplinary methods (Quincy had recently banished an entire class for being disruptive); or about the dismissal of Charles Follen. What we do know is that they judged the education, philosophy, and theology emanating from their alma mater as "very unsatisfactory," needing discussions "in the way of protest and introduction of deeper and broader views."[16]

Ripley agreed to host an initial meeting of "like-minded" colleagues. Emerson provided the rhetorical breath to fan the Transcendentalist conversation into flame. His book *Nature* appeared the next day, beginning:

> Our age is retrospective. It builds the sepulchres of the fathers. It writes biographies, histories, and criticism. The foregoing generations beheld God and nature face to face; we, through their eyes. Why should not we also enjoy an original relation to the universe? Why should not we have a poetry and philosophy of insight and not of tradition, and a religion by revelation to us, and not the history of theirs?[17]

Behind those middle sentences lies the image of Moses encountering the divine in a fiery bush that burned but was not consumed (Exodus 3). If back then, why not also now?

In that autumn of 1836, *Nature* was only the first of a remarkable number of Transcendentalist publications. Reviewers found it evocative and inspirational, if rather mystical: more in need of elucidation than refutation. There were other publications from other members of the new group, however, that later that year drew more critical, negative responses. These thwarted Hedge's hope in Channing's spirit to make the new group become one that could truly transcend differences, be "catholic" and inclusive, and bring more reformers together in common cause.

Yet Hedge wanted the group to consist only of clergy and those studying to succeed them. Emerson, having left the pastorate, wanted to define ministry broadly and made a special plea to include the educator Amos Bronson Alcott, then thirty-seven, calling him "a God-ordained priest."[18] Alcott, in fact, was either the source or the inspiration of the enigmatic utterances about spirit with which Emerson had ended *Nature*: thoughts that helped him deal with the death of his brother Charles, and of Ellen. Spiritual friendships were especially needed in the face of grief and loss.

The first meeting of the Transcendentalist circle took place ten days after Emerson's *Nature* appeared, on September 19, 1836, at the house George and Sophia Ripley rented at 3 Bedford Place in Boston. Only ten men were present. Some were even younger than the four organizers, among whom only Putnam was absent. Emerson brought a recent graduate considering the ministry and an undergraduate helping with an American edition of Carlyle's *Sartor Resartus*.[19] Cyrus Bartol, then twenty-three, had just finished at the Divinity School and was about to be called to Boston's West Church. His classmate Theodore Parker, twenty-six, was still seeking a parish. James Freeman Clarke, also twenty-six, was pastor to the Unitarians of Louisville, Kentucky, where he had initiated the *Western Messenger* as a journal of free faith out on the further frontier. Like Hedge, he came to Boston as often as he could.

Ripley had included his friend Orestes Brownson, thirty-three. An imposing man, standing six feet two, he was a distant cousin of Alcott and, like him, quite brilliant but entirely self-educated. Born in Vermont and raised in poverty in upstate New York, he began in Calvinism but soon found the "no-hell" doctrine of the Universalists. They saw his charisma, intelligence, and eloquence, and then ordained him. For a time, he edited one of many Universalist journals. He lost that post by showing less interest in theology than in economic justice. Supporting the Workingmen's Party, he advocated shorter working hours, greater financial security, universal male suffrage, educational opportunities, and an end to debtor imprisonment. When he also supported the Workingmen's radical allies, freethinkers Fanny Wright and Robert Owen, tied in the public mind to free love and socialism, Universalists lost patience with him. Having read Channing's "Likeness to God," Brownson then shifted to the Unitarians but maintained a strong interest in the plight of labor. As pastor of the Unitarian church in Canton, Massachusetts, he gave a July 4 address suggesting that perhaps chattel slavery in the South and industrial wage slavery in the North were not that far apart. Local men of property objected. He resigned. By the time of the meeting at the Ripleys', Brownson was leading a preaching mission to workers in Boston, the Society for Christian Union and Progress. Channing backed him but suspected that he might be too abstract in his thinking to attract many workers. That soon proved to be the case.

Chosen as moderator for the meeting at Ripley's was Convers Francis, the learned, amiable minister in Watertown. At forty, he was the oldest man present. He had endeared himself to the others by publishing a pamphlet on *Christianity as a Purely Internal Principle*; that is, as a faith transcending creeds, forms, and rites to aim at developing personal and social virtue.

What we know about this meeting and those that followed comes from the journals and letters of participants. No one at the meeting served as secretary, nor were there any minutes, dues, or fixed membership. The characterization of the group as a "club" is therefore misleading. As with Channing's group of teachers, a tacit assumption was that hosts and regular participants were free to invite any guest they felt could contribute to a fruitful discussion. Those present agreed to invite other local Unitarian clergy; Dr. Channing and James Walker, editor of the *Christian Examiner*, received explicit mention, while Follen, they knew, would be in New York. The only rule was that "no man should be admitted whose presence excluded any one topic."[20]

Alcott then offered to host the next meeting. He must have felt rather glad to be able to do so. For the moment, with the income from the Temple School, he and his family were not boarders in someone else's home. They had rented an entire house, however modest, at 26 Front Street in Boston.[21] The topic at this second meeting, on October 3, was "American Genius— the causes which hinder its growth." Only the host and the same seven ministers attended, it seems. "The Symposeum," as some called it, was never large. Over the next four years, in twenty-nine meetings, the average attendance was eleven. Clergy leaders attempted to keep the group to a size in which all those present might easily offer at least one good insight. The group met next on October 18 at Brownson's, deliberating "The Education of Humanity," a theme on which he had written a review article.[22] There was evidently a fourth meeting in November but at an unrecorded location on an unrecorded theme. Then none seems to have occurred until the following May.[23]

Winter weather may have been one factor. Yet there is reason to suspect that the autumn meetings did not go well. Brownson irritated some with his brusque intensity, large physical presence, tobacco chewing, and appeals for his failing ministry to the working class.[24] That fall he published his *New Views of Christianity, Society and the Church*.[25] Much of what he said there, others could easily embrace. He offered a critique of contemporary Unitarianism and of current culture as split between empty piety and spirituality on the one hand and privileged materialism on the other, while slighting the material and spiritual needs of the many. He then called for a "Church of the Future" to transcend this division. Yet in speaking of the Gospel as proclaiming Christ as the God-Man bringing the needed healing between the spiritual and the material realms, he also transcended Unitarian ideas in a direction that hinted at his eventual conversion to class-inclusive Roman Catholicism. The Ripleys liked Brownson's economic radicalism, but others found it best to say little about his theology. That winter the issues uniting the Transcendentalists were intellectual attacks against two of them, Ripley and Alcott, as made by Andrews Norton.

In early November 1836, Ripley published a review in the *Christian Examiner* of a book by the English Unitarian James Martineau. In it, he denied any need for miraculous proofs for what the Enlightenment had framed as "the evidences of Christianity." He argued that the moral teachings and spiritual authority of Jesus were simply self-validating. This idea that the authority of Christ did not rest on such suspensions of natural law as his miracles and his resurrection from the dead simply incensed Norton, who fired back not in private, nor to the *Examiner*, but in an open letter published in the *Boston Daily Advertiser*. There he almost dissociated himself entirely from the *Examiner* for having printed Ripley's ideas, which he called "injurious to the cause of religion, because tending to destroy faith in the only evidence on which the truth of Christianity *as a revelation* must ultimately rest."[26] Ripley also published a series entitled *Discourses on the Philosophy of*

Religion. In them, he declared all humanity as "partakers of the Divine Nature," a theme later taken up by Emerson in his "Divinity School Address" and in the radical theology of Theodore Parker.[27] Boston-area Unitarians began to ask one another, "Which side are you on?" With Norton and the authority of biblical miracles, or with those holding such "new views"?

At the very end of 1836, another Transcendentalist publication drew even more scorn from conservatives like Norton. This one came from Bronson Alcott. His Temple School was an experiment in what we today might call "child-centered education," then inspired and supported by Channing. Rather than furnished with hard benches or desks, the classroom was open in the center, used at times for exercise or dance. Around it were comfortable study areas. Conversation replaced lectures; and moral persuasion, physical punishment. If a pupil repeatedly behaved very badly, Alcott might call that child to his desk and ask him to cane his teacher for having failed him. Most, as quite expected, were too ashamed to do so. His students included children of Boston's best families. Channing's daughter Mary was there, as was a son of Chief Justice Lemuel Shaw, a grandson of Josiah Quincy, and other young notables. Elizabeth Peabody, assisting Alcott, kept copious notes and had published *Record of a School: Exemplifying the General Principles of Spiritual Culture* (1835). The next year, however, Alcott, over Peabody's strong objections and warnings, used her notes to publish his own book, *Conversations with Children on the Gospels* (1836).

In it, he showed how he had led students to question whether to take biblical miracles literally; suggested that all human beings are parts of God; considered Jesus an exemplary teacher but as only one among other spiritual guides. One young boy, told that humans are primarily souls, asked where they then get their bodies. Alcott, playing Socrates, asked the boy's own opinion, who then replied, "from the naughtiness of other people." However indirect the allusion to sex, one letter writer in the *Daily Advertiser* criticized Alcott's "flippant and off-hand conversation about serious topics," such as the virgin birth of Jesus and circumcision. Norton called Alcott's book "one-third . . . absurd, one-third blasphemous, and one-third obscene."[28] Families began to withdraw their children. James Freeman Clarke defended Alcott from afar in the *Western Messenger*; and others said he was misunderstood, but this gave little material help. During the late spring of 1837, the financial panic of that year began to deepen the school crisis. Even Channing withdrew his daughter, asking Peabody to become her governess. By the following fall, with only eleven students remaining, the school moved to a smaller room. Then it moved to the Alcott parlor, as a school for children of the poor. The final straw came when Alcott boldly admitted Susan Robinson, a black girl. That did it; the school dissolved. Depressed and destitute, by April 1840, as Channing was effecting his resignation in place with the Federal Street congregation, Alcott felt forced to accept financial assistance from his friend Emerson, and to move his family out to Concord. Channing admired his attempt to combine spiritual life with labor grounded in the earth. He himself was too ill (and privileged) to do anything similar.

The so-called Panic of 1837 initiated a decade-long economic-political crisis in the United States—the first, but hardly the last, in our nation's history.[29] As with most financial crises, it began with unregulated speculation: first an "irrational exuberance," in this case in new cotton fields and field hands to work them, and then in a collapse of credit. President Andrew Jackson had ended the Bank of the United States, the predecessor to the Federal Reserve. This allowed state chartered banks in the South and West to issue currency backed only by their own shaky loans. Many loans were to speculators in new cotton lands in Alabama, Mississippi, Louisiana, Arkansas, and Texas. The rise in land values there also drove up the value of enslaved field hands to work that land. Overproduction then caused the price of cotton to fall, and when British banks saw this, they then called in their loans to American banks. If speculation in subprime mortgages to those unable to repay them led to the global financial crisis of 2007–2008, similar speculation led to the crisis of 1837. As with our recent experience of the Great Recession, it took the US economy a decade to recover from the collapse of an unregulated market.

Among the literati of the Transcendentalist circle, there were two economic reactions. The first was toward a greater emphasis on publishing and lecturing. The intellectuals involved in the circle simply needed the profits and the fees. This lessened the incentive just to converse. Once again,

George Ripley led the way. He initiated *Specimens of Foreign Literature,* a series of European works in translation, most taken from influential French and German writers. He himself could translate French social thinkers such as Victor Cousin and Benjamin Constant, who had inspired both Brownson and himself, but he did not read German well. Neither did Emerson. Hedge was busy in Bangor; Follen, in New York. James Freeman Clarke agreed to translate a German novel by Wilhelm de Wette, *Theodore, or the Skeptic's Conversion,* while Theodore Parker took on de Wette's commentaries on the Hebrew Bible. Margaret Fuller, recently admitted to the Transcendentalist circle, agreed to translate Johann Peter Eckermann's *Conversations with Goethe in His Later Years.*

The Transcendentalist circle first welcomed women to their midst on September 1, 1837, with Emerson serving as the host. He included Fuller, Sarah Alden Bradford Ripley, the learned wife of his uncle Samuel, and Elizabeth Hoar, who had been engaged to his late brother Charles. Five days later, Clarke, hosting at the home of his mother and sister in Newton, included not only his sister, Sarah, but also Fuller, Hoar, and Elizabeth Peabody.[30] These two meetings marked a peak in attendance, with seventeen and fifteen persons, respectively. Some of the participants—Hedge, Follen, Fuller, Clarke, Peabody, Parker, Sarah Ripley—were valued for their facility with German, that literature having inspired the core discussion. Emerson could read German a bit, but preferred translations. Brownson had stopped attending and in launching a periodical, the *Boston Quarterly Review,* offered it as the voice of the Transcendentalist circle. Others, however, distrusted his ability to balance the group's spiritual focus with his own political-social concerns. Hedge had long favored having a group publication, however. Thomas Carlyle, asked to serve as editor from a distance, had declined. The group realized that Margaret Fuller needed an income. She agreed to serve as editor in hope of receiving something. (She never did.) Alcott proposed to call the journal the *Dial,* thinking of the way a sundial uses light to reflect the time and season.

Meanwhile, the general discussions of the Transcendentalist circle, about a spiritual rather than a material approach to philosophy, religion, and education, had devolved in several directions with more practical implications.

One set of discussions, led by George and Sophia Ripley had to do with growing economic inequality, the impact of industrialization, and the need for a new form of community life. A second set of conversations, led by Fuller, reflected the unequal educational, social, and vocational opportunities for women. The third involved the church, the terrible treatment of Channing by his trustees and the tensions in other congregations. Could the church be reformed and morally and spiritually renewed? And if so, how? All three conversations simmered in the winter of 1839–1840, both before and after the death of Charles Follen.

In the fall of 1839, with the support of both Channing and Peabody, Fuller tried to earn something for herself and her family by leading a paid series of "Conversations for Women." They took place at 13 West Street, the new home of the Peabody family. Fourteen women were present, including Peabody and Fuller. Twelve others paid up to twenty dollars each to take part. What Fuller had to offer was a mastery of the Greek and Latin classics known typically only to college-educated men, but not to their wives. In witty, entertaining, yet proper conversation, she used some of the more titillating stories of Greco-Roman myth, such as that of Psyche and Eros, to challenge issues of gender polarity and subordination assumed in Puritan culture. Her goal was to draw out the participants, to encourage them to give voice to their own insights and experience. Ten of the women enjoyed considerable privilege and probably had no difficulty paying the fee. They included Eliza (Mrs. Josiah) Quincy; Elizabeth (Mrs. George) Bancroft; Miss Marianne Cabot Jackson, daughter of Judge Charles Jackson; and Anna (Mrs. John) Park, whose husband had founded the Boston Academy for Young Ladies. Others also came from other prominent and relatively affluent Boston families (Sturgis, Hooper, Shaw, Goddard, Gardner). Two less economically privileged women must have struggled a bit to pay to join in such conversation with the erudite Miss Fuller.

One was Lydia Maria Francis Child.[31] Perhaps the most neglected female Transcendentalist of her whole era, she was the sister of the same Convers Francis who had presided at the first meeting of the Transcendentalist circle at the Ripleys' home. Remembered today, if at all, for a jaunty Thanksgiving Day song, "Over the river and through the woods, to grandfather's house we go." Maria, as she called herself, was, in fact, a more creative and productive intellectual than her ordained brother. They had grown up in Medford, just northwest of Boston, children of the local baker. Exceptionally intelligent, they caught the attention of the local minister. He helped Convers to enter Harvard and to go on to become a minister. Maria, after their mother died, went to live with a married older sister in central Maine to prepare to work as a teacher. There she met and admired some of the few surviving groups of Native Americans in New England. Later, while living with Convers, she read a review article commending the early history of the region as a fruitful source of important fiction. Encouraged by her brother's reaction to a trial chapter, she then completed *Hobomok: A Tale of Early Times* (1824) in just six weeks. The novel sold well, despite challenging the dominant narrative of the inevitable and almost providential erasure of the native population—represented in the same era by James Fenimore Cooper's *The Last of the Mohicans* (1826). Child's story, by contrast, ended with a rather startlingly antiracist, romantic alternative: intermarriage and mixed-race children. She also launched the *Juvenile Miscellany*, America's first periodical for children, and married David Lee Child, a politically active attorney and journalist. Equally idealistic, Child was Quixotic in his choice of clients and causes. He and Maria never had children, which may have been just as well, since he was forever disastrously in debt, twice sued successfully for libel in challenging conservative opponents. She then turned necessity into virtue by publishing *The Frugal Housewife: Dedicated to Those Who Are Not Ashamed of Economy*. Successive editions earned her more than editing, fiction, or essays ever could, much less her antislavery argument, *An Appeal in Favor of That Class of Americans Called Africans*, which so moved Channing.

Not long after participating in Fuller's "Conversations," Maria moved to New York City, to edit the *National Anti-Slavery Standard*. David was nominally the editor, and she his assistant. By this time, however, she had separated from David, both financially and geographically. He remained on a farm in western Massachusetts, futilely trying to launch a domestic sugar beet industry to free Americans from cane sugar grown on slave plantations in Cuba. She relaunched her own literary career with a series of "Letters from New York," first published in the *Standard*. Fuller soon followed her to New York and became both a fellow journalist and spiritual friend.

Another participant in the "Conversations for Women" who, despite a privileged upbringing, may have worried over the fee of twenty dollars, was Sophia Dana Ripley. After the Panic of 1837, George's ministry at Purchase Street was more than a pastor and his wife could easily deal with. The waterfront neighborhood around the church was filling with the poor, the unemployed and the unemployable, women who had turned to prostitution, and hungry children. Their middle-class congregants too often wanted simply to avert their eyes. She and George could not do so. Instead, they initiated a new series of conversations. Once again, no one kept any clear records. The theme was quite clear, however—what to do about growing social and economic inequality? In an era of growing industrialization, economic competition, and increasing immigration, how should good Christians, trying both to preach and to practice the Gospel, try to work for and realize the kingdom of God here on earth? George then began to visit religious communities transcending the model of a local congregation, such as those of the Shakers.

Elizabeth Palmer Peabody was simultaneously facilitating another set of conversations that, for understandable reasons, went on rather quietly. These involved members of Channing's family, his friends, and as many as fifty congregants, all appalled at how the trustees had treated him in the matter of the Follen memorial service. Their questions were parallel to those the Ripleys were raising. Could a religious community be differently organized and better embody the social principles of the Gospel? They were not inclined to leave Boston, however, or help establish an agricultural commune in West Roxbury, as Ripley soon proposed. Yet like the original disciples in an upper room following the death of Jesus, their minds were on fire with a desire to inspire even unknown strangers toward realizing a future church and commonwealth of all here on earth.

PART TWO

Water

Many waters cannot quench love . . .

SONG OF SONGS 8:7

In the first half of the nineteenth century
no aspect of life suffered such cumulative deterioration as did public health . . .
As towns grew, polluted water became an increasingly pressing problem . . .
the cause of many diseases . . . and death.

RICHARD BROWN[1]

1. Bowdoin Sq. Courthouse	6. King's Chapel
2. Faneuil Hall	7. Federal St. Church
3. Boston Music Hall	8. Purchase St. Church
4. Peabody House	9. Hollis St. Church
5. Channing House	10. Child House

Map of Boston, 1842

CHAPTER IV

Dissolution of the Pastoral Relation

*In which an urban church tries to dismiss its activist minister,
another minister leaves his church to found an experimental community,
the Transcendentalist circle dissolves,
and the life of Channing, mentor to reformers, comes to an end.*

IN 1840, THREE BOSTON UNITARIAN MINISTERS were at odds with the leaders of their congregations. The ill-treatment of Channing at the Federal Street Church was a scandal only among his family and friends, thanks to his decision for a quiet resignation-in-place. The discontent of George Ripley with his pastorate and people at the Purchase Street Church had not yet become public. By far the most notorious dispute between a pastor and a congregation's lay leaders was at the nearby Hollis Street Church. John Pierpont, by then the pastor there for two decades, was yet another of Channing's disciples. He was no radical in his theology but had become a strong social reformer, firmly antislavery and an adamant advocate for temperance. The dispute was over his preaching on the latter subject.

*George Ripley (1802–1880)
Circa 1850, photo by Matthew Brady.*

The Hollis Street trustees had leased the cellar of the church as a warehouse for rum dealers. From the pulpit above, Pierpont persistently denounced not only the use of "ardent spirits," and the dissolute behavior stemming from them, but also the complicity of his people in enabling such a nefarious trade. The trustees asked him to stop speaking in a way they found offensive. Pierpont refused, citing a New England pastor's traditional freedom of the pulpit. Claiming their own traditional authority over temporal affairs of the congregation and uses of its meetinghouse, the trustees then called for a church council to resolve the dispute. Among the congregational churches of the Standing Order in Massachusetts, councils of clergy from related churches examined the fitness of candidates for ordination, and advised and presided over installations of new pastors. The parish or the pastor could then call for such a council again if tensions arose. Tradition also assumed that pastoral settlements were ideally for life.[1]

The very idea of storing firewater in the church basement may seem almost comical to us today, but in 1840, it exposed some serious social fault lines. Brahmin Boston always had two distinct sub-castes, intermarried but not always in harmony: the clergy and the merchants. Now they were at odds. Church disestablishment had contributed to the tension. While the First Amendment to the US Constitution prohibited a *national* church establishment, Massachusetts maintained its Standing Order congregational churches, now both Unitarian and Trinitarian, as the established churches of the Commonwealth until 1833—the last state in the Union to end its religious establishment. This can seem astonishing in today's understanding of church-state relations. Yet the loss of publicly collected taxes to support the Standing Order ministers as "public teachers of morality" made parish finances suddenly more dependent on contributions, pew fees, and building rentals. It also made many clergy in the Standing Order more hesitant to say things that might offend their people. But not John Pierpont. He was not about to keep silent about alcohol.

Since the rural Whiskey Rebellion of the 1780s, alcohol use per capita had only increased in America, chiefly in the form of distilled spirits. Urban ministers saw the results clearly: increased public drunkenness, domestic abuse, family dysfunction, poverty, prostitution, and crime. Boston's leading Calvinist evangelist, Lyman Beecher, had cofounded the American Temperance Society in the city in 1826. Some advocates favored total abstention from alcohol: teetotalism and legal prohibition. Compromise, however, centered on temperance, a stance that exposed class divisions in which the wealthy could retain access to their genteel wine and sherry, while denying the poor their grog. Maine's temperance movement, for example, passed a "Fifteen Gallon Law," prohibiting the sale of distilled spirits in any smaller quantity. Only the rich could afford such amounts. Just as in Prohibition, or laws today about access to marijuana or to firearms, class-related antagonisms complicated public debate.

"The Hollis Street Council" became a cause célèbre in Boston church circles. Channing felt strongly that all clergy, not just his protégé, Pierpont, should be free to speak their convictions. He himself advocated temperance. Yet he did not bring his own temperate voice to the council, having surrendered his public ministry to his junior colleague, Ezra Stiles Gannett. The council generally supported Pierpont. It found no reason for any "dissolution of the pastoral relation," as Channing had phrased it in his letter to his own trustees. Not surprisingly, the council also suggested in its report that Brother Pierpont might do well to moderate the tone of his sermons. The result pleased no one. Some wealthy laypeople left the Hollis Street Church. Yet the very suggestion that a minister should ever "prefer expediency to truth," as Hedge had once put it in comments about the Boston ministers, incensed other reform-minded ministers.

Having agreed to the duty before resigning himself, Channing gave the Charge to the Minister at the ordination of a young minister who had trained with Ripley. Like so many Transcendentalist clergy, Ripley himself had been Channing's disciple. As a seminarian, he read everything that Channing had ever written and went to hear him preach whenever possible. That day, his sermon at the ordination, "The Claims of the Age upon an Evangelist," was, in fact, an homage to one Channing had once given— essay-like, ready for publication, but not at all fiery. When his mentor then charged the young minister, he told him to preach with moral courage or not all: "Fear no man, high or low, rich or poor, taught or untaught. Honor all men; love all men; but fear none. Speak what you account great truths frankly, strongly, boldly. Do not spoil them of life to avoid offence. Do not seek to propitiate passion and prejudice by compromise and concession.

Beware of the sophistry, which reconciles the conscience to the suppression, or vague, lifeless utterance of unpopular truth."[2]

That did it. Dissatisfied with his own preaching, not only that day but also at Purchase Street, and aware of how he always felt obliged to be kind rather than courageous in addressing his people, Ripley concluded that—like Emerson and now Channing—perhaps the most courageous thing he could do would be to resign his own pastoral charge. There were just too many "defects to the church now existing," as Emerson had put it in his 1838 Divinity School Address. They could never all be remedied only with "first, soul, and second, soul, and evermore, soul." At least not through his poor soul, and not from the pulpit at Purchase Street. For some time now, he had been more and more discontent with how his largely middle-class congregants retained a sense of superiority over their poorer sisters and brothers, whose misery was apparent in the streets around the downtown church. Yet if he even alluded to such matters, it only exasperated his people. They clearly did not know what to do about increasing economic inequality and urban poverty, and frankly, neither did he. He only knew it was time to find the courage to dissolve his own pastoral relation and to try a new approach to the moral questions most on his conscience.

For almost two years, he had been visiting egalitarian communities based on religious values. Shaker communities in Massachusetts and New York had impressed him with their simplicity, equality, economic success, and commitment to Christian brother- and sisterhood, if not with their demand for celibacy and the separation of the sexes. At a German pietistic community in Zoar, Ohio, he found a better reception than Follen had had at a similar community in Pennsylvania. Ripley admired their commitment to cooperation rather than competition, and to the avoidance of invidious class distinctions. He was still pondering how to combine the Transcendentalist values of creativity and original thinking with communal labor.

Initially, he tried telling lay leaders that he was resigning because of the poor financial condition of the Purchase Street society. When they then tried to keep him by presenting him with a plan to raise more money, he knew that he would have to be more explicit, courageous, and systematic in laying out the reasons behind his decision.[3] He did not want to abuse his spiritual authority by telling others how to think on economic or political matters, but neither was he convinced, as Channing had always seemed to be, that individual reformation, through the church, could bring about all the needed reforms in society. Channing had laid out his theory of social change in his 1838 Franklin Lectures to the Mechanics Institute, made up of the aspiring workingmen of Boston. He spoke of "Self-Culture," by which he said he meant "the care which a man owes to himself, to the unfolding and perfecting of his nature."[4] He himself had helped to initiate several voluntary associations for good causes, but he also had reservations about the role of associations except as a means to the moral mobilization of individuals.[5]

Ripley, by contrast, was increasingly open to experimenting with deeper forms of association, with greater levels of commitment and in potentially far greater spiritual and practical power. The meetings that he and Sophia led on "the social problem" of growing economic inequality are even less well documented and more difficult to reconstruct than the general meetings of the Transcendentalist circle. We do know, however, that Elizabeth Peabody and Rebecca Clarke, mother of James Freeman Clarke, attended at least some. The latter wrote to James about doing so. She had visited him in the West that summer. On returning home, she encountered, quite by chance, a leading advocate for what some now called "Associationism." Albert Brisbane had grown up with some wealth, traveled to Europe, and become a disciple of the French utopian socialist Charles Fourier. Rebecca met him as he was returning from a visit to Robert Owen's utopian community at New Harmony, Indiana. He had with him copies of his new book, *The Social Destiny of Man* (1840). He devoutly believed, as he later put it, that "Association will establish Christianity practically upon Earth. It will make the love of God and the love of the neighbor the greatest desire, and the practice of all men. Temptation to wrong will be taken from the paths of men, and a thousand perverting and degrading circumstances and influences will be purged from the social world."[6] He gave Rebecca a copy of his book. She then shared it with Ripley.

He composed a lecture and wrote an open letter to his congregation. He said that his duty as a Christian minister required him to become "hostile to all oppression of man by man," and to show that "his sympathies are with the down-trodden and the suffering poor." He again chastised them for the class distinctions shown in their own social lives, describing a true Christian church as a "band of brothers who attach no importance whatever to the petty distinctions of birth, rank, wealth, and station." He regretted the sale of pews and declared that he desired a church in which "we should offer a more spiritual worship, enjoy a more sincere communion . . . even if we came together, as the disciples did, in a large upper room . . . or by the shore of the sea. The minister should [then] take his stand where he can freely speak all that is in his soul . . . The basis of worship in such a church would be feeling, not speculation; the platform would be broad enough to welcome every seeking spirit."[7]

Not long thereafter, the Transcendentalist circle convened twice more, then dissolved. Theodore Parker served as the host on September 2, 1840, in West Roxbury.[8] The final meeting took place just a week later at Elizabeth Peabody's home on West Street. The topic at both meetings was church reform: Is it even possible? If so, what is necessary? Might some entirely new form of community better serve? Peabody reported on the discussions in a long letter to John Sullivan Dwight, at whose ordination in Northampton Ripley and Channing had spoken. Peabody reported that Ripley had given up on reforming the church as an institution. Nothing could redeem it. Like the corrupt, soul-destroying, money-grubbing society it had far too often condoned and blessed, he proclaimed it "vicious in its foundations." Hedge, on the other hand, she said, "eloquently defended the Church." He admitted that "the social principle was yet to be educated—the Church of Humanity yet to grow." Yet if its ministers themselves were to lay waste the historic church, to try to build on the ruins, there would be no living trunk left on which to graft the renewed spirituality so clearly needed. The church of the future, of course, must emerge, "but as another branch from the same trunk."[9]

This argument for historical continuity was striking in a group whose early theme was the need for a break with tradition. Theodore Parker wrote in his journal that Hedge's argument seemed "wedded to the past." He, too, loved the old but "would as soon wed my grandmother whom I love equally well."[10] Emerson almost agreed with both. Despite his preference for *individuals* to break from past models—a theme in his Divinity School Address that would soon reappear in his essay "Self-Reliance" (1841)—he too was done with discussing church reform. He wrote Peabody that if people were "democratized & made kind & faithful," there would be no need to be "always laying the axe at the root of this or that vicious institution."[11] It was then clear that the three initiators of the Transcendentalist circle—Ripley, Emerson, and Hedge—had no further shared interest in any general discussion concerning the role of institutional religion in social change. No two of the three "like-minded" now thought enough alike to be able to go on. With that last meeting at 13 West Street, the group dissolved.

The breakup of the Transcendentalist circle followed the launching of the *Dial* in the summer of 1840, but the new journal was not its cause. It too suffered from the disagreements. Ripley was busy founding Brook Farm. Emerson had expressed interest in that project, but he ultimately declined to join or invest in it. Hedge remained a stalwart churchman. Despite great affection for Fuller, he told her not to expect him to write much for her, since he did not want to be associated with those who had given up on historic Christianity, and the hope of the church continually reforming itself. His 1841 Phi Beta Kappa address at Harvard, "Conservatism and Reform," argued that the vocation of the church was to conserve that part of culture without which further reform could not take place. That disappointed Transcendentalists like Emerson. He then went on to teach church history, to provide the best-known English translation of Luther's reformation hymn ("*Ein Feste Burg*," rendered as "A Mighty Fortress"), and to call for "oecumenical" cooperation among Christians transcending differences in doctrine—perhaps the first use of that term in its modern sense. He did ultimately send Fuller a few new poems to print. She found herself begging the very men who had launched the journal to write for it. The *Dial* then disappointed even Channing. It became more literary than either religious or reformist.

In the winter of 1840, however, some members of the Transcendentalist circle were not giving up on church reform, Elizabeth Peabody chief among them. As she hosted the last meeting of the group, she found that she agreed with Ripley on "the social principle" as central to the teachings of Jesus but not about giving up on the church. There, she was closer to Hedge. As for Emerson, well, she had long worried that he was too much of a privileged individualist. The person whose comments at those last meetings of the Transcendentalist circle had most impressed her was Theodore Parker, whose "deep organ-like voice" had come in now and then with an apt sentence in support of both sides. She had gone to hear him preach a sermon that would later appear in the *Dial* and "again the deep music of his earnest voice moved me as I am seldom moved. He is really inspired. . . . He proves that the 'organization' yet admits a living spirit—& that God yet visits his church."[12]

Peabody had already begun conversations with unhappy members of Federal Street about the same theme taken up at the final gatherings of the Transcendentalist circle: "the organization of a new church," one transcending differences in social class. Channing and even Gannett both supported experiments in that direction. Channing saw Brownson's "Christian Union" mission trying to spread the liberal gospel beyond Boston's well-heeled Brahmins. When that effort failed, Brownson began doing three things at once. He defended Transcendentalism, asking Andrews Norton, in an essay in the *Quarterly*, how, without a direct intuition of the divine available to all, his historical-critical approach to Christianity could be possible for anyone outside of an intellectual elite. Second, in the same issue, he defended "The Laboring Classes" in terms that both rejected Channing's idea of "Self-Culture" and almost anticipating Karl Marx. Finally, he saw himself as defending democracy itself by supporting the Democratic Party and the reelection of President Martin Van Buren. The conservative Whigs, much like Republicans in 2016, had found a candidate more populist than the incumbent, Van Buren. General William Henry Harrison, victor over a coalition of Native Americans led by Tecumseh at the Battle of Tippecanoe (1811), had John Tyler, a slave-owning former Democratic senator from Virginia, as his running mate. When the Whigs then won, Brownson began to give up on electoral politics, even on democracy and Transcendentalism, and then to turn toward Roman Catholicism.

Other Transcendentalists also wondered how to transcend the gap between manual labor and the so-called educated "elites" (often also poorly paid) in creative and cultural production. This included even Channing. When Alcott closed his school and moved to Concord, he wrote to Peabody:

> One of my dearest ideas is the union of *labor* and *culture*. The present state of things, by which the highest and almost the only blessings of life are so often denied to those who bear its heaviest burdens, is sad, and must be changed. I wish to see labor honored and united with the free development of the intellect and the heart. Mr. Alcott hiring himself out for day labor, and at the same time living in a region of high thought, is perhaps the most interesting object in our Commonwealth.[13]

Yet when Brownson's concern for "the masses" went on to condemn the very structure of modern society, including inherited property, banks, monopolies, and even wage labor, Channing called it "absurd" and likely to set off such class warfare as would leave everyone in "universal poverty and woe." He was sorry that a onetime protégé, Brownson, had so easily "thrown away" his potential influence with such a publication. By supporting the 1840 Democratic Party, despite its enmeshment with what we today would call white supremacy, Channing also saw that the Whigs he was trying to convert to antislavery would use this intemperate tract for partisan purposes. In that, he proved correct. Van Buren went so far as to blame his defeat on being associated with Brownson's anticapitalist radicalism.

If Brownson began to turn away from politics after 1840, Channing now used his role as a "public teacher of religion and morality" more freely outside the pulpit, despite his failing health. He had felt too unwell to deliver his second lecture to the Mechanics Association and had sent it to be read for him. He was now working with his younger brother, George Gibbs Channing, to collect, edit, and publish the best of his writings, just as he had advised Eliza Follen to do with her late husband's writings. He also told her that he had begun a new lecture on antislavery with the title *Emancipation*.[14] "Not that I expect it to be heard very widely," as he wrote in its introduction. "No one knows, more than I do, the want of popularity of the subject." Elizabeth Peabody was to publish it. He now declared that "the idea of Human Rights, that great idea of our age, and on which we profess to build our institutions, is darkened, weakened, among us" by the complicity with slavery. He encouraged more women to become involved in the issue, to see it as an "intolerable evil, because its chief victims are women." He also made a more explicit political statement than ever about the "duties of the free states" in relation to slavery. The North should flatly refuse to return fugitive slaves. He also called for amendments of the federal Constitution, and for the abolition of slavery in the District of Columbia. The federal government should also repent of having opened its unsettled territories to slavery. It should refuse to support the claims of slaveholders against foreign governments. Previous generations had carried on slavery in willful blindness. New light had come to reveal the horrors of slavery: "the sacked and burning villages, the kidnapping and murders of Africa" and "the crowded hold, the chains, stench, suffocation, burning thirst, and agonies of the slave-ship." He spoke of "the enormous waste of life" in the Middle Passage, of the "wrongs and sufferings of the plantation, with its reign of terror and force, its unbridled lust, its violation of domestic rights." He praised Britain for having emancipated nearly a million slaves and said that "the first results have exceeded the hopes of philanthropy." Then he concluded, "To shut our eyes against all this light; to shut our ears and hearts against these monitions of God . . . this, surely, is a guilt which the justice of God cannot wink at, and on which insulted humanity, religion, and freedom call down fearful retribution."[15] *Emancipation*, this final jeremiad, to Channing's surprise, and Peabody's, sold out quickly. His role as the conscience of Boston grew even larger. He had long counseled and encouraged those seeking to ameliorate various forms of social injustice.

One was his parishioner and friend Dorothea Dix.[16] When Channing's poor health in 1831 required a winter rest in the Virgin Islands, Dix came along as governess to the children. The approach of the British to ending slavery in the Caribbean then took hold in his thinking. Once back in Boston, Dix suffered a depressive crisis tied to her need for a meaningful vocation. She gradually began to find one in ending another form of slavery: the abuse, exploitation, and neglect of the mentally ill, intellectually challenged, and indigent. A Unitarian student minister had tried to teach a class for women in the Charlestown jail, and felt he had failed. Dix took over, quickly seeing that many of those incarcerated were there not for crimes but only because they were unable to care for themselves due to some mental handicap. Channing and others arranged for her to spend a year with reformers in Britain. Her Unitarian hosts there, the Rathbone family, acquainted her with new and more humane approaches to the care of the mentally ill. After her return in 1840, Dix spent a year inspecting nearly every jail and poorhouse in Massachusetts. Most towns, she found, dealt with those unable to care for themselves by contracting with farmers to board them. The system was underfunded, unregulated, and rife with abuse. Many of the mentally ill and disabled were treated like slaves, if not worse. In early 1841, she prepared a fiery report or "memorial" to the legislature, declaring, "I proceed, Gentlemen, briefly to call your attention to the *present* state of Insane Persons confined within this *Commonwealth,* in *cages, stalls, pens! Chained, naked, beaten with rods,* and *lashed* into obedience."[17] Eventually she went on to replicate this advocacy for the mentally ill in nearly every other state in the Union, and took part in the founding or the expansion of some thirty public hospitals for the mentally ill. So respected was she for her even-handed humanitarian work that during the Civil War, as superintendent of army nurses for the Union Army, she was more than once allowed to cross enemy lines. Considered the founder of the American mental health movement, Dix was just one of the many social reformers inspired by Channing.[18]

That spring Channing traveled to Philadelphia to address the Mercantile Library Company there on "The Present Age." He emphasized the urgency of people coming together to advocate for and effect social reform. "Associated benevolence," he now declared,

gives eyes to the blind and ears to the deaf . . . Benevolence now shuts out no human being, however low, from its regard. It goes to the cell of the criminal with words of hope, and is laboring to mitigate public punishment to make it the instrument, not of vengeance, but reform. It remembers the slave, pleads his cause with God and man, recognizes in him a human brother, respects in him the sacred rights of humanity, and claims for him, not as a boon, but as a right, that freedom without which humanity withers and God's child is degraded into a tool or a brute.[19]

On the same trip, he preached for the Unitarians of Philadelphia a carefully prepared discourse on "The Church."[20] A true church, he said, "according to its true idea and purpose, is an association of sincere, genuine followers of Christ." It is also wide and embracing of differences, such that "no man can be excommunicated from it but by himself, by the death of goodness in his own breast." Forms and doctrines, rituals and traditions, may vary but should never be reason for Christians to refuse fellowship or cooperation with one another in the doing of good works: "We must shun the spirit of sectarianism as from hell." He also argued that the need for effective yet humble spiritual leadership is central. Channing returned to the Federal Street pulpit only once, at the insistence of his successor Gannett, for his sixty-second birthday, on the Sunday following Easter in 1842. This time, his text was from 2 Cor 4:18: "While we look not at the things which are seen, but at the things which are not seen: for the things which are seen are temporal; but the things which are not seen are eternal." He was increasingly thinking of the church as only an imperfect aid to the cultivation of the character of Christ, whose true disciples must learn to follow in his faithfulness unto death.[21]

That summer, he gave his last public address, "delivered at Lenox on the first of August, 1842, being the anniversary of emancipation in the British West Indies."[22] His hosts, the Sedgwicks, thought him vigorous and in good spirits as he ended by saying, "Mighty powers are at work in the world. Who can stay them? God's word has gone forth, and 'it cannot return to him void.' A new comprehension of the Christian spirit,—a new reverence for humanity, a new feeling of brotherhood, and of all men's relations to the common Father,—this is among the signs of our times. We see it; we feel it. Before this all oppressions are to fall."[23] Weeks later, while visiting Bennington, Vermont, he suddenly fell deadly ill. His murmured last words were, "I've received many messages from the spirit."[24]

At the start of his memorial service, all the church bells in Boston solemnly tolled—including those of Catholic churches—because Channing did the same when Bishop Cheverus died, and because he, almost alone among Boston clergy, had condemned the mob attack on the Ursuline convent in Charlestown back in 1834. Gannett gave the eulogy. He had inherited the leadership at Federal Street. Among Channing's many ministerial disciples, however, two others would divide the larger role that he had played in Boston religious life. Theodore Parker, Elizabeth Peabody's "organ-toned" favorite preacher, would succeed him as Boston's leading preacher of progressive and prophetic religion. Yet the disciple who most embodied Channing's inclusiveness, pastoral patience, and determination to combine social reform with a commitment to historic continuity in the church was James Freeman Clarke, the young minister who had first invited Peabody into the Transcendentalist circle. By the time Channing died, he had organized, in her home, the Church of the Disciples. Clarke was then thirty-one and back in Boston after seven years of spreading progressive religion west of the Appalachians.

*Margaret Fuller as a young
woman, sketch by James
Freeman Clarke*

*Young James Freeman Clarke,
sketch by his sister, Sarah*

CHAPTER V

Affection and Vocation

In which a deep spiritual friendship between
Margaret Fuller and James Freeman Clarke develops
and persists despite distance and differences in vocation.

THE TRANSCENDENTALISTS FELT that only by helping others realize their spiritual, moral, and creative potential can one fulfill one's own potential, or develop more egalitarian social relations. Spiritual friendship was central to their ideals and method. Margaret Fuller and James Freeman Clarke had the epitome of such a friendship. It began when they were both only twenty years old, studying together. It outlasted their separation by distance, their marriages to others, and even Fuller's tragic death in a shipwreck twenty years later, with her infant son and his Italian father. Clarke would then help to salvage her public reputation, her literary legacy, and her witness for the freedom and equality of women.

The sketch that he made of Margaret in her young adulthood seems somewhat idealized. Undeniably brilliant intellectually and engaging as a conversationalist, she herself often felt homely and awkward. No one ever considered her a beauty. She was gangly and a bit bent over, suffering from scoliosis. The sketch of young Clarke by his sister Sarah makes him look heavy-eyed, insecure, and pensive. This may be accurate for periods of his young adulthood. Yet it does not reflect his robust athleticism as a youth nor the self-confidence that Fuller helped him to find, much less his mature dignity as a leading Unitarian minister, popularizing the emerging field of comparative religion.[1]

In the spring of 1830, however, James and Margaret were young romantics. They read German together, studying Goethe especially. They walked along the banks of the Charles River near the Fuller home. They rode horseback to Newton to have tea with Clarke's grandparents. They went together to parties hosted by Harvard professors. They corresponded or met almost daily. James then went back to his room at Divinity Hall after these encounters with Margaret and tried to set down, almost verbatim, in his "Journal of Understanding," her piercing, challenging, even coquettish remarks. It begins with an entry dated May 9 that gives the flavor:

J. I do not wish to come here when I have no ideas to tell you when my mind is vacant.

M. But do you feel it necessary to tell me ideas; why not be as you feel?

J. I do not feel it wanting to my own comfort, but I do not wish to be such an unsatisfactory and unprofitable visitor to you—to take your time from pleasanter occupations.

M. Ah! Now you deceive yourself. Why do you veil your motives in so pretty a dress [?]

J. Do you think that it cannot be the true motive?

M. Yes! I do not believe in such disinterestedness. Tell me the truth. Is my talking too much for you?

J. No, I should be gratified always with silently listening to you, but I think it too unequal—yet here I suppose you will doubt of my sincerity.

M. Yes. Do you come because you think I expect you [?] I do not. I expect you to consult your own wishes.[2]

Margaret enjoyed entertaining Harvard students like Clarke and showing that she was, if anything, more adept at conversation, more erudite, and wiser than they. Her father had transferred some of his high standards and ambitions to his eldest child.

Timothy Fuller was the son of a minister who had responded to the American Revolution by going into politics. The son used his Harvard education to study law and then to do the same, representing the Middlesex district of Massachusetts in the US House of Representatives for four terms,

1817–1825. He helped to vote John Quincy Adams into the presidency in the first election not decided in the Electoral College, but in the House. He then returned to state politics and briefly became Speaker of the Massachusetts House. Hoping for appointment to a diplomatic post in Europe, he moved his family from their modest home in Cambridgeport to the Dana mansion in the fashionable area west of the college to give a ball there for the new president. Adams attended but left early, without dancing, then still grieving the recent death of his father. No diplomatic post resulted for Fuller.

He had long encouraged his eldest child in learning languages, as if she were a son preparing for college. When she was not yet four, and when she and her mother were mourning the sudden death of a baby sister, he wrote home, "My love to the little Sarah Margarett. [Tell her] I love her if she is a good girl & learns to read."[3] By six, she had started Latin, and by eight, she could recite Virgil. By her teens, she had dropped the name Sarah, and learned to "read a book, rock a cradle, and peel an apple," while helping her mother (also named Margarett, with two *t*'s, one of which the daughter also dropped) to cope with her younger siblings. Only one, Ellen, ten years younger than Margaret, was a girl, leaving five brothers in need of care, lessons, and supervision.[4] The only customary path out of the paternal household was through marriage; but by the age of twenty, Margaret was already beginning to wonder if that were even possible.

For a time, a Harvard classmate of Clarke's, George Davis, showed an interest in her, and she reciprocated. The courtship went as far as him writing to inquire about her religious beliefs. In that era, this inquiry signaled a man's intention to propose marriage. Not only did suitors aim to assure parents of a proposed partner's piety but also to assure themselves. The assumption was that if the potential bride knew enough of her own faults, and of God's blessings toward her, to have turned toward Christ, then perhaps she would regard *him* as another sign of God's favor. Margaret candidly told Davis that she was "singularly barren of illusions" in matters of faith, and unwilling to have her deepest "feelings soothed" by any doctrine.[5] Davis never replied to her. After graduating, he left Cambridge without even saying goodbye—going on to a career in law, marriage, financial success, and even a term in Congress.

James could commiserate with her. He, too, had been frustrated in a romantic attraction—to a friend of Margaret's named Elizabeth Randall. The beautiful but haughty daughter of a prosperous Boston physician, she had alternated between accepting his professions of affection and paying him no more mind than she did any of her many other young suitors. James quarreled with her but quickly wrote a note of apology. When she did not reply, he spoke to Margaret about what to do. She advised letting the relationship die. What she did *not* confess was that she herself had intercepted the note. Randall had never received it, because Margaret had decided, unilaterally, both that her friend was not worthy of Clarke, and that he was in no way yet ready for marriage. Interestingly, when this later emerged, he accepted that her judgment was sound.[6]

His own childhood had made him sensitive to the feelings of strong women. His mother, Rebecca, was the child of General William Hull—a Revolutionary War veteran turned lawyer and politician who had the misfortune to be governor of Michigan Territory at the start of the War of 1812. His surrender of Fort Detroit to British forces led to his court-martial. Convicted, but pardoned by President Madison, he retired to a family farm outside Boston, in Newton. Rebecca felt very strongly that her father had been misjudged.[7] Eventually, she met and married Samuel Clarke, the stepson of James Freeman, minister of King's Chapel in Boston. When their third child, named for his step-grandfather, was born, Samuel was studying medicine at Dartmouth. Sam Clarke, however, never successfully established himself as a physician but instead opened a pharmacy near his stepfather's church.

James Freeman had helped make King's Chapel a unique religious body: Anglican in worship, in using a form of the Book of Common Prayer; Congregational in polity, in having ordained him with no bishop involved; and Unitarian in theology, having replaced references to the Trinity with verses from scripture. Despite leading a church in central Boston, Freeman loved country life. Except in the winter, he lived on a farm in Newton. The Hulls and the Clarkes both lived nearby. When Samuel opened his pharmacy, the younger James remained with the grandfather whose name he shared. As he recalled later in life, "it is an infinite blessing when little children grow up in a church which teaches them that God is, in his essence, not wrath, but love."[8] He also praised the role of nature in shaping his Transcendentalism: "Happy child! The roof of whose school room is the blue heaven with its drifting clouds, and mellow tints of sunrise, and glories of evening; whose bench is the soft grass, the gray stone, the limb of the apple-tree; whose books are all illustrated with moving, living forms, waving trees, dewy leaves, wild flowers, all varieties of birds and insects and fishes and animals, how fast he learns!—finding 'tongues in trees, books in the running brooks, sermons in stones, and good in everything.'"[9]

The grandfather also tutored young James by taking cues for the day's instruction from the boy's own questions, giving him the run of his library, and starting him on the basics of mathematics and the classical languages he would need for admission to college. At ten, James moved into Boston to attend the Latin School there and live with his parents. Yet his mother's frustrations with his father's failures in business made his grandparents' home a wonderful refuge during holidays and vacations. Just as he was to enter Harvard, his grandfather retired from ministry. Before turning his role at the chapel over to an associate, he helped to organize, on May 25, 1825, the American Unitarian Association—to support liberal missions and tracts promoting "pure Christianity."

Starting Harvard at fifteen—an age then typical—James was athletic, good-looking, outgoing, yet inwardly insecure. Classmates raised in clergy families became lifelong friends. Oliver Wendell Holmes was the son of the orthodox minister of the First Church in Cambridge. The future physician, poet, and author of the essays, *The Autocrat of the Breakfast Table*, later became a Unitarian himself, at King's Chapel.[10] William Henry Channing was the handsome, earnest nephew of Dr. Channing.[11] Like Clarke, he too became a Transcendentalist minister, today also much neglected. Among their teachers, James especially followed Charles Follen. What drew him most were the outdoor gymnastics exercises. These centered on a seventy-foot mast supported by guy wires, with a platform halfway up reached by a ladder, below a knotted rope for the bold to climb to a tiny disk at the summit. Clarke enjoyed proving that he could climb the mast and then balance himself at the very top. He also played sports; went hunting, fishing, and riding; and studied German. Only as a senior did he begin to think much about choosing a vocation. He had read Coleridge, whose transcendental philosophy clearly regarded "the religious affections" as part of higher, intuitive reason, as opposed to mere understanding. Then, suddenly, the issue of a profession became urgent.

His father had risked all of the family funds to buy a gristmill in Newton and transform it into a factory for bleaching beeswax and producing pharmaceuticals. In doing so, he also let the insurance lapse. When fire struck, everything was lost. Rebecca Clarke had already resorted to operating a boardinghouse in downtown Boston, aided by James's older sister Sarah. While Sam and Sam Jr., the eldest Clarke child, worked at rebuilding the mill. James realized that he now needed clear plans to earn his own living. His grandfather's role as a minister seemed daunting, but Follen, his favorite teacher, was now also at the Divinity School. He doubted that he was pure enough for the pulpit, since his feelings for Elizabeth Randall felt more carnal than spiritual. He also doubted himself as a leader. Yet Margaret encouraged him, despite her own skepticism about doctrinal religion.

Spiritual life of the kind that they had come to share transcended that. The bond between them only seemed to deepen as they also both confronted the grief that flesh is heir to.

First, Margaret's youngest brother, Edward, born in 1829—placed in her special care—died of unknown causes, despite her efforts to be a second mother to him. Then, Samuel Clarke Jr. barely survived a fever and seemed paralyzed. Rebecca and Sarah cared for him in the boardinghouse, while James suspended his studies to find work. The Fullers helped, finding him a teaching position at a private Cambridgeport grammar school that they had started.

Yet that winter, he somehow felt strangely content. "*Travaillons sans raisoner*," says a young man in Voltaire's *Candide*, "*c'est le seul moyen de rendre la vie supportable.*" "Let us work without trying to understand; that is the only means to make life bearable." He and Margaret had discussed this. They heard in it a biblical verse that Goethe deemed his favorite: "Whatsoever thy hand findeth to do, do it with thy might; for there is no work, nor device, nor knowledge, nor wisdom, in the grave, whither thou goest."

(Ecclesiastes 9:10 KJV) Whenever he had a break from teaching, James tried to visit his father, who had a room at the Freemans' while working to rebuild the mill in Newton. On one such visit in November, when he was alone with his father, Sam Clarke, only fifty-one, had a massive stroke and died. It fell to James to break the news to his mother and siblings. When he arrived at the boardinghouse unexpectedly, Rebecca asked if his father was now better. He could only mutter, "Worse." She read the truth on his face, turned, went up the stairs, shut the door to her room, and began sobbing. He then went to fetch the minister, leaving Sarah to convey the full details.

Margaret herself disliked most ministers and even going to church, easily finding fault with the sermons and with outward piety. On Thanksgiving Day 1831, her father made her come along and sit in the family pew. She obeyed but despised demanded gratitude when she felt both ambitious and hopeless about her future. Leaving the church, she ran in the twilight into a grove, thinking of how often she had asked what it meant for her to be herself, with no clear answer. Then a clear revelation came to her: "I saw that there was no self; that selfishness was all folly," she phrased it in her journal, "that I had only to live in the idea of the ALL, and all was mine."[12] This moment of enlightenment, almost Buddhist in tone, prompted her also to give thanks for her "communion with the soul of things."[13] Hurrying home, she stopped in the churchyard to pray. What she most wanted, however, was not so much acceptance as a vocation. In living her life, she wanted it *all*—not just insight, but a way to add to life. For *that*, she might sacrifice "self," but not for less.

James had *his* vocation. She heard him preach his trial sermon at the church in Waltham, on the text from Ecclesiastes. She thought well of his effort. He, on the other hand, felt that he had said in one sermon all he knew. They had different casts of mind, Margaret's like a grasshopper, he felt, able to gather its energy and then make great leaps, his own cautious, more like a daddy longlegs, making one tentative step, then another. He considered nearby Unitarian churches seeking new pastors. Most seemed either difficult or dull. Margaret agreed. He then decided to try a leap of faith. He would be ordained as an "evangelist" and go as a liberal missionary to the growing West. There was a new Unitarian group in Louisville.

The first minister had fallen ill. Clarke agreed to go there. Not that he expected success. After all, men, if not women, could always change their direction or vocation, as his father had.

Margaret's father was another case in point. His political career over, and hating law practice, he sold the Dana mansion. His new plan was to become a gentleman farmer in rural Groton. The Fullers moved just before James left for his new ministry. He called to say goodbye, shared his trepidation, and found Margaret grieving the social and intellectual life of Cambridge. With her mother depressed, she now had to run the entire household and teach all of her siblings. After the leave-taking, their correspondence became intense. Reading and writing when she could, she told James that she had no one with whom to discuss matters beyond the commonplace. He asked her to keep a journal and send it to him; he would do likewise.[14]

He too felt lonely. One early letter included this striking confession:

My courage is oozing out at the ends of my fingers . . . In the midst of my sermon yesterday half a dozen women got up and walked out. And the whole congregation did not amount to thirty, and I was convinced from first to last that my words were falling like water on a rock . . . I was sure that not a soul there felt anything but tedium from what I was saying. And yet, it was necessary that I should go on, putting my whole heart into it, and shouting at the top of my voice. How could I? The whole was a complete failure . . . But as to giving up, I dream not of it . . . I wonder how this letter will strike you. Will it degrade me in your eyes? If it does, so be it.[15]

She replied, "'Degrade yourself in my eyes'—why should you think it probable—possible? I will to see you with your feelings *controlled* but not *subdued*."[16] She began sketching out sermons for him. He wrote, "You envy me my situation without which your powers are useless. I envy you your abilities without which I cannot fulfill the demands of my situation. You are the Bengal tiger confined in a cage to leap over a broomstick for the amusement of staring clowns. I am a broken-wing hawk, seeking to fly at the sun, but fluttering in the dust."[17]

As she began to write essays, rejected by the *Christian Examiner*, he tried to assure her that she had found her vocation in writing. She replied in anger, as if he were trying to limit her. She still wanted it *all*: a life as both a writer and more. In order to write a biography of Goethe, who had just died at eighty-two, she needed to go to Europe. Without crossing the Atlantic to visit Weimar and to talk to those influenced by him, how could she ever do that? She then contracted typhoid fever. Her father worried, but after her crisis passed, Timothy Fuller became feverish too. Having worked to drain a wet field, he had contracted not just typhoid but cholera. Dying suddenly at fifty-five, with no will, he left his tangled financial affairs in the hands of his brother Abraham, tightfisted and unsympathetic to young women and their literary ambitions. That ended, for now, Margaret's dream of going to Europe. Like James after his brother's illness and his father's death, she now needed work.

At first, she replaced Peabody in teaching French and Latin at the Temple School. Then Alcott's candid *Conversations with Children* caused the school to collapse. She defended his integrity and methods. So did Clarke, in the *Western Messenger*, the journal he ran, along with Unitarian colleagues in the West, "devoted to religion, life, and literature."[18] As Fuller moved to the progressive Greene Street School in Providence, Rhode Island, Clarke helped to confirm her calling as a writer by publishing her first critical essays. Emerson also contributed. So did Clarke's Louisville congregant George Keats—the brother of the poet—who contributed some of his brother's unpublished prose and poetry.

Then in 1837, as the financial panic hit, Clarke made a serious error as a young pastor. He did not stay in Louisville that summer, but rather returned to Boston, as he had every year. He was seeking money for the *Messenger* and to reconnect with friends in the Transcendentalist circle formed a year before, asking them to provide more content. He had a young Unitarian colleague substitute for him in his absence. When he returned, that minister said he had heard complaints—that Clarke was gone too often; gave too much time to the *Messenger*; needed to work more on his sermons; sometimes neglected calling; the church was not growing rapidly, while Louisville was; and so on—as well as great affection for Clarke personally.

That fall, before the church's annual meeting, a proposal emerged to cut his salary. Clarke then wrote a letter of resignation. His friends, led by George Keats, intervened. The congregation voted to reject his resignation and ask him to stay, leaving his salary intact. He agreed. He had more to learn from friends and congregants in Louisville.[19]

Keats hosted an influential salon and chaired the local Louisville lyceum. He and his wife, Georgina, were nominally Anglicans, but became Unitarians out of admiration for Clarke. Like many others, Keats hated slavery but felt trapped in it. With a shortage of white labor, he had felt forced to lease slaves from their owners to work in his sawmill and other enterprises. There was also Judge John Speed, who had an estate outside Louisville, built in Jeffersonian style for a wife whose grandfather had been guardian to young Thomas Jefferson. Speed admired Jefferson most for the Northwest Ordinance of 1787, banning slavery north of the Ohio. Now, like many Kentuckians, he followed Henry Clay in calling for a gradual end to slavery south of the river as well, through voluntary or compensated emancipation and resettlement or aid for freed slaves. He opposed any expansion of slavery, yet felt a duty to his family—his eleven children, field hands, and servants—to wait for God to show the way to freedom. One of his sons, Joshua, on reaching twenty-one, left for Springfield, Illinois, and in 1835 opened a store and a newspaper, sharing his room above the store with another native of Kentucky, a lawyer named Abraham Lincoln, who also admired Clay.

Clarke was more ambivalent about Clay, "the great compromiser." He agreed with Channing, who in 1837 published an open letter to Clay urging him to oppose the annexation of Texas if he truly opposed the expansion of slavery.[20] Two years later, when Clay gave a speech on the Senate floor, telling the North to stop agitating the issue of slavery, Channing wrote another public letter, claiming the moral right and duty of all citizens to speak against slavery.[21] Like Channing, Clarke considered immediate abolition, without compensation or transition, both unlikely and impractical. He had also lost faith in his ability to end slavery through persuasion, but not in his ideals. What he most lost was public support for the *Messenger*. Some thought its stance too antislavery; others, not enough so. Was its purpose to bring the Unitarian argument against Calvinism to the frontier, or something broader? Defending Alcott, and then Emerson's Divinity School Address, not only lost him Unitarian supporters in the East but also made subscribers in the West ask for more focus on *their* religious issues.

Religious issues on the Western frontier were as tense and dramatic as North-South issues about slavery. They had been ever since the revivals of 1804 at Kentucky's Cane Ridge. Those helped to spark "the Second Great Awakening" in American spirituality. One drive was to transcend sectarian distinctions (Presbyterian, Methodist, Baptist, etc.) and unite directly with the spirit of Christ, restoring the inclusiveness of the early church. Another increased sectarian competition about how best to do that. Unitarians, saying with Priestley that *The Corruptions of Christianity* began with the Trinitarian creeds, resonated with the "Restorationists" in aiming to restore the simple faith and egalitarianism of Christ's earliest disciples. A Restorationist group known as "the Christian Connexion" also had migrated west from New England. Yet as the Restorationists evolved in the West as "Campbellites," under the leadership of Alexander Campbell, they soon became a new denomination, grounded in biblical authority, the Apostles' Creed, believers' baptism, and communion presided over by duly ordained clergy. Clarke admired their inclusive name, "Disciples of Christ."

As he assessed his own spiritual life, Clarke realized that he needed a partner in ministry, a wife. His Unitarian colleague in the West, William Greenleaf Eliot, out in St. Louis, Missouri, certainly had a fine one.[22] He confessed his loneliness to Margaret, as he had years before, even as they comforted one another with hand touches, caresses, and words of endearment—all while recognizing that she could never agree to be a minister's spouse. Teaching in Providence, Margaret kept up her Transcendentalist faith by starting each day reading, not from scripture, but rather from Alcott's *Conversations with Children on the Gospels.* Yet she too felt very lonely. Not only was her work poorly paid and exhausting, but her recent romantic life had crushed her.

Samuel Gray Ward, seven years her junior, handsome and wealthy, and a would-be Transcendentalist, had paid admiring attentions to her. Margaret was then devastated when he transferred his affections to her beautiful young friend Anna Hazard Barker. This was especially hard since she had also felt a love for Anna that she had only been able to discuss with intimates like James. What the younger couple had together, she knew, was what she and James lacked—economic security. Sam Ward stood to inherit his father's lucrative role as the US agent for Barings Bank of London. Anna was the child of a wealthy merchant. When James went to Providence in 1838 to visit her, Margaret spoke of all this, and the more she said, the more her bitterness appeared. He had always before been open with her. Now he could not tell her that he had met his own Anna, and that she, too, came from a wealthy family.

Anna Huidekoper lived in Meadville, Pennsylvania. It lay on an early route to the West: via the Erie Canal to Buffalo, then by lake boats to Erie, Pennsylvania, overland via Meadville to the Ohio River at Pittsburgh. Her father, Harm Jan Huidekoper, born in Holland, as an agent for the Holland Land Company had bought land for himself cheaply and made a fortune.[23] Success tends to sow doubt about predestination, and Huidekoper, raised in Calvinism, had his children tutored by young Unitarians from Harvard, started a Unitarian church, and built an estate called Pomona, named for the Roman goddess of abundance, fruits, and orchards. Despite his support for the *Western Messenger*, Clarke had not stopped there in his first years of travel from Boston to the West. He first met Anna, her mother, and her brother when they passed through Louisville in the winter of 1837–1838, on their way to a winter vacation in Mobile, Alabama. Asked by the American Unitarian Association to explore possibilities for liberal religion in the Deep South, Clarke then followed them there. The next year, he stopped at Pomona on his way to Boston. Anna, four years younger than he, seemed to him pretty, smart, capable, and devoted to the cause of spreading liberal religion—just the sort of woman he needed for a wife. He proposed after visiting Margaret. Yet even then, he did not write to Fuller about his engagement. The news must have reached her through a friend of his sister. She wrote, fuming, about receiving "the news of circumstances so important to you from a stranger," yet promising that she hoped to "love your Elect, if I can, and shall wish to win her regard."[24]

Worried about providing for Anna on a minister's salary, James took added part-time work overseeing the Louisville public schools. Father Huidekoper then promised a thousand dollars a year to supplement his son-in-law's income.[25] By then, James had invested in helping a widow in his church set up a boardinghouse. He and Anna would live there. Rebecca, after all, had achieved some security by doing so. Anna, trained to run a large household herself, tried to be a good minister's wife, but hated being a mere boarder. Shortly after she found that she was pregnant, her mother died. Clarke then took her to Pomona to both grieve and wait for the birth of their child. It was time to resign his pastorate and explore better opportunities back in Boston.

He knew all about Ripley leaving the Purchase Street Church to establish Brook Farm. Yet neither that church, nor the conflicted parish in Waltham, where Emerson's kinsman, Samuel Ripley, was seeking a successor, seemed open to much change. Talking to Elizabeth Peabody at her home on West Street, he heard all about the last meetings of the Transcendentalist circle: the divided opinions over church reform; the hope to form a more egalitarian church. Peabody must also have told him about discussions on the same theme with members of Federal Street Church, upset about Channing and the Follen memorial. His informal and unrecorded conversations in Boston then ended abruptly. A note came from Huidekoper saying that Anna had given birth to a baby boy. He rushed back to Meadville. They named him Herman, after his grandfather Harm. After Christmas, Clarke returned to Boston. The Louisville church had found a new minister. Everyone he had consulted, including Channing, agreed that Boston needed a new church, and that he was right minister to try it, by combining "new views" and church reform with reverence for tradition and an egalitarian approach to discipleship.

Very near his grandfather's church was the Swedenborgian Chapel. Clarke hired it for three Sunday evenings in January and early February 1841. Interest was high. The hall was full to overflowing for each talk, "The Essentials of Christianity, or What Shall I Do to Be Saved?" "Justification by Faith," and "The Church as It Was, Ought to Be, and Can Be."[26] In each, Clarke emphasized the need to transcend divides of class and creed.

George Ripley, resigning his ministry, had written that "the poor widow, who leaves the daily toil by which a suffering family is kept from want to gather with the faithful in the house of worship" should be equal to those "arrayed in costly robes, or who come from the heights of office or the abodes of luxury."[27] Clarke, whose idea of widows began with his own mother, echoed those ideals. As for continuity with the historic church, however, he was closer to Hedge than to Ripley or Emerson. It pained him to see Boston Unitarians so divided over both social and religious issues. Clarke aimed for a stance that, like Channing's, might transcend both divides: a reverent spirituality, but aimed at practical social reform; respectful enough of Christian tradition to restore the non-creedal simplicity and egalitarian spirit of the early church; an inclusiveness that would maintain spiritual friendship among all those willing to unite.

Too many Unitarians, after Emerson's Divinity School Address, seemed ready to be illiberal, excluding from fellowship those who interpreted biblical miracles as symbolic rather than literal. Clarke, again like Channing, had come to see that at issue in all such debates was not whether Jesus was human or divine, but rather whether he was a radical or a conservative. They felt sure he had been both, having said, "I have come not to abolish the law but to fulfill it."[28] The church of the future should be similar, conserving the best of tradition while radical enough to work to fulfill the will of God on earth, here and now.

There were three principles Clarke wanted his new church to follow. The first challenged "the purse principle" still in use even in the liberal churches, with control by trustees or a standing committee elected by those who owned pews. "The voluntary principle" meant a church organized around "elective affinities," with its ministry and mission and governed by all who gave of time or treasury, however much or little.[29] The model of a true church was *not* any longer to be that of a joint stock company, however the law might treat it as such. Rather it should be more like a voluntary spiritual family. All children of God, and disciples of Christ, who covenant together to work to realize God's rule here on earth, were to be equal members. One key text for him was Matthew 12:46–50:

> While He was still talking to the multitudes, behold, His mother and brothers stood outside, seeking to speak with Him. Then one said to Him, "Look, Your mother and Your brothers are standing outside, seek-

ing to speak with You." But He answered and said to the one who told Him, "Who is My mother and who are My brothers?" And He stretched out His hand toward His disciples and said, "Here are My mother and My brothers! For whoever does the will of My Father in heaven is My brother and sister and mother."

The hope to transcend class distinctions in the church is deep rooted and persistent, but in 1841, it had overtones of the anticapitalist Christian socialism of Orestes Brownson. The appeal of a historically grounded and class-inclusive church was drawing Brownson in the direction of a Roman hierarchy with whom he soon quarreled, but Clarke's model was even more nonhierarchical than the Campbellite effort he had seen trying to restore the simplicity of the early church. To transcend sectarianism, he drew from contrasting church traditions. What Peabody called "the social principle" meant emulating evangelicals not only by engaging with social issues but also by meeting, not just for worship but in regular prayer or "social meetings," where members of all classes could come to know one another, read the signs of the times, and consider how best to respond. This was common among Methodists and other evangelicals, but not yet with New England Congregationalists and Unitarians. They held meetings such as those Channing had with his lay teachers, but those were both new and a bit exclusive. Under Clarke's "social principle," *all* church members were urged to meet regularly, at least fortnightly, to share concerns and discern together how best to work not only for their own salvation but for the wholeness of society.

On the other hand, his upbringing in participatory prayer book worship at King's Chapel led him to advocate what he later called "the liturgical principle," with *liturgy* understood in its root sense—worship as "the work of the people."[30] In almost all congregations of the New England Standing Order, even in 1840, worship was often passive on the part of parishioners: "Dr. Channing went to the desk [pulpit] and *read* a hymn." Congregations sang little. Many considered organs rather "high church." The first in Boston, in fact, was at King's Chapel. Music was often paid and sparse, and clergy did almost all the talking. Sermons might last an hour and a half.

Earlier Puritan practices of lay testimony or spoken prayer had largely fallen out of use. The liturgical principle meant participation by all. Clarke believed that the office of a minister was the humble one of promoting the spiritual/moral development and leadership of all one's fellow disciples. Laypeople could not only do the readings and lead prayer, but they could also preach and administer baptism and communion. He did not say all this in his organizing talks. Then they might have caused a distracting, doctrinal controversy. Yet subsequent practice showed his true radicalism.

Lay preaching among the Disciples would come to include preaching by women. Clarke knew the scriptural texts often cited to forbid it. He simply found it inconsistent with the spirit of Christ and the historical testimony of the early church. The idea that even nonordained leaders could administer the Lord's Supper came from his grandfather's experience of not doing so until ordained and then questioning that prohibition. Clarke also wanted a Quakerlike period of silence in worship, as well as a liturgical calendar based not just on the traditional church seasons but also on key occasions in the progress of the church: Reformation Sunday, Forefather's Day (December 22) for the landing of the Pilgrims, and so on.

After his three lectures and many positive responses, he met on February 17 with a group of lay leaders, most of whom came from Federal Street with Channing's encouragement. Clarke said that he was willing to minister to them on the principles that he had described if they would secure a place to hold Sunday services. They found an upper room at Amory Hall on Washington Street that was suitable, around the corner from the Peabodys on West Street. Used as a theater on other days, it seated two hundred and seventy-five. Sunday morning services were so crowded that some people were unable to enter. Evening services were also quite full. Dr. Walter Channing, the eminent physician and brother of the other Dr. Channing, hosted the first social meeting. A draft order of service was set forth. Two weeks later, at Dr. David Weld's, Clarke proposed a church covenant:

> Our faith is in Jesus Christ, the Son of God, and we do hereby unite ourselves into a Church of his Disciples, that we may co-operate together in the study and practice of Christianity.

Finally, at an April 27, 1841, meeting at the Peabody home, Clarke signed his own name beneath the pledge and asked others to join him. Forty-seven did so, led by Dr. Nathaniel Peabody, his wife, and his daughters, Elizabeth, Mary, and Sophia; Dr. Walter Channing and his daughters, Mary and Barbara; his brother George Gibbs Channing; Dr. Samuel Cabot Jr. (brother of Eliza Cabot Follen) and his wife, Elizabeth Perkins Cabot; Rebecca and Sarah Clarke; and others. Far more people attended Clarke's services than became committed to full membership, but that was typical of the time. The new congregation owned no property and so sold no pews. Clarke and his Church of the Disciples kept faith with the calling of the church to promote social change, but by staying in an urban setting.

The same month in the 1841 that saw its founding, George and Sophia Ripley moved from Boston to the dairy farm in West Roxbury they had earlier rented from the Ellis family, starting Brook Farm. Ironically, they purchased it in the name of a new joint stock company—the same model as that of a traditional church society. All Transcendentalists showed interest in their effort, but few joined them. Brook Farm, which ended after only six years, was a noble, if flawed, social experiment. Transcendentalists favored experiments. "All life is an experiment," wrote Emerson. "The more experiments you make the better."[31] Not all worked out.

Margaret Fuller was also experimenting. She had agreed to include men in a third series of conversations on mythology, in the winter/spring of 1841. James was among the first to enroll. The Ripleys hosted, before they moved to West Roxbury. Then meetings moved to West Street. Both Hedge and Emerson took part, among others. The conversations, however, did not go well. While James deferred to Margaret as the leader, other males had a tendency to take the floor and then to hold it. Emerson, in particular, observed young Caroline Healey, "pursued his own train of thought. He seemed to forget that we had come together to pursue Margaret's."[32] Caroline, at times, may have done the same. Peabody had to admonish her, too, to listen more and talk less.[33] Margaret concluded that she would not include males in any further conversations.

Clarke had to wonder just how his own experiment would work out. Healey came to one of his first services in early May and loved much of it: the participatory worship, his voice and extemporary prayer, and the long silence that followed. She had also heard Theodore Parker preach his iconoclastic "Sermon of Idolatry" at the Purchase Street Church the month before and found it startling but likely to offend others.[34] Parker was to exchange pulpits with Clarke in a few weeks. The Disciples would then begin to face a new challenge. Since they shared no creed, but only a covenant, how truly inclusive could they be as a church? Could they welcome to the pulpit someone so iconoclastic as to be considered by many as no Christian at all?

Theodore Parker
(1810–1960)

CHAPTER VI

Division Because of Inclusion

*In which two Transcendentalist experiments
find that inclusion can lead to division,
while the deep spiritual friendship between two ministers
transcends their differences in doctrine,
and endures.*

THERE WERE MANY REASONS for George and Sophia Ripley to choose West Roxbury as the site of their experiment in communal living. They had spent two lovely summers there, "leading a life of extreme self indulgence in the most positive retirement," as she said.[1] The tract they later named "Brook Farm" was 170 acres on the Charles River, only eight miles from their home in Boston. Later absorbed into the city, West Roxbury in 1841 was still a rural village, linked to town by stagecoach. Their fellow Transcendentalist and friend Theodore Parker had been there since 1837, living just two miles from the farm, near the church on Spring Street. Although Parker would eventually become the most influential—and divisive—Transcendentalist minister, there was also division in his own home. He and his wife, Lydia Dodge Cabot, shared their home with her ailing, unmarried, and rather censorious Aunt Lucy, who had bought the house for the three of them.[2] Parker was often glad to get away, to make visits, or to go on walks with friends.

So it was that on a hot August morning in 1840 that Parker sauntered out to the farm to go with George Ripley on "a little foot journey," as the latter put it.[3] They set off for Groton, some thirty miles northwest, via Concord, for a so-called "Christian Union Convention" of reform-minded religionists. They stayed overnight at Emerson's commodious house. Every minister then tried to maintain a "prophet's chamber," where visiting col-leagues, often supplying the pulpit, might spend a night. Waldo invited Al-cott, now his neighbor, to join them for supper and conversation. Parker found Emerson rather dull that evening, but he was glad when both he and Alcott agreed to walk on with them the next day.

The gathering of religious idealists at Groton was neither conventional nor at all unified. It included all manner of spiritual rebels, each eager to manifest the realm of God here on earth, rejecting the materialism, greed, and conflict of present society. Some from Cape Cod were "Come-Outers." Like the Separatists who founded the Plymouth Colony, they had left ex-isting churches as complacent and corrupt, hearing the biblical injunction, "Wherefore come out from among them and be separate."[4] Others were "Second Adventists"—following prophecies of a farmer from upstate New York, William Miller, who declared current tribulations to portend an imminent Second Advent of Christ. In New England, Miller's prophecies went out through a paper called the *Signs of the Times*, spread by the min-ister of Boston's Chardon Street Chapel. The Gospel admonition, to "read the signs of the times," was one with which Transcendentalists resonated. Emerson later lectured on the theme.[5] A well-known essay on the topic by his friend Carlyle began, "Were we required to characterise this age of ours by any single epithet, we should be tempted to call it, not an Heroical, De-votional, Philosophical, or Moral Age, but, above all others, the Mechanical Age. It is the Age of Machinery, in every outward and inward sense of that word; the age which, with its whole undivided might, forwards, teaches and practices the great art of adapting means to ends."[6]

In 1840 the signs of the times seemed indeed troubling in America. The Panic of 1837 had resulted in speculators buying up depressed assets and doing well, while others, already close to the bottom, either materially or spiritually, were so eager for hope as to be willing to put faith in almost any prophet, plan, program, or politician that seemed plausible.[7] The "hard cider and log campaign" of the 1840 presidential race was without shame in its populist pandering.[8] No wonder religious idealists of all persuasions felt called to come together that autumn.

It was at the Groton convention that George Ripley met Adin Ballou. Like Brownson, Ballou was a onetime Universalist minister who had become a Unitarian. Like Garrison and many abolitionists, he had taken up the nonviolent Gospel ideal of "non-resistance."[9] Ballou wanted to abjure all political structures using violence or even the threat of death to enforce laws. He was planning a community in which "Practical Christians" could live together on that basis. His fellow pacifist, Garrison, was also there at Groton and heard him. There would be not one, but four new communities founded after the Groton meeting.

Followers of Garrison in western Massachusetts set up the Northampton Association for Industry and Education in 1842. There, a former slave who called herself Sojourner Truth would find her voice and transforming mission.[10] Alcott would return to the Groton area in 1843 to found a small, short-lived "consociate family" in the nearby town of Harvard, on a farm he called "Fruitlands," which his daughter Louisa May would later recall in her satire *Transcendental Wild Oats*.[11] Ballou and Ripley talked seriously about joining forces. Yet negotiations broke off when the former Universalist insisted upon an affirmation that each member would have to sign. Ripley, despite respect for Ballou, resisted agreeing to any "creed." Parker, for his part, saw most attendees at Groton as "yet in bondage to Sectarianism," damning existing sects only to make room for their own, "which will probably be worse than its predecessors," he told his journal.[12] As plans for Ballou's Hopedale community emerged, some thought them more practical and likely to endure than Ripley's experiment. That proved to be true.[13] Organizational principles were certainly clearer.[14] People and resources that might have gone to Brook Farm instead went to Hopedale. Both began as joint stock companies: members (and others) purchased shares; both later suffered from lack of capital. Hopedale, after a decade, went bankrupt, but then rose again as a textile company town controlled by the two brothers who were its largest investors. Brook Farm's acreage on the Charles River was poor for field crops and only fit for pasturage, as farmers might have seen. Parker, having been raised on a farm, doubted the Brook Farm business plan from the start, but stayed quiet. Having it nearby met some of his spiritual needs. No need for a discouraging word on economics, not in a depression. He was depressed enough already.

When Parker finished divinity school in 1836, he aspired to become colleague-successor to aging Ezra Ripley in Concord. Instead, that parish called Barzillai Frost, an attentive pastor but a dull preacher. In his 1838 address at the Divinity School, Emerson never named Frost but alluded to him with dripping disparagement, saying

> I once heard a preacher who sorely tempted me to say, I would go to church no more. Men go, thought I, where they are wont to go, else had no soul entered the temple in the afternoon. A snow storm was falling around us. The snow storm was real; the preacher merely spectral; and the eye felt the sad contrast in looking at him, and then out of the window behind him, into the beautiful meteor of the snow. He had lived in vain. He had no one word intimating that he had laughed or wept, was married or in love, had been commended, or cheated, or chagrined. If he had ever lived and acted, we were none the wiser for it. The capital secret of his profession, namely, to convert life into truth, he had not learned.[15]

Parker, on the other hand, who heard that address in person, aimed at a powerful and persuasive persona in the pulpit, and achieved it. Having grown up in relative poverty, however, he lacked the family connections other ministers had. He had learned that ill-paid ministers should marry into wealth. Lydia Dodge Cabot came from a different branch of that large clan than her cousin, Eliza Lee Cabot Follen, but still a Cabot. And clearly attentive to her elders—an attractive trait in a minister's spouse. Yet along with Lydia came her perpetually ailing, unmarried, and unhappy Aunt Lucy, for whom she had become the clan's designated caregiver. Lucy was self-deprecating and generous but always controlling, with both connections and money. She used the former to pave the way for the rural parish in West Roxbury to call Parker and then purchased a house there for them to all share. It was a small and conflicted parish; student ministers preaching there referred to it as "Skunk's Misery." Parker acceded to the call, telling himself that at least it was close enough to Boston and Cambridge that he would be able to reach libraries, meetings, and lectures. After all, he had grown up in another village, also ten miles away, in Lexington.

His grandfather, Captain John Parker, led the Lexington Minutemen on the Battle Green on April 19, 1775. His father, also John, was a thoughtful farmer, pump-maker, and skeptic who never joined the church. Theodore ("the gift of God") was the last of eleven children he had with Hannah Stearns Parker, who "assented to the Covenant" and had her younger children baptized in the winter of 1812, two days before a then twelve-year-old daughter died. Family legend said that Theodore, then only one and a half, cried "Oh, don't!" as the baptismal water fell upon him. The death of another sister, when he was five, also affected him. Six years later, their mother also died; each spring Theodore would go to her grave and leave violets. Yet he never spoke about these losses. The faithful had to accept the will of God. In late 1836, as he began his ministry, his marriage, and his meetings with the Transcendentalist circle, his father also died.

John Parker had encouraged his youngest son to be studious and to learn Latin, but when he gained admission to Harvard—no one in the family had ever been to college—he had to say that he could not afford the fees. Theodore promised to pay the costs from out of his own labor, which he did, first by living at home, working on the farm, and walking into Cambridge, often setting off before dawn to hear lectures and borrow books without paying tuition or room and board. Then he began to teach in the poorly financed common, or public, schools. His father did not want him to become a minister—perhaps a lawyer. Yet an inner need to resolve the issues posed by his mother's piety and death, and by his father's skepticism, kept drawing him toward deeper theological concerns. By age twenty, living in Boston, teaching at a school in Blossom Street, he went regularly to hear the preaching of Lyman Beecher—the Yale-educated, Trinitarian evangelist who came to Boston to counter the influence there of Unitarianism.

Just how those emotional appeals affected Parker's spiritual development is uncertain, but by the time he heard Emerson, he was also a critic of Unitarian preaching as too dry and rationalistic. He agreed with the call for a deeper, more personal faith, grounded not in arguments about the past, but in personal, transcendent truths apparent to the soul in the eternal present. Yet he also shared with Waldo this trait: he could be a difficult friend. One of his Divinity School classmates, John Sullivan Dwight, offered him this critique of his character:

> You distrust those who are unlike yourself. You fancy them restraints upon you and then your faith in your own energies and ideas speaks out in a tone of almost bitter contempt for the world and those who do not think and feel as you do. You feel such sentiments as you cherish ought to triumph, but you find the world courting men who pursue inferior aims. Coupled with your high ideal is an impatient wish to see it immediately realized, two things which don't go well together; for the one prompts you to love, the other soured by necessary disappointments, prompts to hate, at least contempt.[16]

George Ripley was another friend. When Parker was ordained, he offered the traditional "Right Hand of Fellowship." When Andrews Norton then attacked Emerson as having promoted "The Latest Form of Infidelity," Ripley replied with an open letter to their professor that he first read aloud to Parker, who gave him his support. Then taking his turn among Boston-area ministers to deliver the traditional Thursday lecture at the First Church in Boston, Parker also emphasized direct inspiration over biblical authority.[17] Still, he was not yet himself good at responding to direct criticism. When a senior Unitarian minister present berated him, accusing *him* of infidelity, he quickly turned and "went weeping through the street."[18] The more Parker felt attacked by traditionalists and unsupported at home, the more brittle he became even toward friends and colleagues in the ministry.

Parker kept a spiritual journal in which he recorded his responses to personal, pastoral, and political events, and pondered scriptural texts for future preaching. Lydia sometimes read it. Entries expressing troubles in his domestic life she tore out. When he wrote resolutions to himself about how to try to get along with Lydia and Lucy, he did so in Latin. Sometimes he resorted to using Greek or Hebrew letters.[19] Some such passages survived. The depth of his estrangement from Lydia reached a point where he used Greek letters to call her a "devil," and to add emphatically, "I have no hope in life."[20] This was the antithesis of any Romantic idealization of marriage as a perfect union between a man and woman, in both body and soul.

In the 1840s, the spiritual covenant of marriage was still almost indissoluble legally—even when women (as rarely happened) held economic power. Covenants between a minister and a parish, were only slightly less so, as Channing knew. His Philadelphia defense of freedom of the pulpit came just eleven days after Parker unwittingly escalated the growing controversy over inclusiveness with a sermon on "The Transient and the Permanent in Christianity."[21] On May 19, 1841, he gave it at the ordination of Charles Shackford at the Hawes Place Unitarian Church in South Boston. Shackford meant his ordination to be, as Hedge might have put it, "oecumenical," with three South Boston ministers present: a Baptist, a Methodist, and an orthodox Trinitarian Congregationalist. No one reacted strongly to Parker's sermon; it was not his best work. Needing dental work and ill, he had been busy with other writing and preaching. Yet what Parker said was certainly provocative. He described traditionalists as often making idols out of transient elements of Christianity—forms, rituals, and doctrines. Those had varied through the ages, often trying to stand on an ahistorical literalism that would not bear much scrutiny when viewed through critical biblical scholarship. The permanent in Christianity, on the other hand, he defined as the pure, ideal religion *of* Jesus, not doctrines or rituals *about* him: "absolute, pure morality; absolute, pure religion . . . The only creed it lays down, is the eternal truth recognized by all religions."[22]

That last phrase implied that Christ himself was only one path to ultimate truth, among others now equally worthy of recognition as also valid approaches to the transcendent. Within hours, some said that Parker was little more than a deist, an infidel, and that what he said was "blasphemy." This was no light charge. As recently as 1838, Abner Kneeland had spent sixty days in a Boston jail for that crime. Another onetime Universalist preacher, Kneeland had denied the authority of the scriptures and become a freethinker, accused of atheism. His right to do so had drawn support— from Channing, Garrison, Emerson, Ripley, and Parker, among others— so that he became the last American ever jailed for blasphemy.[23] Yet in early June, the orthodox clergy present at Parker's sermon used the evangelical press to ask Unitarians to say whether they still considered him a Christian or a blaspheming apostate. Many soon disavowed him. Parker's response was to edit his text to prepare it to be printed.

The next Sunday, May 23, he kept a previously arranged pulpit exchange with his friend James Freeman Clarke, whose new Church of the Disciples was just over a month old. Several charter members came to Clarke worried that the exchange was inexpedient, that Parker was now too controversial, the new church too fragile. Clarke declined to cancel, saying that his reasons for proceeding, as well as their concerns, were open for discussion at a meeting after the morning service that day, before Parker preached in the afternoon. His reasons were simple. It is not beliefs that make a person a Christian, Clarke felt, but rather intentions and actions. Jesus himself had said, "Whosoever wishes to do the will of God, the same is my brother." (Mark 3:35) Brother Parker deserved to be both welcomed and heard. After all, his infamous sermon had been on a text thrice repeated in the Gospels: "Heaven and earth shall pass away, but my word shall not pass away"[24] Moreover, exclusion never ends disagreement; declaring some "heretics" only makes them martyrs.

Elizabeth Peabody had heard Parker preach at Shackford's ordination; Clarke had not. She wrote to their friend John Sullivan Dwight that she herself had winced when Parker said, "'The New Testament has parts that *revolt* the moral sense.' . . . I want him to *point them out* because these are so few places that most people do not notice them."[25] But the meeting of the Disciples before Parker preached on May 23 went relatively well. Clarke explained why he would not cancel the exchange. To do so would be to excommunicate a friend and colleague as a heretic without even the semblance of a trial. This did not mean that he, or any other Disciple, had to agree with all of Parker's views. When he finished, Walter Channing rose to say that he and, he hoped, all other Disciples were "perfectly satisfied." He then moved to conclude the meeting. That passed unanimously. Parker that afternoon preached on "Sympathy and Antipathy." Nothing he said was objectionable. Peabody declared that he had simply "charmed."

Yet when Parker learned that the congregation had met to discuss his preaching for them, he responded with a testy letter to Clarke, asking him to share it with all the Disciples. Clarke did so at their next social meeting. The letter attributed far more resistance to the exchange than had actually been the case. Its offended tone had a further divisive effect, provoking "warm talk," as Peabody put it, despite closing with thanks for the Disciples' efforts "to form a new & more liberal church of our common Rel[igion]."[26] By June, Peabody wrote Dwight that a member of the Disciples had told her Parker would give a series of lectures in Boston expected to draw "an overflowing audience."[27] Indeed, four Bostonians had invited him to do so, saying that his "stirring words," heard when he had preached on exchange, had increased their faith in "the unseen & eternal . . . [their] love to God & man."[28] As Peabody put it, he had made "a prodigious impression on people in spite of clerical opposition." She felt that Clarke should apologize for holding any meeting about Parker preaching and immediately arrange another exchange.[29] Since some of his own people had asked Parker to lecture in Boston, he had not done so. Yet he also did not break with his purportedly blasphemous and heretical colleague.

Other Unitarian ministers did. They began to refuse pulpit exchanges with Parker, lest their more pious people say he had insulted belief in their more traditional approach to the truth of the Gospel. Shackford and several ministers not serving congregations still gave Parker what the clergy then called "a labor of love"—that is, a sermon given freely and not in exchange. Ripley, despite reluctance to perform clerical duties, preached for Parker. So, too, did Dwight, now at Brook Farm after a brief and rather unhappy pastorate in Northampton. To Parker, however, these kindnesses from a few felt outweighed by the refusal of others, such as Convers Francis, who had preached at his ordination, to treat him as a colleague. Most Unitarian pulpits and journals were now closed to him; he had to supply the West Roxbury pulpit with very little help. This meant writing new sermons that few heard. His resentment grew. Parker felt compelled to defend his intellectual integrity and did so in defensive, extensive correspondence. He also finished translating de Wette's *Critical and Historical Introduction to the Old Testament* and prepared the lectures that his listeners at the Disciples had asked for. These "Discourses on Matters Pertaining to Religion," given at Boston's Masonic Hall in late fall 1841, attracted—as Peabody had predicted—overflow crowds. She herself was present. So were Orestes Brownson and Caroline Healey. Their reactions differed widely.

Peabody heard Parker revealing a rational inconsistency in Unitarianism: if human beings are morally capable, why do they still need a supernatural Christ as a savior or mediator? Caroline, then nineteen, reacted more emotionally. The daughter of the Boston banker Mark Healey, raised a Unitarian Christian at the West Church on Cambridge Street, pastored by Charles Lowell and his younger, Transcendentalist associate Cyrus Bartol, Caroline now had a real conversion experience. She wrote Parker a long letter about it. He replied and then called on her at a poignant moment when her baby brother was dying. Empathizing, he also recommended books to read. That spring Caroline told the women of her Bible study group that she was now entirely a "humanitarian" in her idea of Jesus and, "in part," a "disciple of Theodore Parker."[30]

Peabody published a review of Parker's "Discourses" in Brownson's *Boston Quarterly*.[31] She said that he implied in his phrase, "Absolute Religion," that God was, either as law or love, whether in the Hebrew Bible or in the Gospels, one of "Inexorable necessity," rather than a *"relative"* God, "the Living God, revealed [first] in the face of Jesus Christ" and thereafter also to his disciples, then and now. Brownson went further, agreeing with Parker that "the origin and ground of religion is in a religious sentiment natural to man . . . therefore removing what had been my chief difficulty in the way of accepting super-natural revelation." Yet Brownson also heard Parker making "his starting point for reducing all religion to mere naturalism." As Parker's biographer puts it, "the shock would propel [Brownson] with breathtaking swiftness [from Transcendentalism] toward conservatism and Rome."[32] Yet it is worth noting how all agreed on one thing— wanting to be true disciples of Jesus Christ.

This included Parker. He recognized the many varied paths toward "Absolute Religion." Yet he soon dropped theorizing about religion generally. He had decided to fill his own pulpit each Sunday with one old and one new sermon, including parts of the "Discourses." He wrote a prodigious number of essays. Almost all had one aim: to prove his own discipleship. His review of *The Historical Development of the Doctrine of the Person of*

Christ, by J. A. Dorner, rejected by the *Christian Examiner*, appeared in the
Dial, April 1842, and ended with his translation from Leibniz:

> We must demonstrate rigorously the truth of natural religion, that is, the
> existence of a Being supremely powerful and wise, and the immortality
> of the soul. These two points solidly fixed, there is but one step more
> to take,—to show on the one hand, that no known religion can com-
> pare with the Christian. The necessity of embracing it is a consequence
> of these two plain truths. However, that the victory may be still more
> complete, and the mouth of impiety be shut forever, I cannot forbear
> hoping that some man, skilled in history, the tongues, and philosophy,
> in a word, filled with all sorts of erudition, will exhibit forever all the
> harmony and beauty of the Christian religion, and scatter forever the
> countless objections which may be brought against its dogmas, its books,
> and its history.[33]

Parker clearly wanted to be that very man. Yet most of his colleagues
now considered him no Christian at all. He had both denigrated biblical
authority and characterized Jesus as at times wrong and even morally imperfect. Only Clarke and a few others felt that if Parker still claimed to
want to *follow* Christ, then he should be included in exchanges whether
they agreed with all his views or not. John Pierpont of the Hollis Street
Church had good reason to identify with Parker's sense of persecution. He
did not agree with his theology, but he exchanged pulpits with him in March
1842. That August, Clarke also scheduled Parker for a second exchange.
Again, conservative Disciples objected, calling a church meeting. Someone
moved that pulpit exchanges were at the discretion of the minister alone.
That passed. The exchange took place. Parker again preached a sermon
that offended no one. Then one of his writings did offend.

Emerson had succeeded Fuller as editor of the *Dial*, asking Parker to
help fill its pages. Parker sent him a review of the recently printed *Proceedings* of the Hollis Street Council. It was scathing. Parker not only identified
with Pierpont as an embattled reformer but also excoriated the ministers on
the council, comparing them to Jewish Sanhedrin who dealt with a popular

prophet (Jesus) by trying to "speak him fairly with our tongues, but with our actions cut him to the soul."[34] Emerson did not agree with Parker's tone or conclusion, telling him, "I think the people almost always right in their quarrels with their ministers, although they seldom know how to give the true reason for their discontent," and chiding him for wasting ink defending "that most unpoetic unspiritual & un Dialled John Pierpont."[35] Yet he ran the review.

Unitarian ministers who were on the Hollis Street Council took personal offense; one had already told Parker that he should resign from the Boston Association of Ministers for holding views his colleagues felt brought scandal on them. Yet they were loath to expel him, since that felt hardly in keeping with their own inclusive values. That winter they discussed how to deal with Parker, who stopped attending meetings. Some proposed disbanding the association itself. After much debate, Pierpont agreed to ask Parker to meet, not on matters of doctrine, but on his relations with his colleagues. The confrontation was on January 23, 1843. Some told him they found his preaching, lecturing, and writing to have "Deistical & Infidel character & tendencies." Others found his article "unjust and ungenerous to his professional associates." Parker replied that they were making unwarranted inferences, retracted nothing, and said he would remain a member unless expelled.[36]

The meeting ended as the council had: feelings high, nothing resolved, no one satisfied. Parker collected records of every word against him and became hyperactive in his own defense. In twenty-eight months after his South Boston sermon, he "preached 221 times, lectured at least 64 times, wrote 194 sermons and 14 lectures, and published over 2,000 pages of material, including 3 pamphlets, 5 lengthy articles for the *Dial*, and 3 books."[37] His friends felt he was near collapse.

In September 1843, with financial aid from supporters, he and his wife, Lydia, left on a yearlong trip to Europe. In a lengthy farewell sermon, he dared to compare his own experiences as a minister to the sufferings of Christ.[38] His marriage, away from Aunt Lucy, improved during the absence. His relations with colleagues did not. After his return, in December 1844, he undertook an exchange with John Turner Sargent, a minister to the poor for the Benevolent Fraternity of (Unitarian) Churches. When the ministers overseeing that mission heard of the plan, they told Sargent to decline the exchange. Like Clarke, he went ahead with it. When censured for doing so, he then resigned. This provoked Clarke to preach a sermon condemning the exclusion of Parker. He reminded the Disciples that Unitarians had always maintained that moral character, not mere creed or personal belief, was the core of Christianity. They had always said as much in resisting their own exclusion by orthodox Calvinists. Clarke did not hold with Parker's theology; he made that clear in a series of articles. Yet it was time to prove the inclusive character of his view of discipleship. He arranged a third exchange with him for the last Sunday in January 1845. Two important things were at stake: a minister's freedom of conscience and of the pulpit, and the Transcendentalist goal of reforming the church so that it might work to reform society.

Who would stand up for Parker if not Clarke? By this time, his Church of the Disciples had achieved some success. Services, now at the Masonic Temple, attracted up to seven hundred worshippers. Only about two hundred, however, had signed the covenant and helped with the work of pastoral care, music, Sunday school, or social projects. Social meetings were open to all, but attended chiefly by fully covenanted members. George Gibbs Channing, keeper of his deceased brother's legacy, opposed a third exchange with Parker. So did most of the Pastoral Committee, considering Parker deliberately divisive if not an outright infidel. While they wanted to defer to Clarke's authority over exchanges, they tried to persuade him against it. The Sunday before the scheduled exchange, Clarke preached on the basis for "Christian Union." He said that all regular worshippers with the Disciples were welcome at an afternoon meeting on the issue. Nearly four hundred people stayed. Some covenanted Disciples objected. The session became a debate over participation by individuals who had not yet signed the covenant. The meeting reconvened on Wednesday evening. The issue was the same, but ended by declaring covenanted members *only* would meet the next evening in a private home. Some one hundred Disciples crowded in to debate if Clarke should keep the exchange. Soon it became clear the majority did not support limiting his authority over exchanges and also that others would leave the congregation if he did again exchange with Parker.

John Albion Andrew, then only a twenty-seven-year-old attorney, but later the Civil War governor of Massachusetts, rose to speak. He, too, deemed the exchange "inexpedient," but said the Disciples had not come together in covenanted spiritual friendship to be so easily divided over whether to listen to someone they might disagree with. He was eloquent:

I do not believe in the principle of come-out-ism. I am not a come-outer. I am a stay-inner. I shall not leave this church because the majority differ with me on this or any other questions. You may indeed turn me out, but you cannot make me go out of my own accord. This is my religious home; and if you turn me out of your meetings, I will stand on the outside and look in through the window, and see you. If I cannot do this, I will come the next day and sit in the place where you have been, and commune with you. I belong to your communion and must belong to it always.[39]

Clarke closed his own remarks by saying that Romanism had tried crushing heresy; Protestantism, excluding it; but that only "the principle of Union . . . can save the church. I think in this question is involved the question of whether hereafter there shall *be* any Church of Christ on earth."[40] Then he sat down. Dissuading Clarke from the exchange was clearly futile, and the majority wanted to support his authority and avoid a vote on the conservatives' resolutions. It was late. Several Pastoral Committee members resigned. Sixteen of those most opposed to Parker resigned from the Disciples altogether, including Henry Rogers, the wealthiest member; William B. Sumner, another man of means, with all his family; and George Gibbs Channing—all people Clarke considered very dear to him. He vowed to try to remain friends with all of them.

Three days later, Parker preached to the Disciples at the Masonic Temple. His sermons, in both the morning and the afternoon, were again deliberately inoffensive. Yet Clarke in his own journal called it "Black Sunday." Rogers and others had hired Amory Hall, where the Disciples had begun.

That day they met to form a new "Church of the Savior." Sitting behind the pulpit of Parker's church in West Roxbury, Clarke thought tearfully of the dear friends leaving his care. He was unable to begin the service for several minutes. Later that week, he and the remaining Disciples wrote the departing members graciously, accepting their decision, pledging continued spiritual friendship. Defending inclusion had led to division, yet a church covenant, like the covenant of marriage, begins in gratitude for mutual trust and shared aspirations. Among fallible human beings, shared purpose can sometimes change and then trust erode.

That same month, January 1845, members of Brook Farm were also engaged in debate. Some original members, such as Hawthorne, had left, unable to combine manual labor with any real creativity, and were asking to redeem their investment. Nonetheless, the community had grown, now including some 120 associates and probationers. Brook Farm had built more housing and invested in new enterprises. Previously, only the school had provided income. Unprofitable farming had given way to light industry, supported now by a new steam engine. Mortgages had financed it all. Debts and dissension were high and morale low. Even new resident John Sullivan Dwight felt it was as awful as the church he had served in Northampton: it had no real clarity of mission.

When Brownson visited, he wrote, "[T]he atmosphere of the place is horrible."[41] The January meeting was about whether to end the original joint stock model and to take up Fourier's model of a "phalanx" community. Never mind that Fourier's theory had some dubious premises: First, that an ideal community needed 1,600 members, distributed among the various "affinities" inherent in humans. Second, that "elective affinities" could involve relations between men and women transcending marriage. The latter issue George and Sophia Ripley kept out of discussion, even as Brook Farm revised its constitution to become a Fourierist "phalanx." That spring, they again borrowed heavily to build a huge new wooden dormitory and community center, called the "Phalanstery." When Margaret Fuller visited, she reported, "The wheels seem to turn easily, but there is a good deal of sound to the machinery."[42] This echoed what Carlyle had said on the "Spirit of the Times" in an 1829 essay: that the times were less moral than mechanical, subordinating ideal ends to proximate means. In the winter of 1846, the Phalanstery burned to the ground. That ended Brook Farm's experiment challenging the problem of material inequality.

Without Clarke risking his own ministry by exchanging pulpits with him, Parker might never have been "heard in Boston" but simply have remained in rural West Roxbury, influential at Brook Farm until it burned, but nowhere else. Instead, he became something of a martyr to the cause Channing had championed: a minister's freedom of the pulpit. Now "Friends of Theodore Parker," many from Sargent's Suffolk Street Chapel, the Hollis Street Church, and the Disciples, organized to have the "organ-toned" radical speak in Boston. As we shall see, Parker's move to Boston then played a role in the Disciples losing their own church home and seeming to die when their own pastor fell deathly ill. Yet their devotion to spiritual equality served them well, and they survived. The same was true of many friendships and even difficult marriages among the Transcendentalists.

Elizabeth Palmer Peabody
(1804–1894)

CHAPTER VII

Unequal Union, or Marriage in the Nineteenth Century

In which spiritual equality clashes with social and economic inequality, both in marriages and in a nation moving toward disunion.

IT MAY SEEM ODD TO OPEN a chapter on marriage by depicting Elizabeth Palmer Peabody, who never married. Especially with an image from late in her life. In 1886, when she was eighty-two, Henry James published *The Bostonians*, a novel offending many of that city's proper citizens. First, because it satirized Boston's claims to moral superiority, taking as its hero/protagonist a visiting Southern conservative. Second, because its character "Mrs. Birdseye," overseeing others, seemed a clear caricature of Miss Peabody. Third, because James, himself homosexual (but not openly), alluded to "Boston marriages" between pairs of women. Elizabeth, mind you, never seems to have enjoyed that form of marriage either. As a lifelong educator, she was indeed observant of others. Today often remembered chiefly for her late-life role in promoting early childhood education and bringing the German kindergarten movement to America, she was also adept at identifying gifted grownups who needed spiritual friendship in order to become more creative and fulfilled. These included the men who married her younger sisters: Horace Mann and Nathaniel Hawthorne.

In late 1832, Elizabeth, twenty-eight, and her sister Mary, twenty-six, were sharing a room in the boardinghouse on Beacon Hill run by Rebecca and Sarah Clarke. They conducted a small school there by day. Elizabeth also taught an evening history course for women. It was a congenial place for two bright women intent upon marrying but hoping for a male partner of true genius. Other residents included the historian and Unitarian minister Jared Sparks, whose wife was slowly dying, taking her meals in her room. A future president of Harvard, he was then writing a biography of George Washington. Elizabeth could borrow freely from his large library. George Hillard, a young attorney and journalist, later the law partner of Charles Sumner, was also there. James Freeman Clarke might drop by, perhaps with Margaret Fuller. So did Waldo Emerson, Elizabeth's onetime tutor in Greek, or his brother Charles. Conversation could be lively. When Horace Mann moved in, both Peabody sisters showed intense interest in him. Tall, handsome, and at thirty-six, already a reform-minded leader in the legislature, he was recently widowed, both clearly brilliant and deeply depressed.

Death had stalked the life of Horace Mann. A farmer's son from rural Franklin, Massachusetts, where the common school met only six or seven weeks in winter, he had devoured books from the local library, donated by the town's namesake. When he was just beginning adolescence, his father died suddenly. An older brother skipped church on a summer Sunday to go swimming—and drowned. At the funeral, the Calvinist minister bemoaned the eternal punishment he now faced. Horace was bright enough to get help to prepare for college at Brown, where the president not only took him under wing but also allowed him to court his daughter. Once Mann had completed law studies and established himself as an attorney in Dedham, between Franklin and Boston, he married Charlotte Messer. Sadly, her delicate beauty, like that of Emerson's Ellen Tucker, disguised consumption. She, too, died, within two years of their marriage. Mann then fled the house they had shared for Rebecca Clarke's boardinghouse near the State House. He could join in table banter with acerbic wit, but his sadness was clear. Both Peabody sisters tried to help. Mary Peabody saw him as lonely, as he surely was. In the evenings, she would sing or read for him. Her kindness broke down his defenses, and he even wept in her arms. She began to dream of him as "my husband." She also felt overpowered by her older sister. Elizabeth had more accurately diagnosed Mann as not just lonely, but in spiritual distress. She talked with him about issues of fate and free will. This was even more effective. Soon he was crying on her bosom as well, agreeing to a secret pact of emotional honesty. Then, as the anniversary of Charlotte's death neared, he fled both sisters, moving into his law office. Elizabeth persisted. She saw him as retaining Calvinist fatalism but without any redemptive faith. She then took him to Channing, who knew Mann for his work on behalf of prison reform and a state hospital for the mentally ill.

On Easter Sunday 1834, Mann heard Channing preach concerning "The Future Life."[1] The minister was trying to address death and grief in his own family. His brother Walter was the leading obstetrician in Boston. His first wife and the mother of his four children, Barbara Perkins Channing, died of tuberculosis in 1822. Nine years later, Walter married again. Eliza Wainwright Channing hoped, even at age forty, to have a first child of her own. During a long labor, Walter rightly perceived that the baby would be stillborn. He intervened surgically, but to no avail. Eliza hemorrhaged to death, saying she was prepared to die, feeling sure that spiritually, with Christ, they would meet again in heaven. Walter was devastated, but his brother's sermon reiterated Eliza's faith. Peabody, seeing Mann present, wondered how he would react. He was "lost in exaltation," he said, "or found rather." "The veil is lifted," Elizabeth wrote to Mary. "He does not feel any longer fettered to the grave—but has risen."[2]

She was only partly right. Mann's grief went on. It would be some years yet before he would feel able to remarry. It was more as if a dam had burst, and he was now better able to discern what to do with the freer flow of his life. He and Channing continued to talk. Both opposed slavery but also agreed that there was no easy solution to that source of America's original sin. They also shared a concern for those deprived of the opportunity to unfold their full potential—and especially the need to provide access to education so that even poor children might become responsible citizens. In 1837, when he was president of the Massachusetts Senate and expected to become either governor or a US senator, Mann stepped entirely away from electoral politics. He instead became the first secretary of the Massachusetts Board of Education, charged with making improved common schools more accessible and supplied with trained, professional teachers. Like the efforts on behalf of the mentally ill launched by another Channing disciple, Miss Dix, this campaign soon went nationwide. In 1840, Mann even traveled to Louisville, where James Freeman Clarke was then superintendent of schools and met with him.

On May 1, 1843, in the parlor of the Peabody house at 13 West Street, Clarke officiated as Mann exchanged vows with Mary Peabody, Elizabeth having long since stepped aside. The couple then joined another reformer, Dr. Samuel Gridley Howe and his young bride, Julia Ward, in sailing on the steamer *Britannia*. The men wanted to see what Britain and the Continent might have to teach them about medical, social, and educational reform. Clarke would continue his pastoral friendship with both couples across difficulties and distance.

He and Elizabeth played parallel roles in the marriage of the youngest Peabody sister, Sophia. In 1837, as Mann was withdrawing from politics, the Peabody sisters adjusted to the economics of the day by retreating to their hometown, Salem. That winter Elizabeth cultivated a relationship with another man who seemed in need of an encouraging wife: the shy, handsome author Nathaniel Hawthorne, then thirty-three and unmarried, as was she. The two families had long lived near one another, but the Hawthornes never socialized. Nathaniel's father, a ship captain, had died in South America of yellow fever when his son was four. His widow kept perpetual mourning and retained emotional control over her son and two daughters. At Bowdoin College, in a class with Franklin Pierce and Henry Wadsworth Longfellow, Nathaniel made an odd wager with another classmate. Envious of Hawthorne's good looks, that friend bet a cask of Madeira that Nathaniel would marry before turning thirty-two.[3] Hawthorne won. He knew his family, and himself, rather well. He returned to Salem and lived with his mother and sisters, reading, and writing a first novel and some stories, all anonymously. Two of them, "The Maypole of Marymount" and "The Minister's Black Veil," included themes of Puritanism and grief casting a pall on the potential joy of a wedding. When he allowed the stories to appear in a volume titled *Twice-Told Tales*, under his own name, his friend Longfellow praised them in the *North American Review*. Finding them to be original and inspired, Elizabeth invited him and his family to visit the Peabody home for an evening. Hawthorne arrived with a sister on each arm.

Elizabeth settled them in the parlor and then tried to get Sophia, who had gone upstairs early, to dress and come down to meet them, saying, "Mr. Hawthorne and his sisters have come, and you never saw anything more splendid—he is handsomer than Lord Byron!"[4] She declined, as the invalid of the Peabody sisters, suffering frequent migraines. Elizabeth then proceeded to make Hawthorne her own project. She learned that he was beginning to consider marriage. Salem gossip reported that he had been courting a prominent, wealthy, flirtatious young woman. Mary Silsbee, daughter of a former US senator, reportedly told Hawthorne that she would marry him when he had an income of three thousand a year. Since he had no hope of that, she became the second Mrs. Jared Sparks, first lady of Harvard. Whether Elizabeth helped with that match as well is unclear, but making matches for others surely exceeded her interest in one for herself.

She used all she knew to draw Hawthorne out of his protective shell. This was not easy. Oliver Wendell Holmes later commented that trying to converse with Hawthorne was rather like "love making." His "shy, beautiful soul had to be wooed from its bashful prudency like an unschooled maiden."[5] Yet Elizabeth succeeded. She flattered him; she promoted him; she sent his book to Wordsworth in England, and to Mann, suggesting that Hawthorne might work for the state board of education writing stories for young people. Once Sophia finally met handsome Hawthorne, she got up from her sickbed only if she thought he might be coming by. If not, she might still have a migraine. She began to talk constantly about him. Elizabeth saw that he also seemed more drawn toward the vulnerable, artistic Sophia than to her own strong personality. Rumors evidently arose in Salem. Hawthorne joked in a letter to his friends: "I have heard recently the interesting intelligence that I am engaged to two ladies in this city."[6] Around this time he also wrote a story, "Edward Randolph's Portrait," in which the female protagonist far more clearly resembled Sophia than her older sister: ethereal, pale, sickly. This says much about ideals of female beauty in the Romantic era.

As the eldest Peabody sister, Elizabeth was always practical, but not above resentment. She went away for a time. Then she resumed meddling—trying to get Hawthorne a sinecure that would allow him both the income to marry and the time to write. Knowing that Hawthorne was a Democrat, like his classmate Franklin Pierce—and not a Whig like most politicians she knew—she connected him with Boston's most influential Democrat, George Bancroft, then collector of customs for the Port of Boston. He appointed Hawthorne as a "measurer," where he could make more than he could editing the *American Magazine of Useful and Entertaining Knowledge*. He soon left the post, however. Instead he decided to join Brook Farm, hoping both to save money for marriage and to write there.

Elizabeth promoted the idea without joining herself. Hawthorne bought two five hundred dollar shares in "Mr. Ripley's Utopia," one for himself and the other for Sophia. He had secretly proposed, and she had accepted. During their engagement, she was painting romantic landscapes of idyllic living in the country. He hoped to earn enough from his writing that she could join him there. Yet he soon realized his mistake. He hated farm labor and high-minded communal living and had no leisure to write anything more than his letters to Sophia. He asked for his investment back. Ten months before the Mann wedding, on July 9, 1842, Hawthorne and Sophia Peabody were married, also at 13 West Street, with Clarke officiating. The newlyweds then had a yearlong honeymoon in the Old Manse in Concord, Emerson having arranged a lease at a low rent. Hawthorne wrote his *Tales from an Old Manse*, and Sophia and he wrote love notes on the window glass with the diamond of her ring. On their first anniversary, he wrote to her, "We were never so happy as now—never such wide capacity for happiness, yet over-flowing with all that the day and every moment brings to us. Methinks this birth-day of our married life is like a cape, which we have now doubled and find a more infinite ocean of love stretching out before us."[7]

After marrying Mann and Hawthorne to her sisters, Elizabeth next turned her attentions to her favorite Transcendentalist: Theodore Parker. The gap between his ideals and the reality of his marriage to Lydia, given her Aunt Lucy, was apparent. Peabody never questioned Parker's fidelity to his marriage, but others did. He was close to two near neighbors in West Roxbury, Francis George Shaw and Sarah Sturgis Shaw. Their son, Robert Gould Shaw, was later the martyred colonel of the black Fifty-Fourth Massachusetts Volunteers. Wealthy progressives, they supported both Brook Farm and abolitionism. Sarah's sister, Caroline Sturgis, was a friend to both Emerson and Margaret Fuller. Even closer to the Parkers were George Russell and his wife Sarah, the sister of Francis George Shaw. Parker's visits were most frequent when Mrs. Russell or her brother was hosting their unmarried sister, Anna Blake Shaw, who had attended some of Fuller's "Conversations." Sarah Clarke described her as "gentle and wise, beautiful and modest, with ringlets like the daughters of Odin, and a slightly Transcendental cast of intellect. This is something in a belle and an heiress, is it not[?]"[8]

Parker's attraction to Anna Shaw was obvious. Aunt Lucy Cabot accused him to his face of paying improper attention to another woman, to which Parker replied that she knew nothing of true *"friendship*—the friendship of two souls."[9] Elizabeth Peabody, when she heard rumors of Parker's temptation, not only deflected suggestions of impropriety, but then also arranged for Anna to meet the dashing, intelligent William Batchelder Greene. He was a West Point graduate then studying for the ministry as a liberal Baptist. He had come into her bookshop and made insightful comments that caught her attention, and showed interest in Brook Farm. Once again, Elizabeth played matchmaker. Greene met and won Anna, and went on to become first a Unitarian minister, then an early socialist.[10]

Another development helped to improve the Parker marriage. For whatever reason, they had no children together. In 1842, however, Lydia learned that her brother, John Cabot, who had led a dissipated life and died prematurely, had apparently fathered a son out of wedlock, acknowledging paternity by paying support. The boy was now six and in need of a new home. Aunt Lucy and other Cabots rejected the boy as related to them in any way. Lydia did not. If she could not have a child of her own, she would raise her brother's son. Parker asked a court to make him guardian for "Georgie." Over the objections of other Cabots, they had the boy's name legally changed to George Colburn Cabot, placing him at nearby Brook Farm for his board and education.[11] This alignment of Lydia and Theodore in opposition to Lucy helped the Parker marriage and their trip to Europe. When they returned, admirers in Boston asked him to lead a church there organized on Clarke's "voluntary principle." They moved into the city, with Georgie, but without Aunt Lucy. Their relationship remained complicated, but more harmonious. They used their home to help both other children and fugitive slaves. As he later said of marriage, in a passage often quoted at weddings,

It takes years to marry completely two hearts, even of the most loving and well-assorted. A happy wedlock is a long falling in love. Young persons think love belongs only to the brown-haired and crimson-cheeked. So it does for its beginning. But the golden marriage is a part of love which the bridal day knows nothing of. A perfect and complete marriage, where wedlock is everything you could ask and the ideal of marriage becomes actual, is not common; perhaps as rare as personal beauty. Men and women marry fractionally, now a small fraction, then a large fraction. Very few are married totally, and they only after some forty or fifty years of gradual approach and experiment. Such a large and sweet fruit is a complete marriage that it needs a long summer to ripen in, then a long winter to mellow and season in. But a real, happy marriage of love and judgment between a noble man and woman is one of the things so very handsome that if the sun were, as the Greek poets fabled, a god, he might stop the world and hold it still now and then, in order to look all day long on some example thereof, and feast his eyes on the spectacle.[12]

If marriage in the mid-nineteenth century challenged men like Parker, it was far more difficult, even dangerous, for many women. No one needed to explain that to Elizabeth Peabody or to Margaret Fuller. Both knew it from experience in their own families. The Palmer family of Elizabeth's mother was full of men who were violent, unfaithful, or unable to provide for a wife and children—as was her own father, the improvident Dr. Nathaniel. While Margaret's father, Timothy Fuller, was disguising the gap between his ambitions and his finances, his wife wrote to him, "I have long thought that the constant care of children narrowed the mind."[13] Her eldest daughter had seen her endure eight further pregnancies and the deaths of two children, and then had to help her raise the six surviving younger Fullers.

Yet both women idealized marriage. In late summer 1837, Peabody stayed at the Emerson home in Concord. She liked Mrs. Emerson, whom Waldo called Lidian rather than Lydia. She outlined her "theosophy of marriage," in which each partner has an "original relation to the Universe," but through their partner. She saw Emerson delighting in his son and namesake, and then wrote about the family as "the only divine institution on earth."[14] Five years later, in the late summer of 1842, Fuller also stayed with the Emersons. Waldo was glad to have her visiting, but Lidian was less than enchanted. She was pregnant with a daughter who would be born in November. That January, Lidian was still nursing Edith, when their five-year old son Waldo came down with scarlet fever. Louisa May Alcott, at six, came to the door to ask Mr. Emerson if her playmate could come out to play. Emerson replied, "Child, he is dead."[15]

That loss shaped Emerson's most somber essay, "Experience."[16] Trying to compensate by gathering friends to Concord, he nonetheless found Margaret's return the next summer too emotionally demanding. She also found him distant and aloof, as indeed he often could be. "Most people descend to meet," he said in his essay, "Friendship."[17] Yet they spent so much time conversing that Lidian was provoked to jealousy. She shut herself in her room, and when Margaret came to ask if she was ill, she burst into tears.[18] These conversations, according to Margaret, centered on "Man and Woman, and Marriage." Just what Emerson said is unknown, but a later entry in his journal (September 1848) may come close:

None ever heard of a good marriage from Mesopotamia to Missouri and yet right marriage is as possible tomorrow as sunshine. Sunshine is a very mixed and costly thing as we have it, & quite impossible, yet we get the right article every day. And we are not very much to blame for our bad marriages. We live amid hallucinations & illusions, & this especial trap is laid for us to trip up our feet with & all are tripped up, first or last. But the Mighty Mother who had been so sly with us, feels that she owes us some indemnity, & insinuates into the Pandora-box of marriage, amidst dyspepsia, nervousness, screams, Christianity, "help," poverty, & all kinds of music, some deep & serious benefits & some great joys. We find sometimes a delight in the beauty & happiness of our children that makes the heart too big for the body. And in these ill assorted connections there is ever some mixture of true marriage. The poorest Paddy & his jade, if well-meaning and well-tempered, get some just & agreeable

relations of mutual respect & kindly observation & fostering each of
[the] other. & they learn something, & would carry themselves wiselier
if they were to begin life anew in another sphere.[19]

Margaret was thirty-three during her second visit with the Emersons.
One reason she had come to Concord was out of concern for her newly
married younger sister, then living there. Against her family's advice, Ellen
Kilshaw Fuller had married the rather erratic son of Dr. Walter Channing. "Ellery," as everyone called him to distinguish him from his ordained
uncle, was actually William Ellery Channing II.[20] His mother died when
he was four; his stepmother when he was still a teen. Moreover, to put it
mildly, he had never felt able to live up to the expectations of his name.
In a sense, Clarke was responsible for Ellen Fuller having met Ellery. He
had arranged for Margaret's sister to visit Louisville, staying with the
George Keats family. When her age-mate there, Emma Keats, then married Philip Speed, Ellen was so jealous that she behaved quite badly and
left for Cincinnati. There she encountered Ellery. He was trying to begin
a law practice, but found he had no gift for it at all and would prefer to become a poet. Emerson liked him. Thoreau as well, to a degree—he walked
Concord and beyond with him, noting that Ellery was both conversational
and observational. Yet he found him a rather volatile friend and called his
verse "sublimo-slipshod."[21] Margaret worried about her sister's marriage to
someone so abstracted, impractical, and unpredictable.

She herself simply wanted to get away from where all her age-mates and
even her younger sister were marrying and starting families. Preferably to
Europe, though she had no husband to take her there. Nor did she really
expect to find one. She turned thirty in May 1840. As Louisa May Alcott
later wrote in *Little Women*, "At twenty-five, girls begin to talk about being
old maids, but secretly resolve that they never will; at thirty, they say nothing about it, but quietly accept the fact."[22] At least outwardly. Perhaps she
could travel and write observations the way Harriet Martineau had done in
coming to America. Her earnings from her "Conversations" and from her
teaching were too meager for Europe, however. So when her friend Jamie
Clarke proposed a less costly journey, to the West, Margaret quickly agreed.

She would go with him, along with his mother, Rebecca, and sister, Sarah, on a summer journey to the Great Lakes, as Martineau had with Charles Follen and others some years before. Clarke had brothers in Chicago. Margaret also had a relative to visit: her uncle William Fuller, practicing law in rural northern Illinois. Traveling largely by barge and boat, she was an insightful observer, much as Peabody had trained her to be. She admired the sad dignity of the few remaining Native Americans along the Great Lakes, the Ottawa and the Ojibway, inexorably displaced by what she called "hordes" of immigrants from Germany, Ireland, and Scandinavia who crowded the trains and docks. From Chicago, Clarke's brother William drove her out to the Illinois prairie town where her uncle lived; she tried to discover from him whether her younger brother, Arthur, an aspiring Unitarian minister, might lead a school there using egalitarian innovations in education. The unmarried William showed real interest in Margaret during this time, even copying out her journal.[23] She even dared entertain the hope that the relationship could blossom into a romance and made him promise to see her when he came to visit family in the East.

Going home, she began to imagine an eclectic book of a kind Herman Melville also tried: part travel adventure, part allegory.[24] She returned via Manhattan, where William Henry Channing met her at the dock. Clarke's classmate and dearest friend, Dr. Channing's nephew, he had not lasted long in the West. For one thing, his wife, Julia, had declined to leave her network of Episcopalian friends in New York to join him in Ohio. Then the pew owners of the Cincinnati Unitarian church, despite his spiritual leadership, voted thirty to twelve *not* to allow the local Anti-Slavery Society to meet in the building.[25] Writing to Fuller about his decision to resign, though it meant narrowing his future, he penned a paragraph that, although often later quoted, deserves its original context:

> To live content with small means; to seek elegance rather than luxury, and refinement rather than fashion, to be worthy, not respectable, and wealthy, not rich; to study hard, think quietly, talk gently, act frankly, to listen to stars and birds, to babes and sages, with open heart, to bear all cheerfully, to all bravely await occasions, hurry never. In a word, to let

the spiritual unbidden and unconscious grow up through the common. This is to be my symphony.[26]

Returning East, this younger Channing now tried to emulate both Clarke and Brownson in organizing a new, more egalitarian urban church. His Society of Christian Union in New York advocated Christian socialism and prison reform, among other causes. On the Sunday that Margaret heard him preach, Bronson Alcott and the Englishman Charles Lane were also at his services, fruitlessly trying to recruit more participants for vegan communal living at Fruitlands. During her New York stay, Margaret met the editor of the *New York Tribune*, Horace Greeley. He later called her "one of the most original as well as intellectual of American Women"[27]—this in a review of the book she had produced from her trip to the West, *Summer on the Lakes, in 1843*, both travelogue and fable, with female protagonists.

She finished writing the book on a return visit to Concord in June 1844. The very day that she finished her manuscript, her sister Ellen gave birth to a daughter. She and Ellery named her Margaret Fuller Channing, but called her "Greta." Sophia Hawthorne lived near at hand, nursing a daughter she and Nathaniel named Una, after the personification of spiritual truth in Spencer's *The Faerie Queene*. When Ellen's milk failed, Sophia fed both babies. That July, Lidian Emerson had a second son, the future physician Edward Waldo Emerson. Margaret had written Waldo that she hoped that his next child might be a son, since "men do not feel themselves represented to the next generation by *daughters*."[28] This she knew from experience. While she never wished to be other than a woman, she still felt that "womanhood is at present too straightly-bound to give me scope."[29]

When William Clarke came to Boston to return his brother's visit, he spent time with Margaret as well as with Caroline Sturgis. Whether he paid more avid attention to Caroline, or otherwise disappointed Fuller, is not clear; but there was a rupture in the relationship, and despair arose in Margaret.[30] That summer she stayed with each of three sets of new parents. "I have no child," she wrote in her journal, "the woman in me has so craved this experience that it has seemed the want of it must paralyze me."[31]

As she edited the *Dial*, and male friends failed to submit promised pieces for publication, Fuller had filled an issue with her own essay "The Great Lawsuit: Man versus Men, Woman versus Women." It included a fourfold typology of marriage as she had seen it: (1) household partnership, or marriages of economic convenience; (2) mutual idolatry, where romance shuts out the world; (3) mere intellectual companionship; and (4) religious or spiritual union, in which both partners share a lifelong pilgrimage. She then argued for a future in which "inward and outward freedom for woman, as much as for man, shall be acknowledged as a right, not yielded as a concession. As the friend of the negro assumes that one man cannot, by right, hold another in bondage, so should the friend of woman assume that man cannot, by right, lay even well-meant restrictions on woman. If the negro be a soul, if the woman be a soul, appareled in flesh, to one master only are they accountable. There is but one law for all souls, and, if there is to be an interpreter of it, he comes not as man, or son of man, but as Son of God."[32]

Her friends praised it. Greeley wanted it expanded. It helped recruit paying participants for a fourth series in Boston of "Conversations for Women." Those enrolled included the future suffragist leader Elizabeth Cady Stanton and young Julia Ward, then engaged to Dr. Howe. The profit was very small, however. Margaret decided to act on Greeley's encouragement to expand her essay into a full book, *Woman in the Nineteenth Century*.

She spent late 1844 sharing a rented cottage in the Hudson Valley with Caroline Sturgis. Encouraged by William Henry Channing, she visited women at Sing Sing Prison in Ossining. Many had been prostitutes. She spoke to them not as criminals, but as sisters. She saw their degradation related to the imprisonment more respectable women felt in many proper homes. She also accepted another invitation from Greeley, going to work for him at the *Tribune* as the paper's literary editor. He was difficult at times, but paid her well, better than he had paid her male predecessor. She even boarded in his large home on Turtle Bay, along the East River. She did not enjoy the abstemious Grahamite diet there, but she did like Greeley's wife, Molly, prodding him in the direction of women's rights.

Fuller saw journalism, as she wrote Clarke, as "mutual education."[33] She not only did reviews of literature and the arts but also engaged in what

we today would call "investigative journalism," reporting on conditions in
public institutions designed for education, health, and corrections. Ellen's
husband, Ellery Channing, joined her at the *Tribune* for a time, but briefly;
Greeley dismissed him as lacking the initiative needed for effective journalism. Margaret worried that he would never be able to provide for her sister
and her namesake.

While in New York, she enjoyed attentions from a German-born banker,
James Nathan. Despite being Jewish, he took her to services at Channing's
Christian Union congregation and to arts events. He called on her at the
Greeley home, played guitar, and sang for her. Yet when he wanted a physical relationship, she refused. She knew that he had loved and left another
woman. She was not about to become a fool, nor marry one. She rekindled
a spiritual friendship with Lydia Maria Child, there editing the *National
Anti-Slavery Standard*. Although married, Child had gone from being the
primary breadwinner in her marriage to separating herself entirely from
the unending debts of her quixotic husband. She was also undertaking projects such as her five-volume *Ladies Family Library*, beginning with short
biographies of historic women, including such radicals as Madame de Stael
and Manon Roland. The last two volumes attempted a remarkable survey,
The History and Condition of Women in Various Ages and Nations.

Like Peabody, Child idealized male-female relations. She had found it
expressed in the mystical writings of Emmanuel Swedenborg and joined
Boston's Swedenborgian Church of the New Jerusalem when she was just
twenty.[34] Many Transcendentalists, including Emerson, admired Swedenborg, but her actually joining was also a way of differentiating herself from
her brother, Convers Francis, the Unitarian minister who moderated the
first meeting of the Transcendentalist circle. For whatever reason, David
Child seems to have had little interest in the physical aspect of marriage.
The couple never had children. Yet their partnership endured. Maria not
only praised Fuller's *Woman in the Nineteenth Century* as "a bold book" but
also admitted that it was harder for Fuller to offer a critique of marriage
as an unmarried woman than it would have been for herself to do so as a
wife. Child also gave perhaps the wittiest definition of Transcendentalism
ever penned. In the *National Anti-Slavery Standard*, her column, "Letters

from New York," was so popular that she republished them even after she resigned as editor. There she wrote:

> You ask me what *is* transcendentalism, and what do transcendentalists believe? It is a question difficult, nay, impossible to answer; for the minds so set are . . . without any creed. If a man [*sic*] is a non-conformist to established creeds and opinions, and expresses his dissent in a manner ever so slightly peculiar, he is called a transcendentalist. It is indeed amusing to see how easily one may acquire this title. A southern lady lately said to a friend of mine [Margaret Fuller?], "I knew you were a transcendentalist the first half hour I heard you talk." "How so?" inquired my friend. "Oh, it is easy enough to be seen by your peculiar phrases." "Indeed! I had thought my language was very plain and natural. Pray what transcendental phrase have I used?" "The first time I ever saw you, you spoke of a person at the North as unusually *gifted;* and I have often heard you use other transcendental expressions."[35]

Emerson, giving a lecture in Boston in 1842, just around the corner from 13 West Street, had tried to define Transcendentalism as Platonic, simply as "idealism as it appears in 1842."[36] Child went on to describe the nearer origins of Transcendentalism: in the challenge that Kant had set against the notion that all ethics must depend upon what comes in through the human senses. She then admitted a "slight resemblance" between Quakerism and Transcendentalism in sharing "a doctrine of perpetual revelation"—the former, in their austerity, almost against the arts; the latter, embracing beauty almost promiscuously. "Neither . . . favor the activity of reforms," she complained. This was historically unfair. Quakers split over antislavery, but many were pioneers in that conscientious activity. Meanwhile, Transcendentalists were leading among the Unitarians in the direction of promoting activism for antislavery, women's rights, and social reform. No one was more active than Theodore Parker. The more his colleagues isolated him, the more those concerned for freedom of conscience and radical social change rallied to his voice. The real question then became whether the marriage between Parker's form of Transcendentalism and other Unitarians could endure.

Caroline Wells Healey Dall
(1822–1912)

CHAPTER VIII

Tribulation and Separation

*In which a consummate pastor and family man
still cannot spare friends, congregants, those whom he marries,
or himself, the tribulations of grief and separation.*

IF ONLY SOME TRANSCENDENTALISTS were fortunate enough to find or make truly happy marriages, James Freeman Clarke was surely one. While Margaret Fuller remained single, working at the *New York Tribune*, he settled into a comfortable life in Boston as a pastor, husband, and father. He and Anna now had three young children: Herman (b. 1840), Lilian Rebecca (b. 1842), and Eliot Channing (b. 1843). In starting the Church of the Disciples, he never mentioned a salary. He simply took it for granted that the congregation would support him both spiritually and materially. They did, giving him $1,200 a year—twice what he had made in Louisville or Parker made in West Roxbury. His father-in-law also sent $1,000 more and, in 1844, began distributing his wealth to his five children. Each received gifts worth $20,000—equivalent to perhaps a million dollars today. Just $10,000 bought the Clarkes a house on Beacon Hill's Pinckney Street. James then invested the rest wisely, through his brothers, in high interest bonds in the West. They soon doubled their money.[1] Anna had a governess, two maids, and a hired man for chores. James had a warm fire in his study after he returned from a winter church meeting or lecture. This economic and domestic security helped to buffer the blow of having some of his closest friends and wealthiest congregants leave the Disciples over his loyalty to Parker. He then saw other members, including Elizabeth Peabody, leave to follow Parker.

Amid this division in the Disciples, Parker's greatest admirers met at Marlboro Chapel, where the memorial for Follen had taken place. There they resolved that Parker deserved "a chance to be heard in Boston."[2] Chairing these "Friends of Theodore Parker" was Boston banker Mark Healey. Although conservative, he did this in devotion to freedom of the pulpit and in support of his daughter Caroline, who had heard Parker give his "Discourses on Religion" and had become a convinced follower. Other supporters of Parker came from the Hollis Street Church and from the Suffolk Chapel, where John Turner Sargent had resigned when censured for exchanging pulpits with Parker. All supported a ministers' free expression, as Channing had. They then leased Boston's Melodeon Theater for Sunday morning services. Initially Parker continued his West Roxbury pastorate, preaching in Boston on Sunday mornings to growing crowds, in the afternoon in West Roxbury to the small group of the faithful there.

In early 1846, his city followers organized as "the Twenty-eighth Congregational Society of Boston." Parker asked Clarke to join in his installation. The latter said he would gladly do so, but would feel compelled to make clear their theological differences. Parker then went ahead with an entirely lay-led installation, with no clergy taking part. This simply reinforced his image as shunned by his Unitarian colleagues—a reputation that only made more people want to hear what he had to say. With his eloquence, his new congregation grew rapidly. Even William Lloyd Garrison, a "come-outer" who rejected the church entirely as too complicit with slavery and social sin, came to hear Parker. So did future women's rights advocate Elizabeth Cady Stanton. Then just starting out in her own career, she called Parker's sermons "soul satisfying" and later credited him with introducing her, through his public prayers, to an idea of God not only as heavenly Father but also as Mother. As Parker became a prophetic voice of Transcendentalism in Boston, more and more applying its ideals to social reform, the congregation developed more as a large Sunday morning audience than as a congregation of deep fellowship, although they did maintain a Sunday school and a benevolent committee.

The Disciples, by contrast, took a different approach. At their fortnightly social meetings, they discussed practical social ministry projects. When they discerned a need to shelter women fleeing domestic abuse or prostitution, they established a pioneering "Home for Temporarily Destitute Women" on Kneeland Street, directed by Rebecca Clarke. They raised funds for the black-led New England Freedom Association, to aid fugitive slaves. In the *Christian World*, they emphasized the spiritual basis— a deep and abiding change of heart—for effective, lasting social reform. It also provided a forum for moral reflection on the pressing social issues and politics of the day. In addition to his preaching, Clarke wrote more than two hundred articles for the *World*. He supported the new Protective Labor Union and endorsed what he called its "constructive socialism."[3] He also worked actively on behalf of temperance, through the Washingtonian movement, an early precursor to Alcoholics Anonymous.

While some abolitionists like Garrison refused to vote under a corrupt Constitution, Clarke was more politically pragmatic. In the presidential race of 1844, he came out strongly against slaveholder James K. Polk, as well as against any expansion of slavery through the annexation of Texas. He not only preached against the sin of slavery on public fast days and Thanksgiving Days but also did so wherever he traveled, as far west as Chicago. Because he maintained good relations with most other Unitarian ministers, he organized their antislavery petition to the Congress, signed by 173 Unitarian ministers. He also formed friendships with leaders of the Boston African American community and joined the Boston Vigilance Committee, organized to protect black Americans, whether fugitives from slavery or already legally free. His pastoral prominence as a white ally was such that he officiated at a noted wedding between two free African Americans, Robert Morris and Catherine H. Mason, held at the home of his congregants, abolitionist attorney Ellis Gray Loring and his wife, Louisa. Loring had taken young Morris into his home and his law office, and had mentored him to pass the bar and become one of the first black attorneys in the United States. His bride had been a paid servant in the home of a wealthy neighbor. They were married in the presence of Mayor Josiah Quincy, several leading lawyers, and Garrison, who described in the *Liberator* how Clarke had presided with "elegance, simplicity" but also clear delight in the occasion.[4] While Parker became the successor to Dr. Channing as Boston's leading reform-oriented preacher, Clarke inherited his role as pastor to the city's leaders, literati, and reformers.

On a Wednesday morning in August 1847, Clarke walked a few blocks up Beacon Hill to the home of Lemuel Shaw, chief justice of Massachusetts, at 47 Mount Vernon Street. Later that day he was to officiate at the wedding there of Elizabeth Shaw, then twenty-five, to Herman Melville, twenty-eight. While the couple had known each other only three months, their two families had ties going back to Revolutionary times. Young Melville was a suddenly popular author. His two exotic, titillating novels, *Typee* and *Omoo*, set in the South Seas, were all the talk of Beacon Hill parlors. He had dedicated *Typee* to Chief Justice Shaw. Both fictions drew on adventures Melville actually had on the island of Nuku Hiva, after deserting a whaling ship there. He depicted the Polynesians as leading an idyllic life, spoiled only by the arrival of Western traders and missionaries. No romantic himself, Lemuel Shaw had doubts about Melville as a son-in-law. At first, he refused his blessing. Elizabeth then persuaded her father to relent, but she must have had some worries herself. She asked Clarke to come before the wedding to pray with her and give her communion. Those worries proved prophetic, and the Melville marriage, worthy of a tragic novella.[5]

Clarke also became pastor to the wife in another marriage so troubled that it resulted in a permanent, long-distance separation that her biographer has called "a Boston divorce."[6] Later much neglected, Caroline Wells Healey Dall was a forceful woman, extraordinary diarist, and the author of some twenty-two books. Once considered Margaret Fuller's likely successor as the leading advocate for women's rights in Boston, she had married Charles Henry Appleton Dall, a Unitarian minister and fellow Transcendentalist. He, however, spent the last thirty years of his life in Calcutta, India, as a Unitarian missionary and teacher, while she stayed in Boston with their children, becoming a leader among the Disciples despite an early admiration for Parker.

Caroline grew up in Boston's West Church, on Cambridge Street. As she came of age, young Cyrus Bartol, a member of the Transcendentalist circle, began his ministry there. He both encouraged Caroline to do social ministry among the poor and to keep a journal. She did so for over seventy years. Elizabeth Peabody reinforced the value of the practice. Caroline was the youngest participant in a series of Fuller's "Conversations"—the one that had included men. Peabody had to tell Caroline also to try to talk less and listen more. She gradually learned to be almost as observant as Elizabeth was. When she heard Parker give his "Discourses on Religion," she noticed beads of sweat on his brow, as he said that the authority for his religion was not in the past but in the Transcendent that he felt in confronting the moral and spiritual realities and tribulations of the present. She wrote to him that she agreed but felt he had used unfair shock tactics to present his ideas. When he wrote back to her, treating her as a spiritual equal, then visited her at home, just after a baby brother had died, Caroline became a devout Transcendentalist.

Her banker father had kept his finances afloat after the Panic of 1837 only by borrowing. In 1842, he found it necessary to declare temporary bankruptcy. Suddenly the man who had been courting Caroline seemed to lose interest. She herself took work as a teacher, moving to Washington, DC, to teach at a school for girls. At the Christmas service for the Unitarians there, the preacher was Charles Dall, then minister-at-large to the poor of Baltimore. Caroline spent the following day with him, visiting the poor of Washington. She liked his earnestness and attention and kept seeing him and writing to him. When he began to talk of marriage, however, she told her diary that she had once told a friend, "No! I will never marry Mr. Dall. He has not strength enough. I wish to *lean* upon my husband."[7] Yet when he proposed, she accepted. It can be hard to know when to trust an intuition.

Dall proved unable to raise the funds to support his vocation for a ministry to the poor. Having failed to do so in three different settings, in 1847 he accepted the pastorate of a small church outside Boston, the First Parish in Needham. It was then the only church in that rural town. While most leaned to the Unitarianism of previous ministers, others were more conservative. There the twenty-seven-year-old minister's wife stunned the farmers' wives by publishing a book of *Sketches and Essays*: one against the Mexican War, one calling for the abolition of slavery, and another on "sisterhood" and women's rights.[8] She also went through the trauma of giving birth to a child born both deformed and dead. Her physician, a Calvinist and the senior deacon of the parish, called it God's judgment on the Dalls for their heretical beliefs. Parish leaders then reduced Dall's salary to force his resignation.

Although he soon found a new pastorate in Toronto, that ministry did not succeed either. The Dalls hosted Dorothea Dix on one of her many trips to inspect mental health facilities—and found they had made an enemy of the Unitarian physician who ran the local asylum. Charles sank into depression and self-blame. Caroline began to overcompensate. After an evening when she had tried to carry the conversation with congregants and visitors, he told her angrily that he wished she would not "*seem* to lead." Some blamed Caroline for the failures of Mr. Dall as a pastor. Her biographer suggests that he probably could have failed all by himself. Her own father wanted Caroline to leave Charles, saying that he would support her financially only if she did so. She declined. Then Dall stunned her, and others, by suddenly announcing that he had accepted a post as a missionary teacher in Calcutta, India, where the British Unitarians ran a school for girls. He went alone. Caroline and their children stayed in Boston. He initially sent home part of his stipend. Over thirty years, he returned five times, chiefly when their three children graduated or married. The Dalls never legally divorced or resumed married life.

Caroline found her vocation in women's rights but managed to offend other women in the movement by wanting to talk not just about equality in the abstract, or suffrage, but also about the concrete social realities faced by women—including domestic abuse, lack of access to employment, and the related issue of prostitution. She produced some of the first studies about access for women to higher education and to the professions, and went on to cofound the American Social Science Association. She received her most consistent spiritual support from Clarke. In the Church of the Disciples, she began to occupy some of the female leadership role that Elizabeth Peabody might have had, had she remained in the congregation.

The Disciples, despite the defections of some conservatives and the loss of others to Parker's society, had grown into a real force in the spiritual and political life of Boston and beyond. Clarke not only opposed the annexation of Texas, as Channing had. He also predicted that it would lead to war with Mexico and said so in the *Christian World*. This stance then influenced his colleagues. After the 1844 election, a series of fifteen well-reasoned, anonymous letters on the issue appeared in the Boston *Atlas*, and then in other papers around the country. They said that annexation was "derogatory to the national character and injurious to the public interest," but also argued that "no individual in power in Mexico would dare to entertain the idea of surrendering Texas—nor could such a surrender be obtained except by force."[9] The author was actually Clarke's friend George Ellis, pastor of the Unitarian Church in Charlestown and the editor of both the *Christian Register* and the *Christian Examiner*.

The witness of more theologically radical Transcendentalists like Parker also became increasingly ethical and political. Parker's speeches and sermons were printed and distributed widely. In another Parker sermon, given to him by his Unitarian law partner William Herndon, Lincoln found the inspiration for his famous phrase, "government of the people, by the people, for the people."[10] By then, New England leadership against the Mexican War and connections in the West also led to the first truly national antiwar movement in American history.[11]

With Parker's Music Hall flock flourishing, the Disciples began to feel the need to differentiate themselves by having a church building of their own. They did not want to appear to be just another Sunday morning audience in rented halls. Some had even begun to call them "the Church of the Wanderers."[12] Then a prime site on Beacon Hill, between the State House and King's Chapel, just across from the Athenaeum, became available. Dr. Samuel Cabot and his family promised to give $5,000, but the total cost of building would be five times that amount, and there were few other wealthy Disciples. With only half the needed amount raised, they decided to proceed by faith and undertake two mortgages. They surrendered their lease at the Masonic Temple, worshipped for a few months at the Church of the Savior—with the very people who had left them—and then, in March 1848, dedicated a plain brick church seating 650.

At the dedication, Clarke again spoke on "The Church as It Was, as It Is, and as It Ought to Be." Yet the Disciples were not giving enough to continue his salary, other expenses and the two new mortgages. That fall, he arranged for a winter series of lectures to try to raise more funds. Lecturers included Emerson, Horace Mann on education, William Henry Channing on war and peace, John Albion Andrew on prison reform, and so on. It was a commendable series, but not remunerative enough. Resorting to a system they disliked, the Disciples reluctantly agreed to rent out some of the pews, while leaving others entirely free so the poor could worship with them. The cul-de-sac off Beacon Street on which the new church stood was renamed "Freeman Place."

All this effort, plus a constant involvement in social causes, had tested Clarke's strength. At the age of thirty-eight, he had never been seriously ill. Now he contracted influenza. When he tried to return to his duties quickly, his exhaustion was so apparent that the Disciples insisted that he take some time away. He repaired to a "water cure" spa in Brattleboro, Vermont. Anna and the children joined him there in the summer. The social set there included both prosperous Bostonians and fellow Transcendentalists, including William Henry Channing and young Thomas Wentworth Higginson, a Divinity School graduate who had both joined the Disciples, marrying one of its charter members, Dr. Walter Channing's daughter, Mary Elizabeth, and begun a search for his own first pastorate. The following winter, Clarke's eight-year-old son Herman caught scarlet fever. He died quickly, on February 15. As Clarke's biographer puts it, "The suddenness was bewildering. One day James and Anna went out to call on Henry Whitney Bellows, who was visiting in town, and Herman walked down with them to Walnut Street and sat in Cyrus Bartol's doorway as they went down the street. Less than a week later they carried him out of the house on his way to his grave at Mount Auburn. Ten days after the burial his father could look out of the living room window and still see the path that the boy had dug in the snow."[13]

Clarke leaned on his colleagues and spiritual friends. Higginson, then only twenty-six, read the funeral service for Herman. His youthful energy had made him a favorite with the boy. William Henry Channing gave the prayers. Friends could do only so much to console grief, however. A second son, Eliot, had also caught the fever, but not so severely. Anna was able to nurse him through the crisis. But when he survived, she then gave way, collapsing from the grief, anxiety, and fatigue that kept her in her room for weeks. James also relapsed into the exhaustion that had weakened him the year before. The Disciples again insisted that he go away for a rest.

After the 1848 revolutions in Europe, an International Congress of the Friends of Peace had formed. It had called a Paris Congress that summer, with Victor Hugo presiding. The Disciples sent Clarke as their delegate, voting him the funds to make the journey. Anna stayed behind, spending the summer with their two surviving children at a country cottage. James and Sarah Clarke both wrote to Margaret Fuller, still in Rome, asking for travel advice and when she might come back herself. "O Jamie," she replied, "What come back for?" Rome, like France, had declared itself a republic. She had no interest in "Brownson Alcott and other rusty fusty intel. and spiritual-ities." Europe had given her "a sphere much more natural to me than what the old puritans or the modern bankers have made" in America. What she did not say was that she now had a child, fathered by young Giovanni Ossoli.[14]

In early July 1849, Clarke sailed for Europe for the first time in his life. Other reform-minded friends had gone there to visit slums, hospitals, or prisons or talk with other reformers. Clarke did not have the inclination earnestly to contemplate much more suffering and affliction. He needed to transcend his own grief and mortal sense of limitation. During his first four weeks, he toured England. At Salisbury Cathedral, with its four-hundred-foot tower, he and a friend climbed as far as visitors normally went. Outside the tower window, Clarke saw metal fittings that allowed steeplejacks to reach the metal ball and weathervane at the very top. To his friend's horror, Clarke climbed the rest of the spire. Reaching the ball, he pulled himself up to the top, much as he had done on the mast Charles Follen raised on the Harvard Delta. Taking in the view, he then realized he had lost sight of the way back down. He had to feel around with his feet to find the foothold again. He eventually descended and rejoined his rather terrified companion.[15] The Paris Peace Congress itself, with its earnest speeches on avoiding war, frankly bored him. Then he spent three weeks hiking in the Swiss Alps, pausing at times to sketch a sublime scene. Sadly, there was no possibility of visiting Margaret in Italy. The French, under Louis Napoleon, had sent an army there to retake Rome for Pope Pius IX, ending the republic.

He could only pray that she was safe. Instead he went to Germany, visiting sites of the Reformation and of Goethe, returning via Belgium to Liverpool, to board a steamer to Boston, arriving in late October 1849.

He found the Disciples in some tribulation. Their pastor and preacher had been absent from them for almost eighteen months. Occasional lay preaching was one thing, if an eloquent Disciple, such as John Albion Andrew or George Bond, led the worship, but a long absence of pastoral leadership was another. Attendance had suffered. The Sunday school lacked teachers, social meetings often drew only twenty, and benevolent social projects were suffering from lack of volunteers. Ben Winslow, a Harvard classmate of Clarke's and a Disciple, said their original fervor had succumbed to worldly concerns all around them. Clarke himself felt that was a good diagnosis. The immediate problem, however, was also worldly: paying mortgages on the church. Subscriptions had actually increased enough to cover operating costs, but $12,500 owed on the Freeman Place church was due in full by year's end.

Clarke thought that his time away had restored him enough to return to his usual pace of hyperactivity. In January 1850, however, he experienced chills, vomiting, and a racing pulse. He took a cold shower and then went back to work. One week later, after entertaining the Boston Unitarian ministers at his home, his symptoms returned, but now worsened. Anna then called for Dr. Samuel Cabot, who diagnosed typhoid fever. For some weeks, Clarke's life seemed likely to end before his fortieth birthday. He developed erysipelas, a bacterial skin outbreak, and could not lift his head for two weeks. Fully two months after his first symptoms, his fever finally broke. It was still another two months before he felt able to go outside, to walk from his house to the church and to the Athenaeum.[16]

A few days after leaving his sickbed, he found the strength to walk to the home of Charles Sumner at 20 Hancock Street. Sumner, Clarke, John Albion Andrews, and Ellis Gray Loring met to assess the chances of getting the legislature to choose John Gorham Palfrey, a Unitarian minister and antislavery man, to replace Daniel Webster, who had resigned as US senator to become Fillmore's secretary of state. Although Sumner had helped organize the new Free Soil Party, their conclusion was that the political realities were not looking very favorable. Anna and Dr. Cabot were also insisting that Clarke face the full reality of his weakened condition before returning so soon to a full schedule of ministerial life. Both recommended complete rest and recuperation. Anna felt that best place for that was at Pomona, her family home in Meadville, Pennsylvania. Her father then wrote, virtually insisting that they come. Clarke acceded.

He then advised the Disciples to sell the Freeman Place church to another congregation. Investing the proceeds, they could perhaps eventually resume holding regular services in a less expensive part of the city. Fortunately, the trustees of the Second Church in Boston, led by Clarke's Divinity School classmate Chandler Robbins, needed a new, less expensive building. Having sold their overly large meetinghouse on Hanover Street in the North End, they began negotiations with the Disciples over a proper price for their far simpler building on Beacon Hill. Late in June, Clarke suffered another illness. Dr. Cabot now diagnosed "lung fever," indicating the possibility of consumption or tuberculosis. Although it subsided after two weeks, the time had come to rent the Pinckney Street house and preach a final sermon at Freeman Place. He made it clear that selling the church did not mean the end of the Disciples. At his last service, on August 11, eight devoted families brought forward children for their pastor to christen. Presiding then at communion, he reminded them that offering the holy ordinances did not require clerical ordination. John Albion Andrew and other lay leaders resolved to continue the spiritual life of the Disciples and to continue in communion together. The Disciples would both live on and rise again as an active faith community. Clarke had faith in them.

Almost harder to bear than saying au revoir to dear Boston friends was the sadness of a final adieu to Margaret Fuller. She, her infant son, and husband had died in a shipwreck three weeks earlier. The ship bringing them to America had broken up when a storm drove it aground off Fire Island, east of New York Harbor. Clarke had heard about Margaret's child and his father, but only indirectly. She had written William Henry Channing about Ossoli and their baby Angelo, called Nino. She had also apologized by letter to her mother for not revealing this new descendant sooner, and had written a few others, but not Clarke. A letter Emerson wrote to her, advising that she "stay in Italy, for now," had never reached her.[17] Yet she must have had trepidations about returning to an America culture that she associated with Puritans and bankers, as she had told her friend "Jamie." Giovanni was penniless. Although she styled him *marchese*, he was only a younger son in a lesser line of papal nobility, with an older brother holding the almost worthless title. Had they truly married in some formal or legal way, or merely considered themselves to be married, spiritually? In Italy, it was hard for a Catholic man to marry a "heterodox" woman such as Margaret, as it said on the child's baptismal record. Yet that same document had described Ossoli as married. Church law also authorized taking children born out of wedlock away from a mother who had obviously sinned. Margaret had told Channing that her "tie" to the child's father was a love free from the "corrupt social contract" of marriage.[18] Whatever her marital status, newspaper accounts had provided a vivid account of her last hours. Horace Greeley had assigned his best reporter to the story.

Margaret, Ossoli, and Nino boarded the American merchant brig *Elizabeth* at Livorno, bound for New York. The hold contained a cargo of Italian marble. Near Gibraltar, the ship's captain died of smallpox. Nino also came down with it, but recovered. The first mate who became acting captain did not know the approaches to New York Harbor. When a hurricane arose, he was unable to prevent the *Elizabeth* from running aground off the beach on Fire Island. Two of the three masts came crashing down. As dawn broke, with waves lashing the walls of their deck-level cabin, the six passengers had to join the crew in moving forward, amid howling winds, to the higher forecastle, facing the shore. Among them was Horatio Sumner, younger brother of the future senator. He said to the captain's widow, Catherine Hasty, "We must die." She replied, "Let us die calmly then."[19] A wave nearly swept her away. A mate grabbed her long hair and saved her. A sailor carried Nino forward in a canvas sling. Margaret wrapped him in blankets and held him close. She persuaded the mate to go back and bring her purse and her travel desk, with her manuscript about the Roman revolution. At low tide, some of the sailors decided to try to swim to shore. Sumner also dove in, never to resurface. As the waves crested higher, and it appeared that the ship would break up entirely, the mate proposed tying ropes to planks and towing the women ashore. Catherine Hasty went first, and made it to the beach.

Margaret refused to be separated from her baby and his father. In the early light of dawn, they could see a lifeboat on the distant beach. The mate there, however, could not persuade anyone to help him launch the heavy craft into the huge waves. Many of those who had gathered on the beach were more interested in scavenging among the things then washing ashore than in helping. The acting captain then released his remaining crew to save themselves as they might and swam for shore himself. At midafternoon, some ten hours after grounding, the ship began to break up. All hope of rescue was gone. The last of the crew told everyone to dive, swim, and grab onto anything that would float. The steward took Nino in his arms as a wave broke over the forecastle and brought down the remaining mast, sending them both overboard. The next wave swept away Giovanni and the young Italian nursemaid that they had brought with them. As for Margaret, "when last seen, she had been seated at the foot of the foremast, still clad in her white night-dress, with her hair fallen loose upon her shoulders."[20]

Greeley's reporter found that Catherine Hasty had taken Nino's body, still warm when it washed ashore, to the nearest house. The surviving sailors there crafted a little coffin for him out of a sea chest. They also improvised rough coffins for the steward, nursemaid, and two drowned shipmates. Given the heat of July, all had to be buried in shallow graves in the dunes nearby. Missing were Horace Sumner, Giovanni, and Margaret. Hasty had also rescued a trunk of Margaret's miscellaneous papers, but not the desk with her manuscript. When news of the shipwreck reached her family, her sister Ellen, their mother, and two brothers went to New York. Clarke, ill and ending his pastorate, was in no position to do anything. Emerson responded on behalf of Margaret's friends, paying Henry David Thoreau's expenses to go, to recover her body or writings, if possible. Margaret's sister Ellen's husband, Ellery Channing, went along with him. They met there with his cousin, William Henry Channing, Horace Greeley, and Charles Sumner.

Little was found. Thoreau stayed an entire week, diligently inventorying trunks, clothing, jewelry, and books that he could retrieve from the beach or from the scavengers. Toward the end, an unidentifiable skeleton, shark eaten, appeared nearby. Thoreau felt that it was best to believe that it was *not* from the *Elizabeth*. Emerson told his journal, "To the last her country proves inhospitable to her," while also mourning, "I have lost in her my audience."[21]

Margaret's friends soon realized that what they most needed to retrieve was not her body, nor her manuscript, but rather her reputation. Rumors were already in the air about her union with Ossoli. Even liberal women said that Margaret was rather lucky not to have reached shore. Lydia Maria Child projected from her own experience of marriage and said that Ossoli would have been "wholly unfit to be her husband in this country . . . He would have been nothing here—he could do nothing, be nothing, come to nothing, and he would have dragged her down." Fuller's "only prospect of maintenance was by her pen." Mary Peabody Mann similarly wrote, "When we think of what a laborious and precarious living she would have had to earn, I think that we may well be thankful that they all went to Heaven together, agonizing and melancholy as the departure was."[22] Only Caroline Healey Dall was an exception. In her own journal, she said, "All the particulars of Margaret Fuller's death sadly confirmed. I weep for her. I anticipated her return with lively pleasure."[23]

She knew that while Margaret had been away, writing about revolutions in Europe, another revolution she had helped to spark had broken out at home: a still nascent "second American Revolution," this one involving "the ladies," as Abigail Adams had once called them. Like most revolutions, the American women's rights revolution had multiple origins. Subsequent mythmaking, however, declared that it had begun exactly two years before Margaret's death, on July 19, 1848, at Seneca Falls, New York, when some two hundred women gathered at the Wesleyan Chapel in that village, invited by two women who met in the abolitionist movement, the Quaker Lucretia Mott and Elizabeth Cady Stanton, who had attended Fuller's last "Conversations."[24] The next day in Seneca Falls, men could take part, and some forty did. Frederick Douglass was the only man of color present. Stanton read out a "Declaration of Sentiments and Grievances," modeled closely on the Declaration of Independence: "We hold these truths to be self-evident: that all men and women are created equal; that they are endowed by their Creator with certain inalienable rights." Douglass endorsed those words. It went on to detail the many grievances of women and encourage them to organize and fight for their rights.

Margaret did not know it, because she had never received that letter either, but had she survived, her fellow advocates for women's rights hoped that she would preside at the first truly national Women's Rights Convention, meeting in Worcester, Massachusetts, in October 1850. Had that occurred she would today be remembered as the true founder of the women's rights movement in America. Caroline Dall also hoped to attend, but was still entangled in her highly dysfunctional marriage. After it, she wrote a long public letter in Garrison's *Liberator* to Paulina Wright Davis, the wealthy feminist who did preside in Worcester. Caroline called her address "able, graceful, and prudent," but then went on to offer more thoughts on women's education, equal wages, and the causes of prostitution. She then agreed to help lead the organizing of the next Women's Rights Convention, in Boston, the following year.

Concerned that competition and gossip among other women might dampen appreciation for Margaret's many spiritual, moral, intellectual, and literary contributions to American life, her male friends determined to assemble and then publish the *Memoirs of Margaret Fuller Ossoli*. Greeley first made the proposal. The intention was to pay tribute to her life and literary legacy, while making sure that she was understood to have been duly married and her child legitimate. He then asked Emerson, William Henry Channing, and Samuel Gray Ward, whom Margaret had dared to love before he married her close friend Anna Barker, to serve as the co-editors. When Ward decided that he could not or should not serve, James Freeman Clarke stepped in.

Having largely recovered his health, he had been feeling restless at his wife's family home in Pennsylvania. He had written two little books. He had been doing more reading about non-Christian "ethnic" religions and teaching the subject to students at the theological school in Meadville headed by his brother-in-law. He had even resumed work as an evangelist to the West, visiting Unitarians around the region. He also went to Washington, where Horace Mann was now serving as an antislavery Free Soil congressman. Yet the chance to work through his grief over Margaret's death by helping to shape her legacy had a clear call for him. Returning to New England, he spent three days at Emerson's home with him and with William Henry Channing, going over Margaret's writings and their own memories to present her as unconventional, heroic intellectual but also as a married woman and martyred mother.

Their book became a bestseller. It topped all US book sales and had several printings until displaced, late in 1852, by Harriet Beecher Stowe's antislavery novel *Uncle Tom's Cabin*. Then it went through thirteen more editions before the end of the century. Progressive American women, many of them trapped as Margaret had been in the confines of "woman's sphere," identified with her. One group of women in Knoxville, Tennessee, in 1885 named their club "The Ossoli Circle" as they worked for women's education and suffrage. Proceeds from the *Memoirs* helped to fund a cenotaph in Mount Auburn Cemetery in Cambridge. The family reburied Nino's remains there, even without those of his parents. While all three names are inscribed, the tribute is to Margaret:

> *By birth a child of New England*
> *By adoption a citizen of Rome*
> *By genius belonging to the world*

In early 1851, Caroline Dall was among those who took part in a conversation led by Bronson Alcott to discuss "Margaret Fuller, or, Woman." Others present included Emerson, Higginson, Dr. Walter Channing, and Harriot Hunt. The last was a woman whom Dr. Walter had helped to admit to Harvard Medical School. When virtually all the male students objected to her presence, however, she had been unable to remain. Higginson spoke of Fuller's wide range of intellectual activity. Dall spoke of her discontent with injustice and her "want of serenity." Emerson then passed around a serene daguerreotype image of Margaret made in Rome. It caused Dall to say that in marriage and motherhood, Margaret had at last achieved a beautiful calm previously unknown. When Abby Alcott thanked Dall for her help with a conversation that Dall herself did not think a success, her eyes filled with tears—"for in truth Margaret's death was a private grief to me, & there is no American woman that stands near her."[25]

Through Transcendentalist and related influences, American women were beginning to stand in solidarity with one another, in sisterhood. They were subjecting even the contract of marriage to higher covenantal and transcendent ethical standards. Margaret's male friends were not so much patronizing as realistic in trying to protect her reputation. Like her, they, too, saw marriage as ideally a spiritual, and not just a legal or material union. They also saw another urgent spiritual and ethical question involving legal relationships: namely, the pending divorce between the slaveholding states and those to the North trying to end the South's "peculiar institution" and its exploitation of enslaved women.

Even as they grieved Margaret Fuller, Boston Transcendentalists were shaking their heads and fists over Senator Daniel Webster's speech of March 7, 1850. Twenty years before he had debated Senator Robert Hayne of South Carolina on the floor of the Senate, recalling New England as the cradle of the Revolution and predicting that his region would always defend liberty. He had supported the Missouri Compromise of a decade before with an oration that ended, "Liberty and Union, now and forever, one and inseparable!" Now he endorsed Henry Clay's package of compromises, aimed at preserving the Union. These included, most notoriously, a new Fugitive Slave Law. He also denounced Northern abolitionists, warning that their activity would only lead to war and disunion. Over eight hundred leading Bostonians signed a letter endorsing Webster's efforts at compromise. Emerson felt disgusted. He wrote in his journal, "I opened a paper today in which he pounds on the old strings . . . 'Liberty! Liberty!' Pho! Let Mr Webster for decency's sake shut his lips once & forever on this word. The word *liberty* in the mouth of Mr Webster sounds like the word *love* in the mouth of a courtesan."[26] Webster's financial improprieties, drinking, and philandering were enough a matter of parlor gossip that others agreed. Caroline Dall wrote in her journal that she preferred speeches against the Compromise of 1850 that pointed out Webster's "personal sin."[27] Those two issues—a woman's right to marital divorce or separation occasioned by abuse, neglect, or misconduct; and the question of federal political disunion that might allow the abuse of slavery to continue—were rarely spoken of together, but remained intertwined throughout the 1850s.

Lewis Hayden,
Boston's leading black abolitionist
(1811–1889)

Earth

Those who profess to favor freedom,
and yet deprecate agitation,
are people who want crops without plowing up the ground.

FREDERICK DOUGLASS

Earth to earth, ashes to ashes, dust to dust;
in sure and certain hope of the resurrection unto life eternal.

Book of Common Prayer, BURIAL SERVICE

CHAPTER IX

Collaboration

In which Boston antislavery activists transcend racial lines,
risking their lives to protect the lives of fugitive slaves.

LEWIS HAYDEN WAS ONE OF THE LEADERS of black Boston and perhaps that community's most effective abolitionist and activist.[1] Clarke knew him well. Hayden had first come to Boston in 1845. He quickly became part of an antislavery movement that was far older, more black-led and interracial than has often been recognized.[2] Born a slave near Lexington, Kentucky, in 1812, he saw his first wife and their son torn away as chattel. Sold to Henry Clay and his wife, then to a slave trader, they disappeared into the cotton lands of the Deep South. Hayden could never find them, so he married again. It was with Harriet Bell and her son Joseph that he escaped to Canada in 1844. The Kentucky authorities focused on finding the whites who had assisted the escape.

With attention on their "abductors," the Hayden family quietly recrossed the border to Detroit. The free black community there was growing and building black churches, but it was poor; they sent Hayden to Boston in search of spiritual and financial aid. At a meeting of the New England Anti-Slavery Society, he described his life as a slave and the drama of his escape. Among his listeners was John Albion Andrew, the young lawyer emerging as a leader among the Disciples. Despite differences in race, age, education, and theology, Andrew and Hayden became lifelong spiritual and political friends.[3]

Andrew and others recommended that Hayden become an "agent," or public speaker, for the Anti-Slavery Society, as had Frederick Douglass. Almost everyone meeting Hayden liked him but also recognized that he lacked the inner poise and eloquence of Douglass. As Garrison put it, "His chief embarrassment seems to be to find language to express the facts of his history, and the thoughts and emotions of his mind."[4] On August 1, 1846, Hayden spoke "in a fine grove" in Concord, Massachusetts, for "Emancipation Day," the anniversary of the abolition of slavery in the British West Indies. As the *Liberator* reported, Ellery Channing, Margaret Fuller's brother-in-law, opened the meeting by reviewing the antislavery activities of the previous year. Emerson then spoke, in his "calm . . . philosophical" way, about "the need be of all things." Hayden followed, impressing the crowd by "stammering out touchingly, that which none has power fully to utter, what a glorious thing liberty is."[5] Thoreau and the Concord Female Anti-Slavery Society were the hosts. The "fine grove" overlooked Walden Pond, and the speakers stood in turn on the front step of the little cabin he had built there.

White allies then recommended that Hayden try to find employment in New Bedford. Douglass had found his first refuge in the North there. The first dollars he had earned as a free man were given to him by the local Unitarian minister, Clarke's friend Ephraim Peabody, for whose family he had done odd jobs. Blacks made up a larger proportion of the community in New Bedford than they did in Boston. Friends there may have also helped him to compose a short letter to another antislavery meeting, later published and widely circulated:

> Sir, while sitting alone in my room, thinking of your meeting, my mind has been led to the South, there gathering together my scattered and chattelized relations, but I cannot find them. O, when shall slavery cease? God speed the day I pray, and when I dare to think or bring to mind one dreadful and terrifying fact, that the wife of my youth, and my first born child, is dragging out a life on some tyrant's plantation. I pray you just look at the condition of my wife, driven all day, under the lash, and then at night to be at the will of any demon or deacon that has a white face. How long shall these things be?[6]

That letter may have finally won Hayden the role of agent, but his subsequent speaking tour was not a success. He was often tongue-tied. Wendell

Phillips, the most effective orator among the white abolitionists, drew the difficult task of terminating him. Hayden apologized for his failures as a speaker "jest three years from slavery," saying he was not "a second yourself," but promised to remain an activist for the cause, as indeed he did.[7]

In mid-1849, backed by white allies, Hayden opened a modest store on Boston's Cambridge Street, Boston, offering, said a notice in the *Liberator*, "Men's and Boy's Clothing" at low prices. This was the same business conducted nearby twenty years before by black abolitionist Daniel Walker, whose *Appeal to the Coloured Citizens of the World* (1829) had moved both Garrison and Follen. The ad was also a coded signal: this is where fugitives from the South could obtain warm clothing to prepare for the New England winter. He and Harriet also ran a boardinghouse nearby, on the north slope of Beacon Hill, the center of Boston's free black community. Both the house and the business were to meet the needs of fugitive slaves for shelter, food, and clothing. Although the term "Underground Railroad" implies more organization than was ever the case in the abolitionist network assisting fugitives, the "stations," such as the one run by the Haydens, depended on spiritual and practical alliances crossing racial lines.

Back in Kentucky, a white man who had aided the escape of Lewis and Harriet Hayden still languished in prison five years later. There was no real railroad leadership to help him. Hayden's former owners agreed to join in a petition for his release if they were given $650 in payment for him as their escaped property. Since that man's help was on Hayden's conscience, he appealed to his friends in Boston. Raising the money was easy, but prudence required holding it until the release of the man in Kentucky was confirmed. When that happened, and the money received, Hayden himself was legally free, but Harriet and her son Joseph were both still fugitives—a situation made more perilous after the Fugitive Slave Law of 1850.

To admit Gold Rush California to the Union as a free state, but also to further his own ambitions, Senator Daniel Webster of Massachusetts supported the grand compromise worked out by Henry Clay of Kentucky. In the District of Columbia, slave trading would end, although not slave owning. The new territories of New Mexico and Utah would be nominally open to slavery. Finally, a new Fugitive Slave Law would enforce the return of Southern "property," with criminal penalties (a thousand-dollar fine or six months in prison) for assistance to a fugitive slave, while requiring all citizens to assist in the capture of anyone accused of being a fugitive. Federal commissioners in each district would get ten dollars for returning someone to slavery but only five dollars if they ruled the person was free. Those identified as fugitives could not testify on their own behalf, nor have the right to a jury trial. When it proved impossible to pass the entire compromise as a single package, Senator Stephen Douglas of Illinois pushed through all the related bills. President Millard Fillmore signed the Fugitive Slave Law into effect on September 18, 1850. Many of Boston's commercial leaders and Cotton Whigs felt relieved. They wanted the Union preserved and the cotton trade to go on undisrupted. Conscience Whigs and antislavery leaders were disgusted. In his journal, Emerson fulminated against those who had passed the law and those who found it constitutional, writing, "And this filthy enactment was made in the 19th Century, by people who could read & write. I will not obey it, by God."[8]

Within two weeks of its becoming law, the "Colored Citizens of Boston" convened in a black church on Beacon Hill. The crowd overflowed the hall. They chose Lewis Hayden to preside. Garrison attended and spoke, but the resolutions passed made it clear that the black community had little use for his form of "non-resistance," relying on mere words and moral persuasion, but rather would "defend ourselves and each other in resisting this God-defying and inhuman law, at any and every sacrifice." One speaker, the successful black caterer Joshua B. Smith, brandished a pistol and suggested every fugitive should be given a firearm, declaring that "[i]f liberty is not worth fighting for, it is not worth having."[9] The meeting resolved to call on the clergy to denounce the law and for white allies to join them at Faneuil Hall.

That gathering, on October 14, 1850, consolidated the growing alliance between black and white abolitionists in Boston. Frederick Douglass even came back from Rochester to speak. He said that he knew from his new home in northern New York how many blacks were tempted to flee to Canada, and why he told them to remain in the US to fight slavery. He added that slave owners could gain nothing of value by having a fugitive returned to them because "one who has tasted the sweets of liberty can never again make a profitable slave"; that all they would get would be a chance to inflict torture and murder.[10] Theodore Parker also spoke. He had also been working to bridge the gap between political abolitionists and those who, like Garrison, rejected the US Constitution itself and refused to vote or take any part in electoral politics. His proposal, to form a Committee of Vigilance & Safety, evoked the Committees of Safety in the years just before the American Revolution. With the understanding that black abolitionists would share in the leadership, the meeting adopted his plan. Hayden and Joshua Smith were to be on the executive committee, along with Wendell Phillips and Parker himself, who had written a searing public letter to President Fillmore, a fellow Unitarian, for having signed the Fugitive Slave Law. Robert Morris, the black attorney, joined the finance committee, as did John Albion Andrew. The meeting ended with a final resolution: "Constitution or no Constitution, we will not allow a fugitive slave to be taken from Massachusetts."[11] It was not long before the committee had to take direct action.

Ellen and William Craft were fugitives from Macon, Georgia, with a remarkable story. Because both had skills—he as a cabinetmaker, she as a seamstress—their slave owners had hired them out and allowed them to live together. Having seen children of slaves sold away from their parents, the young couple considered themselves married but vowed not to have children until free. Using the small savings they had been allowed to keep from their earnings, they then made their way northward by rail. Ellen, who was light-skinned, fashioned a disguise for herself. She dressed as a young Southern gentleman, while William pretended to be "his" body servant. Their story was that their journey was for the gentleman's medical treatment in Philadelphia. Nearly stopped in Baltimore, they did reach the City of Brotherly Love. Antislavery activists there sent them on to Boston, where they found a first refuge at Harriet Hayden's boardinghouse. They began to speak at antislavery rallies and attend Parker's congregation, which Ellen joined. When their story appeared in the newspapers,

Georgia slave hunters were able to locate them. Fortunately, Southern slave hunters in Boston were also relatively easy to identify. Black women working in hotels reported them to the Vigilance Committee, which William Craft had joined, but the slave hunters soon confronted him in the carpentry shop he had opened. He and Ellen then turned once again to Hayden and his allies.

Lewis arranged for Ellen to hide, first at the Parker home, then outside the city, while he and William, with a group of heavily armed men, barricaded themselves in the boardinghouse at 66 Southac (later Phillips) Street. They announced that they had two barrels of gunpowder in the cellar below the entrance that would ignite if any slave hunters or marshals ever tried to enter. The Vigilance Committee began to harass the slave hunters both in the streets and in the courts. Abolitionist lawyers filed suits against them for which they would have to post bond, accusing them of slandering the Crafts in various ways. The committee sent Parker to lead a group to confront the slave hunters at their hotel. He said they had thus far been protecting them from outright violence, but that it might be best for them now to leave the city for their own safety—as they soon did. The Crafts now felt that they themselves could only be safe if they left the United States entirely or if the Fugitive Slave Law were overturned. Abolitionist leaders urged them to go to England, to influence British public opinion on American slavery, and raised the funds for them to make the journey. Before leaving, the Crafts asked to be formally married. Parker officiated, in the parlor of the Hayden home. Taking hold of a large knife in one hand, and a Bible in the other, Parker charged William Craft with defending the bodies of both his wife and himself with the one, and their souls with the other.[12]

In his letter to President Fillmore, Parker asked, "Suppose I had taken the woman to my own house, and sheltered her there till the storm had passed by: should you think I did a thing worthy of fine and imprisonment?" Actually, he had already done so. He then defended armed defense of the vulnerable. "There hangs in my study," he told Fillmore, "the gun my grandfather fought with at the battle of Lexington . . . and also the musket he captured from a British soldier on that day. If I would not peril my property, my liberty, nay my life to keep my parishioners out of slavery, then I should throw away these trophies, and should think I was the son of some coward and not a brave man's child."[13]

Parker had indeed kept a loaded pistol and a sword at hand when secretly hiding Ellen Craft, and may have done so on other occasions as well. "Christian non-resistance," the pacifist stance of Garrison and his followers, he saw as inadequate to the armed resistance needed to protect "life, liberty, and the pursuit of happiness" the way his grandfather had. So did most black abolitionists, starting with Frederick Douglass, who never forgot his courageous stance.

In keeping with his Transcendentalist faith, Parker was certain of a higher law, a law made by the universal and transcendent God, to which he was accountable, even if it meant breaking the fallible statutes passed by mere men here on earth. Fillmore, on the other hand, saw his job as one of enforcing the legislated laws of the land and of preserving the federal Union. Addressing Daniel Webster, now his secretary of state, he wrote, "God knows I detest slavery, but . . . we must endure it and give it such protections as is guaranteed by the Constitution till we can get rid of it without destroying the last hope of free government in the world."[14] When Senator William Seward of New York spoke out against slavery and referred to a "higher law," Webster had publicly sneered at the very idea. Emerson commented in his journal (April 1850): "The worst symptom I have noticed in our politics lately is the attempt to make a gibe out of Seward's appeal to a higher law than the Constitution, & Webster has taken part in it."[15] Opponents of slavery in Massachusetts felt betrayed by Webster's support for the Compromise of 1850, and saw in it simply a "profound selfishness," aimed at gaining Southern support for his own presidential ambitions. Instead, he lost the Whig nomination for the presidency and then died just before the next election.

Another sign of the growing bond between black and white activists in Boston was the case of *Roberts vs. City of Boston*, heard before the Supreme Judicial Court in November 1850. Sarah Roberts, a young, free citizen of color, complained, through a suit filed on her behalf by her father, that she had to walk past two other better-housed schools for white children to attend the Abiel Smith School on Beacon Hill, the one shabby school provided by the Boston School Committee for children of color. Her attorneys were the interracial team of Charles Sumner and Robert Morris. Their argument was not only that Sarah's long walk was inconvenient for her and for similarly situated children of color. They also said that "it inflicts upon them the stigma of caste; and although the matters taught in the two schools may be precisely the same, a school devoted to one class must differ essentially in its spirit and character, from that public school where all children meet together in equality."[16]

Chief Justice Lemuel Shaw ruled that the Boston School Committee was free to make decisions about where children should attend school without much attention to racial fairness. The phrase "separate but equal" did not appear in his ruling, but the later US Supreme Court in *Plessy v. Ferguson* (1896) cited his decision to that effect. It put off legal challenges to school segregation for a century, until *Brown v. Board of Education* (1954). Shaw wrote, "It is urged that this maintenance of separate schools tends to deepen and perpetuate the odious distinction of caste, founded in deep-rooted prejudice in public opinion. This prejudice, if it exists, is not created by law, and probably cannot be changed by law."[17] Transcendentalists also argued for an inner change in moral and spiritual empathy. More and more, however, they felt that expecting it to come entirely from within was naïve and might require submitting even the Constitution itself to a higher law, even at the risk of violence and the potential conflagration of armed conflict.

In February 1851, Hayden and his white allies again defied the new Fugitive Slave Law. The fugitive this time was a young man called Shadrach Minkins.[18] He had escaped by ship from Norfolk, Virginia. While he was working as a waiter at the Cornhill Coffee House in central Boston, slave hunters identified him and took him to the courthouse. Members of the Vigilance Committee soon surrounded the building to try to rescue him. As the initial hearing ended, only three hours after his arrest, Hayden saw an opportunity. In a moment of confusion, Hayden, Morris, and other black abolitionists rushed his jailers and absorbed Minkins into their midst, taking him out of the building and into the nearby black neighborhood. Rather than hide him at his own now well-known home, Hayden first hid him in the attic of another house, then in Cambridge, before hiring a large wagon to take him out to Concord and then on to another station stop on the route to Canada.

This escape infuriated Boston's Fugitive Slave Commissioner George Ticknor Curtis, a member of the Federal Street Church, and other supporters of the law. They arrested eight men, four white, four black, including Hayden and Robert Morris. Prosecutors then decided to drop the charges against the whites but to take the blacks, including Morris and Hayden, to trial. Mayor Josiah Quincy then posted bail for Morris, and the Anti-Slavery Society, for Hayden. From Meadville, Clarke wrote to Hayden, expressing his support. John Albion Andrew wrote in reply for him, saying:

> It gratified him, beyond measure, that you should thus remember him. He is bound over to answer to the next term of the United States district court. But I have no idea that he, or any other person, will be convicted. The poorest colored man finds no difficulty in procuring bail at a moment's warning. I think there is a reaction commencing . . . God grant that no man may ever be sent from Massachusetts into the prison house of slavery. I hate war and love peace; but I should less regret the death of hundred men defending successfully the sacred rights of human nature and the blood-bought liberties of freemen, alike cloven down by this infernal law, than I would the return to bondage of a single fugitive.[19]

Public opinion in Boston was rapidly shifting. Massachusetts freemen, black and white, felt invaded by slave catchers. They compared the infringement on their local liberties to those taken by the British that occasioned the Revolution. Despite strenuous efforts by the prosecutors to empanel a jury supportive of the Fugitive Slave Law, Hayden's trial resulted in one juror holding out against his conviction. Similar results freed all the other rescuers. In a similar case, the holdout juror, blacksmith Francis Bigelow of Concord, later admitted being the man who had first hidden Minkins in his home and then driven him to safety in New Hampshire.[20]

The divide among Boston Unitarians, however, only became deeper. Conservatives such as Curtis and his pastor, Ezra Stiles Gannett, argued for upholding enacted law, however much they deprecated slavery. Transcendentalists and abolitionists held to a higher law. At the annual May meeting of the Unitarian ministers, Gannett defended his stance. Theodore Parker replied with scathing rhetoric. He described how he had called their squabble over the Hollis Street Council an "honest difference of opinion," but Gannett had replied, "Not an honest difference," and said he would no longer call him "Brother Parker" nor take his hand. "I attribute no unmanly motive to Mr. Gannett," Parker now declared. "I thought him honest when he denied that I was; I think him honest now. I know him to be conscientious, laborious, and self-denying. I think he would sacrifice himself for another's good." Then he made his case:

> I have in my church black men, fugitive slaves. They are the crown of my apostleship, the seal of my ministry. It becomes me to look after their bodies in order to "save their souls." . . . When a parishioner, a fugitive from slavery, pursued by the kidnappers, came to my house, what could I do less than take her in and defend her to the last? But who sought her life—or liberty? A parishioner of my Brother Gannett came to kidnap a member of my church. Mr. Gannett preaches a sermon to justify the fugitive slave law, demanding that it should be obeyed; yes, calling on his church members to kidnap mine, and sell them into bondage for ever. Yet all this while Mr. Gannett calls himself a "Christian" and me an "Infidel" . . . O, my brothers . . . You [also] have called me "Infidel." Surely I differ widely enough from you in my theology. But there is one thing I cannot fail to trust; that is the Infinite God, Father of the white man, Father also of the white man's slave. I should not dare to violate his laws, come what may come;—should you?[21]

However much Hayden appreciated help from white abolitionists and Transcendentalists, he himself belonged to Twelfth Baptist Church, then referred to as "the fugitive slave church." After Minkins's arrest, that congregation saw over sixty members flee the city, often to Canada. Minkins had settled in Montreal, under a new name. Hayden continued to work in spiritual and practical friendship with whites such as Andrew, Parker, and

Thomas Wentworth Higginson. When a third fugitive slave rescue attempt developed in Boston in early spring 1851, Higginson emerged as another courageous and effective white ally to black abolitionists like Hayden.

Thomas Sims had escaped from slavery in Georgia at seventeen. He was twenty-three when he was arrested in Boston on the night of April 3, 1851. The Massachusetts legislature had by then chosen to deny use of its jails in federal fugitive slave cases.[22] Marshals then took Sims to the federal district court jury room on the third floor of the Bowdoin Square courthouse. Hayden then organized the rescue attempt. When leaders of the Vigilance Committee met in the offices of the *Liberator*, Hayden had his pastor, the Reverend Leonard Grimes, beside him for moral support. Garrison, as a nonresistant pacifist, sat quietly in a corner, trying to set type for the next edition, as the committee debated what to do next. Some, like Garrison, believed in relying on moral suasion, not force. Others were supporters of the new Free Soil Party and did not want to damage its electoral chances nor violate the new federal law. Only Higginson, Hayden and a small minority strongly supported using force to rescue Sims.

Higginson had come from Newburyport for the meeting. He had resigned as the Unitarian minister there after giving a Thanksgiving Day sermon, rather like the one Follen had given in New York City, but much less delicate. He had denounced his congregants for giving thanks for their material bounty while so much depended upon the suffering of others. The merchants of Newburyport clearly opposed his antislavery stance as threatening to their profits from trade. Their reaction led to his resignation, but he then remained in Newburyport to run for Congress as a Free Soil candidate on a "higher law" platform. He said of the Fugitive Slave Law, "DISOBEY IT . . . and show our good citizenship by taking the legal consequences!" Thoreau, of course, had taken a similar stance in his essay "Resistance to Civil Government," now known as "Civil Disobedience."

The Vigilance Committee, however, this time was able to agree only on holding a rally. Higginson was disgusted. He compared their timidity to the courage of black abolitionists, who "had just proved their mettle, and would doubtless do it again." As he later recalled, "On my saying this in the meeting, Lewis Hayden, the leading negro in Boston, nodded cordially and said, 'Of course they will.' Soon after drawing me aside, he startled me adding, 'I said that as a bluff, you know. We do not wish anyone to know how really weak we are. Practically there are no [activist] colored men in Boston; the Shadrach prosecutions have scattered them all. What is to be done must be done without them.'"[23]

After the rally, Higginson wrote to a friend, "It is worth coming to Boston occasionally to see that there are places worse than Newburyport; there is neither organization, resolution, plan nor popular sentiment—the Negroes are cowed and the abolitionists irresolute and hopeless, with nothing better to do than to send off circulars to clergymen!"[24]

Horace Mann, now a Boston-area Free Soil congressman, presided over the rally held at the Tremont Temple. Numerous speeches denounced Daniel Webster, Lemuel Shaw, and the infamous law, but Higginson went further, insisting on an imperative to try to rescue Sims. Samuel Gridley Howe praised him for "bringing the community to the verge of revolution." When no rescue emerged from the meeting, Higginson and Hayden decided to act on their own. The plan was for Pastor Grimes to visit the prisoner for spiritual counsel and quietly convey the plan and signals. Allies would hide mattresses in the offices of sympathetic attorneys around Courthouse Square. At dawn, Sims would crash through the window, land on the mattresses, and then jump into a fast carriage, driven by Hayden. That evening, however, checking on the site, Higginson saw workers installing iron bars on the windows behind which Sims languished.

The rescue was off. What Clarke called "the prayer of John Andrew" was not answered. When dawn rose, a guard of two hundred police and armed men surrounded the courthouse door. They then formed a hollow square around Sims and marched him through the streets of Boston to a federal ship waiting at a wharf. A small crowd of protesters, including Parker, shouted taunts of shame at the guards, especially when the prisoner passed over the spot where Crispus Attucks, a black man, had died in the Boston Massacre that preceded the Revolution. Hayden, Higginson, Howe, and others were clearly ready for a second revolution. Returned to Savannah, Georgia, the fugitive Sims was subjected to a public flogging that nearly killed him.

In the North, the *Liberator* reported that when news of the "man-stealing" reached the textile town of Waltham, outside Boston, the bells of the Methodist, Congregational, and Universalist churches tolled in outrage, but "the bell on the Unitarian Church being clogged with cotton would not sound." On the first anniversary of this outrage, Theodore Parker held a memorial meeting at the Melodeon. Higginson had by then returned to ministry, to lead a nondenominational congregation of antislavery progressives in Worcester, Massachusetts, on a "Free Church" model like that of Parker's.[25] The gap between Transcendentalists and traditional Unitarians was widening.

It was in this context that Clarke once again came back to Boston in September 1851, with his gift for bridging gaps in the service of shared goals. It was a habit. All seven years that he had served in Louisville, Clarke had returned to Boston toward the end of every summer. Now, one reason was to work on the *Memoirs of Margaret Fuller Ossoli*. He, Emerson, and William Henry Channing did much of their collaboration in an odd summerhouse—no longer standing—that Bronson Alcott built for Emerson. With nine arched entrances—one for each of the Muses—and a roof that dipped toward the center, it resembled an exotic, abandoned temple. Emerson had laughingly written about it to Margaret. He referred to it as "Tumbledown Hall." His wife Lidian simply called it "The Ruin."[26] There the three went through Fuller's published works, surviving letters, and journals. They easily agreed that Clarke would write the first section of the memoir—about Margaret's youth and young adulthood, when he had read Goethe with her, and she had had such an influence on him.

Visiting his own publishers, he submitted two manuscripts: one for a short book about his *Eleven Weeks in Europe*, and the other one concerning *The Christian Doctrine of Forgiveness*.[27] The issue of forgiveness must have been much on his mind, at both personal and political levels. Many arguments in the antislavery cause were really arguments about the sin of slavery, the demand for repentance, and the goal of reconciliation. Was it even possible anymore? Only by the grace of God. Perhaps he was also thinking about those who would have judged Margaret.

He was also eager to see his friends and fellow Disciples. Perhaps he hoped that they, too, could forgive him for having left them. They had kept alive the essential spirit of egalitarian discipleship. They had met in one another's homes, rarely in hired halls. They followed Clarke's teaching that no ordained person needed to be present for them to celebrate communion together, and that absolution and reconciliation is an inward work of grace in a priesthood of all believers.

The key lay leaders of the Disciples were two abolitionist attorneys, John Albion Andrew and Ellis Gray Loring, a founder of Garrison's Anti-Slavery Society; the devout and articulate merchant George Bond, the Winslow brothers; and the Chaplin family. Clarke loved them all as much as they loved him. It was poignant to preach to them again at the Freeman Place church that they had struggled so hard to build. Present were both the congregation that purchased it and many of the Disciples. After the evening service, he and some sixty of them then celebrated communion together in the vestry. The following Saturday, he took a friend with him when he went to a marble manufacturer to order a cross and footstone for the grave of his firstborn child. On the cross, he simply had the name "Herman" engraved, and on the footstone, "Dear Boy."

The next day he again preached for the Disciples, this time in Washingtonian Hall on Bromfield Street, hired for the purpose. It was undoubtedly the most gratifying part of the trip. As he wrote to Anna: "The hall was filled with our own people; all the most near and dear. It was delightful to see them again. Theodore Parker and many of his people were there, and some six or eight colored people, including Lewis Hayden. Parker, Hayden [and others] were called out just after the sermon began to attend to a slave mother and child just arrived in a vessel from Virginia. After church some thirty or forty came and spoke to me."[28]

That particular fugitive situation passed without incident. Boston authorities and the abolitionists by that time had reached an uneasy standoff. Most fugitives went undisturbed. Records show that Lewis and Harriet Hayden alone received reimbursement for aiding at least a hundred fugitive slaves in the early 1850s. When Harriet Beecher Stowe visited, she found them currently hosting thirteen fugitives in their small boardinghouse.

Back in Meadville, where Clarke had recovered from his own near fatal illness, Anna had given birth to a fourth child, Ellen, but then doctors diagnosed her mother with dreaded "lung disease," giving her the usual prescription of rest and travel in some warmer place. That spring, he and Anna returned to Louisville, where they had begun their married life. Emma Keats, just a child when James first knew her, had now married Philip Speed, son of the judge and brother of Joshua, Lincoln's intimate friend. They found the Unitarian church there prospering under Clarke's successor, and the city grown larger and more beautiful. Yet Anna still did not feel well. Physicians advised a longer stay, in an even warmer place. The children were well cared for at Pomona, and they had the financial means, so James suggested they go to the Mediterranean. They stopped briefly in Brooklyn, where the Unitarians had tried to entice Clarke to be their pastor, to decline the call politely. They sailed from New York in October 1852. After a few weeks in England, they went to Italy, where he had hoped to see Margaret a few years before. They spent two delightful evenings in Florence with Robert and Elizabeth Barrett Browning. The latter was beginning to write a book-length poem—more like a novel—called *Aurora Leigh*. It centered on a female character like both Elizabeth Barrett and Margaret Fuller, raised in economic and educational privilege. The secondary figure, however, Marian, seems more based on Fuller as she had come to Browning two years before—with a child born out of wedlock, but not through any form of spiritual sin on her part.[29]

Clarke, like Channing, called himself a "catholic Christian," at least among Protestants, seeing redemption as a work of grace and one of voluntary acceptance of a new start in life. From Nice, surrounded by Catholics, yet excluded from communion with them, he wrote the Disciples, expressing his desire to rejoin them, saying, "I am here apart from all communion of worship, but I feel myself more than ever at home in the great universal church of the Lord Jesus. In that church is one Lord, one faith, one baptism. Heresies and schisms are unknown in it. Its creed is a trust in God the Father, and love to man the brother. Its worship is obedience and benevolence, doing good and growing good. From this church no one can excommunicate or exclude us except ourselves."[30]

Clarke knew that he was more privileged by class and economics, more temperate, and more traditional in his theology than Theodore Parker. Unlike his friend, he still believed in the need for Christ's mediating role between human sin and God's infinite perfections. Thanks to his grandfather and the Stone Chapel prayer book, his worship style was also more traditional. When he prayed "Thy Kingdom come, Thy will be done, on earth as it is in heaven," he knew that his goals were the same as those of Parker and the radicals. So he would never exclude such fellow Transcendentalists from Christian fellowship. Perhaps he thought he could play a mediating role between the radicals of Boston and the wider spiritual support that they would certainly need. That would mean returning to work with the Disciples again. After a tour of Europe, including a stop at the ancestral seat of the Huidekoper family in Holland, and a rendezvous with his mother and sister, starting their own yearlong European trip, Clarke wanted to use his gratitude for the renewed health of both himself and Anna to return to his vocation, soon. He and Anna stopped in Boston on their way back to Meadville, so he could preach and celebrate communion with the Disciples again. There were not many left: the same sixty. Yet wonderful friends! No building. Just a small fund left from selling the Freeman Place chapel. He would return in the fall, alone initially, to explore if resurrecting his ministry with the Disciples seemed feasible.

Boston had changed. Downtown, houses once owned by Brahmin families had become tenements for Irish immigrants. Anti-immigrant sentiment was rising. Yet there were hopeful signs. Back Bay, once a stinking cesspool, was now filling with gravel brought in by railway. The city was expanding southward, toward Brookline, Roxbury, and the village of Jamaica Plain. There were also some signs that divisions between the Unitarians need not last forever. Emerson and Parker were still thought heretical. Yet when Emerson gave a new series of winter lectures, or when Parker preached his radical gospel of political and social transformation at the Music Hall, even former conservative critics of Transcendentalism attended.

For Clarke to preach to them again, the Disciples rented Williams Hall, in the South End. Attendance was not large, but it included some new people. Samuel Gridley Howe and his wife Julia Ward Howe began attending regularly. They had been early followers of Parker, but now preferred a more churchlike congregation. Then there was Caroline Healey Dall, also clearly in need of a spiritual community after her husband's departure to Calcutta. She could be difficult and often talked too much at social meetings, but she was willing to do volunteer work with the Sunday school and other projects.

Most promising was the overture made by the congregation of the Indiana Place church, also in the South End, but a bit closer to the Common, and with no pew ownership to deal with. They had followed the voluntary model that Clarke had pioneered. Now their minister wished to retire. The members would consider merging with the Church of the Disciples if Clarke would agree to be their pastor and if the Disciples would assume the outstanding debt on their building. There was a pipe organ to support the singing and the good possibility of a volunteer choir. Clarke agreed to resume his role as pastor of the Disciples as of January 1, 1854. Negotiations with the Indiana Place people took until autumn, but 1854 would prove to be an important turning point not only for the Disciples but also for the antislavery struggle. It would center on an event that Clarke both witnessed and gave a public name: "The Rendition of Anthony Burns." Once again, Lewis Hayden needed collaboration with white allies; even if he failed to rescue a fugitive, he was building momentum for the shared cause of liberation.

Thomas Wentworth Higginson
(1823–1911)

CHAPTER X

Rendition and Insurrection

In which Boston Transcendentalists try to stop
"The Rendition of Anthony Burns,"
radicalize the antislavery movement, and help form
the "Secret Six" behind John Brown's plan
for a slave insurrection.

IN THE WINTER AND SPRING OF 1854, national US politics centered on the "Nebraska bill." So did the political attention of antislavery Boston. As maneuvered along by Senator Douglas of Illinois, the proposal would overturn the Missouri Compromise of 1820 and employ popular sovereignty—the votes of new white, male residents—to determine if any part of the huge Kansas/Nebraska territory would be slave or free. Most Democrats, even in the North, felt obliged to support Douglas as a matter of party loyalty (and patronage). The Whig Party, already split in Boston between Cotton Whigs and Conscience Whigs, would come apart after dividing on this issue. Mass meetings protesting the bill took place in Boston and elsewhere. In Congress, the debate grew so heated that violence was just below the surface. A petition against the bill, started by Harriet Beecher Stowe and signed by over three thousand clergy of all denominations, was to be presented to Congress by Senator Edward Everett of Massachusetts on March 7, the anniversary of Webster's infamous speech favoring the 1850 Compromise. Despite his credentials as a Unitarian minister and as a past president of Harvard, Everett thoroughly bungled the occasion. He somehow failed to vote when an early form of the Nebraska bill came up and passed the Senate. Antislavery Bostonians were outraged, and Everett was forced to resign. The House then passed the bill on May 22; the Senate, two days later. Senator Charles Sumner then re-presented the petition with added signatures on May 25, saying that passing the Kansas-Nebraska Act, which overturned the 1820 Compromise, makes "all future compromises impossible. Thus it puts Freedom and Slavery face to face, and bids them grapple. Who can doubt the result?"[1]

Democrats celebrated. Antislavery outrage in Boston expressed itself in the form of mass protests and an urban riot over the capture of yet another fugitive slave. James Freeman Clarke named it, in a sermon given the following Sunday and widely reprinted, "The Rendition of Anthony Burns."[2] The dramatic events in Boston took place just as the political drama in Washington was also unfolding.

Anthony Burns was nineteen years old when he escaped slavery in Virginia, arriving in Boston by ship in 1853. He found work first in Hayden's haberdashery, then in another clothing shop, and joined the Twelfth Baptist Church on Beacon Hill. On Wednesday, May 24, 1854, as he was just coming home from work, federal marshals seized him, taking him to the courthouse. Almost simultaneously, Boston Democrats celebrating the Kansas-Nebraska Act stole cannon from an armory, dragged them to the Common, and fired a salute. Pastor Grimes did not learn that his congregant was in jail until the next morning. After visiting the prisoner, he alerted Parker as head of the Vigilance Committee. They found Burns already in court, before Judge Edward G. Loring, sitting as a commissioner under the Fugitive Slave Act. Present was the Virginian Charles Suttle, who had identified Burns as his property. Parker, presenting himself as minister-at-large to fugitive slaves in Boston, persuaded the resigned but religiously inclined Burns to accept as his counsel Richard Henry Dana, an attorney on the Vigilance Committee. The judge granted a continuance until Saturday.

The committee obtained Faneuil Hall for a Friday night mass meeting. Handbills went out decrying the "kidnapping" and the lack of trial by jury, invoking the spirit of the American Revolution. Debates over tactics divided the enlarged committee, now numbering over two hundred. Samuel Gridley Howe wanted fifty armed men to try to seize Burns immediately. Others wanted a night attack or a mass assault on the courthouse. Still others opposed any form of violence. The majority voted to await a decision and then, as marshals took Burns to a ship, to assemble a crowd and carry him away in all the confusion. Black abolitionists were to keep the courthouse under constant watch in the meantime. Lewis Hayden took yet another tack: He swore out a complaint against Suttle and a fellow slave catcher for attempted kidnapping. This resulted in their arrest but also their quick release on bail. When Higginson arrived from Worcester, where he was the pastor of the new Free Church, he succeeded in persuading a smaller group, including Hayden, to join him in a forcible rescue. The plan involved axes, a battering ram, and other weapons, and an interruption of the Faneuil Hall meeting.

On Friday at 7 p.m., an estimated five thousand people crowded into Faneuil Hall, including three hundred women. Parker entered with attorney and Disciple John Albion Andrew. His West Roxbury neighbor George Russell presided. The last two speeches were by Wendell Phillips and Parker. Neither said very much about Burns himself. "There is now no law in Massachusetts," Phillips declared, "and when the law ceases the people may act in their own sovereignty." "Fellow-subjects of Virginia!" began Parker. "Take that back!" people cried. "Fellow citizens of Boston, then." He said that hypocrisy lay in mere protest, and valor only in deeds. He then presented the issue as a struggle against the slave powers for the soul and manhood of all descendants of the Revolution. "Now, I want to ask you what you are going to do." Some cried, "Shoot! Shoot!" Taken aback, Parker said there were other means. He called for everyone to assemble at Courthouse Square at 9 a.m. Others shouted about going *now* to the courthouse or to the slave catchers' hotel. Russell got the formal resolutions passed, but the crowd was nearly out of control when one of Higginson's men yelled, "A mob of negroes is in Court Square, attempting to rescue Burns!"[3]

This was not true, but the crowd poured out. The only doors were at the end of the hall most distant from the platform. The leaders were now in the rear. Higginson and his men from Worcester had axes; Hayden and the others, a huge beam with which they began battering down the courthouse door. Shots rang out. Someone put out the gaslight. The newly reorganized Boston police arrived but arrested only one rioter at a time. When the courthouse door gave way, a black man entered first, with Higginson right behind him. The deputies inside used billy clubs. One of them, twenty-four-year-old James Batchelder, shouted that he had been stabbed. He died quickly. Higginson, his chin nicked by a saber, then tried to rally the crowd, but the assault had failed. The mob had begun to pull back. Bronson Alcott arrived just in time to hear Higginson berating them. He then entered the courthouse quite serenely, while the police, astonished at his spiritual composure, simply stood back. Alcott then exited, just as calmly. Howe arrived in time to see both the door broken and the attack fail. Seeing it was futile to stay, he went home to his wife. Julia was pregnant, sick, worried, and worn out, as she wrote the next day, by her "habitual struggle against crying."[4]

The governor called out the militia to keep order. The federal marshal had authority to use troops and marines from the Charlestown Navy Yard. Suttle told Rev. Grimes that he would free Burns for twelve hundred dollars. The money was available, but by then it was Sunday. Grimes had scruples against doing business on the Sabbath. Others pointed out that Massachusetts law forbade buying and selling human beings. Many, including both Garrison and Theodore Parker, were opposed to paying off enslavers and persuaded the largest donor to withdraw his pledge. The rescue had not succeeded. Yet in human rights work, there is such a thing as "failing forward." That strategy depends upon activists staying resolute in the face of failure and then reframing the failure into outrage that mobilizes more moderates. In the Burns case, Higginson and Hayden may have led the failed action, but Theodore Parker led the rhetorical reframing, and John Albion Andrew and James Freeman Clarke provided the resolute voices necessary for persistence.

Loring's order came down on Friday, June 2. It required "many hundreds of constables and policemen, the marines from Charlestown, cavalry, infantry and a light battery with shotted guns, to take Burns to the waiting ship," said Clarke in his sermon two days later. Captain Hayes of the Boston police resigned rather than take part. Along the route, black crepe draped buildings and American flags in mourning. A black coffin labeled "Liberty" hung suspended over the street. Clarke watched from the law offices of his fellow Disciple John Albion Andrew, now lead counsel for the rioters. With him was his congregant, Walter Channing, Higginson's father-in-law. Below the office window, a city alderman held forth, denouncing the mayor's use of military force. People yelled, "Kidnapper! Slave Catcher! Shame!" in the street. What impressed Clarke the most, however, was Andrew, at his desk, "the only calm man in the room," preparing his case in defense of those who felt compelled to follow a higher law rather than that of the one Emerson had called a "filthy enactment."

The trial resumed Monday, which began Boston's annual "Anniversary Week," when churches of all denominations and organizations of all sorts held their annual meetings. Hayden prudently left town. The arrested rioters came before the local courts. The Boston *Post*, organ of the Democrats, called the meeting at Faneuil Hall "treasonable." Higginson, now charged with riot, and further accused of "high treason," wore both as proudly as he did the scar he had acquired on his chin. He boasted to a fellow abolitionist that it was *high* treason because it had "always been considered the crime of a gentleman." In the end, the prosecutor dropped all such charges. Parker was one of six accused merely of "incitement to riot." Andrew served on the defense team that then succeeded in also getting even those indictments quashed.

The Sunday after armed force returned Burns to slavery, Clarke gave his sermon, "The Rendition of Anthony Burns" on Pentecost Sunday. "I blame today the churches and clergy of Boston," he declared, "for if they had been faithful to their Master, this could not have happened." He especially blamed all Unitarians who had supported the Fugitive Slave Law. He then went further: "Last Friday Christ was crucified again in the form of the poor negro slave. This morning I feel in my heart that he has risen from the grave, and that his spirit is poured out on many a mind and heart."[5] His sermon was printed and four thousand copies distributed. That same Sunday, Parker spoke to thousands in the Music Hall. He decried martial law as despotic. When he spoke of the death of Batchelder, he boldly indicted Judge Loring as like Pilate, the one most at fault.

The Burns case converted some of Boston's conservative leaders to the cause of antislavery. Cotton Whig millionaire Amos Abbott Lawrence was certainly one. He later wrote, "We went to bed one night old-fashioned, conservative, compromise Union Whigs & waked up stark mad Abolitionists."[6] Another was Channing's conservative successor in the Federal Street pulpit, Ezra Stiles Gannett. When his own daughter asked him what he, as a Christian minister, would do if a fugitive came to their door, Gannett said he would provide shelter, assist an escape to Canada, and then go prison himself, if need be. When told that the military had already taken Burns back to bondage, he burst into tears.[7]

The Boston merchant class, led by Lawrence, then entered the antislavery struggle through a mechanism they all knew well—by forming a joint stock company. The Massachusetts (later New England) Emigrant Aid Company was to invest in sending antislavery settlers to Kansas. Such emigrants, they hoped, would outvote pro-slavery settlers from neighboring Missouri and the South—while also turning a profit from the rich agricultural lands of the Kansas plains. Lawrence was corporate secretary. The goal was to send as many as twenty thousand emigrants a year, but recruiting idealists to do farm work, just as with Brook Farm, was not that easy, especially in the face of violence. Fewer than two thousand New Englanders joined the company and went to Kansas. Over a third soon left in the face of the violent actions against them by pro-slavery "border ruffians" coming over from Missouri. The American Unitarian Association sent a minister to try to bolster morale. Ephraim Nute arrived at the antislavery town of Lawrence, Kansas, in the spring of 1855 bearing a pistol given to him by colleagues and a shipment of Sharps rifles disguised as Bibles, and began to gather a Unitarian congregation. On May 21, 1856, pro-slavery forces attacked the town. The foundations of the Unitarian church building, not yet built, became a fort. A number of church members died in battle.[8] The Free State Hotel burned to the ground. The news, conveyed by telegraph, reached Boston just as another Anniversary Week was beginning.

On June 3, 1856, Faneuil Hall once again housed a mass protest meeting. A new Kansas Aid Committee resulted, with Samuel Gridley Howe as its secretary. His mandate was to enlarge the committee and to send not just emigrants to Kansas, but more weapons and more funds, this time donated rather than invested. The expanded support group now included not only Dr. Samuel Cabot of the Disciples; but also the wealthy Unitarian industrialist George Luther Stearns of Medford, a follower of Parker; and eager young Franklin B. Sanborn, age twenty-five, Harvard Class of 1855, a schoolmaster in Concord, and admirer of Alcott. Along with Parker, Howe, and Higginson, Stearns and Sanborn would become five of the "Secret Six" supporting John Brown in Kansas and beyond. Serving as agent for the committee, Higginson went to Kansas that September with an armed emigrant group and made a public report in the form of a series of letters printed in Greeley's *New York Tribune*. From Lawrence, he reported, "Ever since the rendition of Anthony Burns, in Boston, I have been looking for *men*. I have found them in Kansas." He went on to describe how two hundred Free State men and a few women had held off a pro-slavery army estimated at twenty-eight hundred or more. "They had no regular commander, any more than at Bunker Hill; but the famous 'Old Captain [John] Brown' moved about among them, saying, 'Fire low, boys.'" He urged contributors to remember that even a few dollars could buy the bullets needed to protect those struggling for freedom. That Sunday he preached a sermon that took for its text "the one employed by the Rev. John Martin the Sunday after he fought at Bunker Hill—Neh. iv: 14; 'Be not ye afraid of them; remember the Lord, which is great and terrible, and fight for your brethren, your sons and daughters, your wives and your houses.'"[9]

Higginson believed in what he called a whole "sisterhood of reforms." The abolition of slavery was his highest priority, but women's rights were not far behind. He had signed the call for the Women's Rights Convention held in Worcester in 1850. He also stood up for immigrant rights and religious freedom. When he defended the right of a Catholic child in a public school to read from the version of the Bible that her priest had approved, he lost his post on the Worcester school board, but won it back. He dared to speak to the all-male Massachusetts Constitutional Convention of 1853 on "Woman and Her Wishes," calling for a range of rights well beyond the right to vote. When the World Temperance Convention that year refused to seat Lucy Stone on the platform, he led a walkout of women's rights supporters to form a *Whole* World Temperance Convention. When Stone married Henry Blackwell, daring to retain her own name, Higginson officiated. Prison reform, abolition of the death penalty, electoral reform, extending the franchise, ending the common law treatment of labor unions as "conspiracies," abolishing imprisonment for debt, elimination of child labor, and free public education for all were some of his other causes. He returned from Kansas predicting that the conflict there "is only the prelude to a severer struggle" to come. After the new Republican Party, trying only to stop the extension of slavery, lost the election of 1856, he initiated a Disunion Convention at Worcester, attended mostly by Garrison and other abolitionists who had lost all hope of ever using or amending the federal constitution to end slavery. Higginson was the epitome of a young Transcendentalist minister as a radical activist, striking for how often he formed spiritual friendships with other crusaders for freedom, black and white, male and female, some quite different from himself, including John Brown.

Brown was no religious liberal, but rather a staunch Calvinist, with the feel of an Old Testament patriarch and the fervor of a prophet. He had endured multiple failures in business and suffered multiple personal losses. By the mid-1850s, he had fathered twenty-two children with two successive wives, but only twelve of them were still living. Born in Connecticut, raised in the Western Reserve of Ohio, he claimed descent from a Peter Browne who had been aboard the *Mayflower* and a grandfather who had died fighting in the Revolution. His Transcendentalist supporters liked to say that he was "a Puritan of the Puritans." His first homestead was in New Richmond, Pennsylvania, near Meadville, land once held by the Holland Land Co., sold by Harm Jan Huidekoper. Having failed with a tannery there, Brown spent the years 1846 to 1850 in Springfield, Massachusetts. There he failed again, this time as a dealer in wool. That only seemed to deepen his commitment to antislavery. Springfield's black abolitionists had formed a nondenominational Free Church, similar to Higginson's congregation in Worcester and Parker's in Boston. Brown joined. There he heard speakers like Sojourner Truth and helped Springfield become a station on the Underground Railroad. In 1847, Frederick Douglass gave a lecture at the church and talked with Brown. Both of them shared the deep feeling that wholly peaceable means would never abolish slavery in America. During the course of his work in the wool trade, Brown had managed to travel to England and Europe in 1849, musing on military history and failed revolutions. When his wool business went bankrupt, he reinvented himself by going to Kansas to fight for the Free State cause.

The burning of Lawrence caused a violent, vengeful reaction in Brown. A few days later, he led what even his most sympathetic biographer has termed "a war crime."[10] He and his followers found five sleeping pro-slavery sympathizers and brutally butchered them. This Pottawatomie Creek Massacre only escalated the violence in "Bleeding Kansas." Brown never took responsibility for the incident; rather he tended to emphasize how God had guided him in all his battles. At Palmyra, Kansas, he and nine followers, plus twenty local men, successfully defended the Free State settlement, taking twenty-three prisoners. After feeding them, Brown signed an agreement releasing them in exchange for two of his sons held captive by pro-slavery forces. When the release of his sons did not happen quickly, his outrage only grew. On August 30, 1856, some three hundred pro-slavery men attacked the Free State settlement at Osawatomie. They shot and killed Brown's son Frederick and another man. Outnumbered seven to one, Brown led only thirty-eight defenders but managed to inflict sixty casualties on his opponents. The day ended in retreat, but gave "Osawatomie John Brown" a reputation for bravery and success in the antislavery cause.

Brown came to Boston in January 1857. James Freeman Clarke met him in the course of a pastoral call. Senator Charles Sumner was at his home in Boston, recovering from a traumatic beating inflicted in May when he was caned and bloodied while sitting at his desk in the Senate. His assailant was Congressman Preston Brooks of South Carolina. Sumner had given a speech on "The Crime against Kansas." In it, he referred to Senator Andrew Butler of South Carolina, one of the cosponsors of the Kansas-Nebraska Bill, as having "chosen a mistress to whom he has made his vows, and who, though ugly to others, is always lovely to him; though polluted in the sight of the world, is chaste in his sight. I mean the harlot, Slavery."[11] Brooks felt that this rhetoric impugned the honor of his relative, Senator Butler, and of all Southern "gentlemen." Long after his wounds healed, Sumner suffered neurological impairment and perhaps post-traumatic stress. Clarke had known Sumner since they were boys together at the Boston Latin School.

The senator was not his congregant, but simply a friend. As Clarke later told the story, "I first saw John Brown at Charles Sumner's house in Hancock street, Boston. I was shown to his chamber, where he was reclining on the bed. Three men were in the room with him, Captain John Brown, one of his sons, and [the journalist] James Redpath. In the course of the conversation, the circumstances of the assault on Sumner were cited, and he said, 'The coat I had on is hanging in that closet.' John Brown went to the closet, took out the coat, and looked at it as a devotee would contemplate the relic of a saint."[12]

Sumner's rhetoric had offended Preston Brooks, not only because it alluded to the sexual exploitation of women of color by their white masters but also because it implied Sumner's own moral superiority as a man. Still unmarried at forty-five, Sumner was drawing on the Victorian-era assertion that men were most "manly" when suppressing rather than indulging their sexuality. This was especially true in the North, among inheritors of the Puritan ethos. Sumner's closest friend, Samuel Gridley Howe, is a good example. He had fought, like Byron, for Greek freedom against Turkish rule and became a Chevalier of the Greek Order of St. George. Warned by his medical training not to contract a venereal disease, Howe became "Chev" to his contemporaries and "the manliest man" to his biographer. He was still a bachelor at forty-two when he married young Julia Ward, having channeled his libido into both reform work and social ambition.[13] James Buchanan, elected to the White House in 1857 at the age of sixty-six, was the only bachelor president in US history.

Brown, when Clarke met him at Sumner's, was in Boston to find friends and funds for his efforts in Kansas. He met with Franklin Sanborn in the grubby garret on School Street that was the office for the Kansas Aid Committee, asking for thirty thousand dollars and two hundred rifles. He was a guest of Theodore Parker at one of Parker's regular Sunday afternoon home receptions. Garrison and Wendell Phillips both attended, but neither felt that they could excuse Brown's extralegal violence. George Luther Stearns, on the other hand, having heard Parker preach on Kansas, felt that Brown was just the Puritan Cromwell that the antislavery cause needed. He invited Brown to stay at his estate in Medford, "The Evergreens," where

Brown's tales of the Kansas atrocities committed by pro-slavery forces prompted Henry Stearns, twelve, to hand over to Brown all his boyhood savings. His wealthy father then agreed to pay for the two hundred rifles. Brown also addressed a committee of the Massachusetts legislature, asking it to join Vermont in voting an appropriation to protect settlers going to Kansas. That failed, but the next month, in Concord, Brown met Emerson, dined with Thoreau, and spoke to the local lyceum on Kansas and "the folly of the peace party" in a way that left a positive impression of his character, even if it did not raise much money.

Pro-slavery forces in Kansas had declared in print their intent "to repel this Northern invasion and make Kansas a Slave State; though our rivers should be covered with the blood of their victims and the carcasses of the Abolitionists should be so numerous in the territory as to breed disease and sickness, we will not be deterred from our purpose."[14] Supporters of Brown were willing to respond in kind, although they characterized their efforts as defensive, not aggressive. Even popular preachers, such as Harriet Beecher Stowe's brother, Henry Ward Beecher of Brooklyn's Plymouth Church, took up collections for Kansas, as did the Disciples. People began to call the rifles sent to Kansas "Beecher's Bibles." *Uncle Tom's Cabin*, Harriet's novel, did much to spread antislavery sentiment in the North. Brown came back to Boston the next year. He had been thinking about slave insurrections, and how to take the struggle beyond Kansas, where it now appeared that Free State forces would prevail. Clarke once again encountered him, this time in the office of Dr. Howe at the Blind School. As Clarke later recalled,

[Brown] said that he was proposing to do something which should alarm the slaveholders along the northern line of slavery, and make them feel that they could not hold their slaves in safety, and so induce them to move South, and he hoped thus, by a series of attacks along the border, that slavery would gradually be pushed further South, and all the rest of the territory would be free soil. That was the plan. He said, "I am proposing to do on a larger scale what I did in Kansas. When I found that the Missouri people were in the habit of attacking us in Kansas, I saw that we must fight fire with fire. So I organized a party and invaded Missouri, and carried off a whole party of slaves[,] some 20 or 30. I took them into Kansas, and marched them through Nebraska and Iowa into Illinois, and finally carried them over into Canada, where they were free. Though the papers told every day where we were, yet on one occasion only was I hindered on my march. I was crossing into Nebraska, when the United States marshal came into the hut or log cabin where I was with only a few men, and ordered me to give up the slaves to him, and to his orders. I took my rifle," said old John Brown, "and I told him I would give him two minutes to leave in, and no more. But if I had known he was one of the men who murdered my friends in Kansas, I wouldn't have given him those two minutes."[15]

The next day, according to Clarke's account of Brown's narration, the marshal with a large posse of men waited for Brown's party to cross the river. John Brown had only about twenty men. He formed his men into two lines; and they charged into the river, and by the time they had reached the other side the marshal's party broke and ran. Brown's men pursued, caught the marshal, made him dismount, and put an old black woman and her baby on his horse, which they compelled him to lead the rest of the day.[16]

Brown certainly knew how to tell a good story, nearly always with himself as the hero. He described his plan to his supporters as "[Underground] Railroad business on a *somewhat extended scale*." He first revealed that it involved a slave insurrection in Virginia to only two men. One was young Franklin Sanborn. The other was the one member of the Secret Six who was neither a Bostonian nor a Unitarian. Gerrit Smith was a wealthy philanthropist, abolitionist, and politician, who had inherited a vast tract of land in the Adirondacks from his father, who had been a business partner of John Jacob Astor. Raised a Calvinist, Smith had absorbed the duty of accounting to God for his undeserved good. He devoted his wealth to the full range of needed social reforms, including building one of the country's first temperance hotels. His first cousin, Elizabeth Cady, met a fellow abolitionist, Henry Stanton, at his home, and married him there.

In 1840, Smith had helped to found the abolitionist Liberty Party. James Birney, its first presidential candidate, became his brother-in-law, and they traveled together to the World Anti-Slavery Conference in London that year. Eight years later, Smith was the candidate of the same party, now competing with a more pragmatic Free Soil movement. He then served a term as a Free Soil congressman, and donated 120,000 acres of land around the village of North Elba in the Adirondacks to the cause. Fifty-acre farms were free to former slaves and to allies like Brown.

On Washington's Birthday, 1858, at his home in Peterboro, New York, Smith and Sanborn heard Brown's plan. Brown said he had studied previous slave insurrections, such as one in Jamaica that helped to hasten emancipation. Those, he found, often involved retreats to mountain country, and guerilla raids from the mountain base. From this came his plan to capture the US armory at Harpers Ferry, Virginia, then to establish a multiracial guerrilla force in the Appalachians, sending women and children northward to safety. Neither Smith nor Sanborn felt that the plan could succeed, but they also sensed that it would be impossible to dissuade Brown from following what he felt to be his God-given mission. "We cannot give him up to die alone," said Smith to Sanborn, "We must support him."[17]

Sanborn went back to Boston and arranged for Brown to meet with other key supporters, who then met in his room at the American House Hotel on Hanover Street on March 4: Sanborn, Stearns, Higginson, Parker, and Howe. They all judged that the time for peaceful efforts to end slavery had passed. The Supreme Court had ruled, in the Dred Scott case, that people of African heritage could never be eligible for citizenship and that residence in free states could not protect fugitives. Like Frederick Douglass, these white allies no longer saw any peaceful path toward ending slavery; they were ready to support a slave insurrection, a Second American Revolution, and what Douglass had called "a conflagration" aimed at slave power in the South.

Brown then attempted, without great success, to get black leaders on board with his radical plan. He had drafted a provisional constitution for the lands that he planned to free, with himself as president. He wanted it ratified by a convention of black abolitionists at Chatham, Ontario, near where many fugitives from slavery had settled. Few attended. Yet Brown did not seem to get the message that black slaves would be reluctant to follow a white leader in a slave insurrection.

Perhaps beginning to envision a Christlike martyrdom, he soon acquired his own white Judas. Brown had hired an English drillmaster, Hugh Forbes, who had served with Garibaldi in Italy. Forbes kept demanding more money, writing to various other antislavery leaders, and criticizing and revealing outlines of Brown's plan. Alarmed, Smith came to Boston on May 24, 1858, and met the others (minus Higginson) at the Paul Revere House in the North End, then used as a tavern. They concluded that Forbes was enough trouble that Brown should delay. He agreed to do so. That winter Brown went back to Kansas. Theodore Parker became so ill with tuberculosis that he left for the Caribbean with Lydia, then to the Mediterranean, and had no more direct ties with Brown. Sam and Julia Ward Howe went with the Parkers as far as Cuba. Brown came to Boston a third time in the spring of 1859. His supporters there, especially Howe, Higginson, and Sanborn, did not have much money to give, but helped him raise the two thousand dollars he said he needed—including twelve hundred dollars and two hundred more rifles from Stearns alone.

Were Brown's plans doomed from the start? Was he crazy? This has been a common later assessment. Higginson may have been closer to the mark when he said to another donor, "He is of the stuff of which martyrs are made. He is of the Puritan order militant." Brown's most recent biographer, the antislavery historian David S. Reynolds, calls him perhaps the truest white antiracist of his generation.[18] Yet he had rigid turn of mind, given to believing his own plans, even for his failed business ventures, to be foolproof. Surely Frederick Douglass was only being prudent when he declined to take part in the Harpers Ferry plan, doubting that any white man could spark and lead a successful slave rebellion. There is no need to repeat here the whole story of what happened when the raid on the federal armory took place in October 1859. Suffice it to say that Brown learned what several generals learned in the Civil War. Set at the confluence of the Shenandoah and the Potomac rivers, with high ground looming all around, Harpers Ferry is relatively easy to capture, but almost impossible to hold. The raid ironically caused the needless death of several people of color, not to mention most of his raiding party and two of Brown's sons. Captured, imprisoned, and tried for treason, Brown met his own death by hanging on December 2, 1859.

Smith, who had said, "We cannot give him up to die alone," was so distraught by fear of his own arrest that when the Chicago *Tribune* said that he had had knowledge of the plan, he sued for libel. When the paper produced proof, in the form of an affidavit from one of Brown's surviving sons, Smith had himself committed to an insane asylum for over a month. Reactions to Brown's capture among his other key supporters varied. Sanborn, alarmed by reports that the army had found letters from himself, Howe, Stearns, and Smith at the farmhouse in Maryland that Brown had used as his base, consulted with John Albion Andrew, who suggested that he leave the country. He took ship for Quebec. Sam Howe told Julia that he, too, had helped Brown, warned her that "men may be coming," and then galloped off, leaving her alone once again, in the last stage of a difficult pregnancy. He rode to Medford, to Stearns, who suggested that they, too, should consult Andrew. By the time they did, the attorney had researched the law of treason. He found that Virginia might prosecute Brown's accomplices for treason, but not Massachusetts. Emerson then wrote Sanborn that it was safe to come home. Howe set about raising funds and finding counsel for Brown's legal defense in Virginia. Only Higginson remained calm, reacting most like a minister. He went to North Elba to Brown's family, bringing his widow, Mary, back to Boston with him. He also conspired with Howe on how to rescue Brown from jail in Virginia. While her husband and Higginson pondered improbable rescue plans, Julia Ward Howe reported in a letter,

I have just been to church and heard Clarke preach about John Brown, whom God bless, and will bless![19] I am much too dull to write anything good about him, but shall say something at the end of my book on Cuba, whereof I am at present correcting the proof-sheets. I went to see his poor wife, who passed through here some days since. We shed tears together and embraced at parting, poor soul . . . [Brown's] attempt I must judge insane but the spirit heroic. I should be glad to be as sure of heaven as that old man may be, following right in the spirit of the old martyrs, girding on his sword for the weak and oppressed. His death will be holy and glorious—the gallows cannot dishonor him—he will hallow it.[20]

The Transcendentalists, with their rhetorical gifts, soon turned John Brown's death into a martyrdom that helped to turn the coming conflagration of civil war into a sacrificial effort to end slavery. On the same Reformation Sunday, October 30, that Clarke spoke, Thoreau addressed the citizens of Concord with "A Plea for John Brown." He was searing about the complacency of most. "I plead not for his life, but for his character," he said, "his immortal life; and so it becomes your cause wholly, and is not his in the least. Some eighteen hundred years ago Christ was crucified; this morning, perchance, Captain Brown was hung. These are the two ends of a chain which is not without its links. He is not Old Brown any longer; he is an angel of light."[21] He repeated this talk before the Parker Fraternity in Boston on November 1, substituting for Frederick Douglass, who, like others who had known of Brown's plan, had found it expedient to leave the country. Emerson then chimed in. In his November 8 lecture in Boston on "Courage," he called Brown a "new saint awaiting his martyrdom, and who, if he shall suffer, will make the gallows glorious like the cross."[22]

On the same day, Mary Stearns, as strongly antislavery as her husband George, raised in Medford with Lydia Maria Child as her "Auntie," wrote Brown a supportive letter. He replied that no letter he had received meant more to him, writing, "[M]ay God forever reward you & *all yours. My love to All* who love their neighbors. I have asked to be *spared* from having any *mock; or hypocritical prayers made over me,* when I am publicly *murdered:* & that my *only religious attendants* be poor *little, dirty, ragged, bare headed, & barefooted, Slave Boys & Girls,* led by some old gray headed Slave Mother. Farewell. Farewell."[23]

In mid-November, Andrew revised his opinion on the legal vulnerability of the Secret Six. There was a statute that would make possible their indictment. Sanborn and Howe then fled again to Canada. Higginson thought such "fugitive behavior" to be both dishonorable and self-incriminating. When a letter from Howe appeared in the *New York Tribune* praising Brown but denying knowledge of his plans, Higginson wrote him to say that it just made him sad. Meanwhile Sanborn composed a dirge for a public service in Concord on the day of Brown's execution. Theodore Parker was by then in Rome, having traveled there from the Caribbean. The last thing he wrote for publication before his own death was a letter defending Brown. He spent the day of Brown's December execution in contemplation, interrupted only by coughing and a visit from an English doctor to whom he said, "I shall be seeing Brown soon. We two have an appointment; my old friend and I are booked on separate trains to the same distant place . . . Hold a séance as old Garrison will most assuredly do." Howe and Stearns sat vigil during the execution on the Canadian side of Niagara Falls, listening to what the latter called "the dirge of the cataract."[24]

The Secret Six were not out of danger even after Brown's death. A Senate Investigating Committee, chaired by Senator James Mason of Virginia, with Jefferson Davis of Mississippi as a member, had power to subpoena them. Higginson escaped a summons, for lack of a letter from him to Brown. On April 3, 1860, five federal marshals arrived at Franklin Sanborn's home in Concord, handcuffed him, and attempted to wrestle him into a coach and take him to Washington. Some 150 local people rushed to his defense. In a letter to a friend, Louisa May Alcott wrote, "Sanborn was nearly kidnapped. Great ferment in town. Annie Whiting immortalized herself by getting into the kidnapper's carriage so that they could not put the long legged martyr in." A judge intervened. Only Howe and Stearns ultimately testified. Both denied knowing that Brown "contemplated anything like what occurred at Harpers Ferry." "I should have disapproved if I had known of it," Stearns defiantly added, "but I have since changed my opinion."[25]

The Mason committee condemned all who had supported Brown, but filed no charges against any of them. It filed its final report in June 1860. Theodore Parker had by then succumbed to tuberculosis, dying in Florence on May 10. In Boston, John Albion Andrew became the governor of Massachusetts. As several observers later noted, the Secret Six and their allies had a relationship with Brown that paralleled that of the original Disciples with Jesus. Like Peter, they had taken up arms for Brown, but then denied really knowing him. After his death, they declared that he was still alive. "He is more alive than he ever was," said Thoreau of Brown. "He has earned immortality . . . He is no longer working in secret. He works in public, and in the clearest light that shines on this land." The work that Brown began went marching on toward its goal: emancipation but also at the cost of conflagration.

John Albion Andrew (1818–1867),
Governor of Massachusetts, 1861–1866

CHAPTER XI

Emancipation

In which an abolitionist disciple becomes governor,
regiments of black soldiers are formed and outfitted,
a battle hymn is composed,
and a proclamation is celebrated
in honor of John Brown.

THE DRAMA AT HARPERS FERRY ended October 18, 1859, with the capture of John Brown. With that news not yet in hand, James Freeman Clarke the same day finished a long letter to his ailing and absent colleague, Theodore Parker. Over the years, he had maintained a warm, bantering friendship with his more radical colleague and friend. He addressed one note to him, "Rev. Theodore Parker, D.D. (degree given by the people)," acknowledging that Parker's scholarship had never been properly recognized by Harvard. Another, referencing Parker's disdain for hierarchy and church tradition, went to the "Rt. Rev. Theodore Parker . . . Bishop of [the] Music Hall." In 1856, Clarke had even collaborated with Parker on a brief effort to revive regular meetings of the Transcendentalist circle. This last letter began: "Did you know that I had the pleasure of preaching to your people in the Music Hall on Sept. 25th? And moreover do you understand, that by their full consent, I talked to them about *you* & your opinions—liking the first pretty well, the last not quite so well. The day was good, the congregation also good, that is to say in numbers, their goodwill in other respects I will not vouch for. But they looked serious, and quite as devout and wide awake as congregations in general."[1]

Clarke then reported on recent events in Boston in the same tone. Wendell Phillips in speaking at the Music Hall had mocked their more traditional Unitarian colleague in New York, Bellows, for wanting a "Broad Church"—when the Twenty-eighth Congregational Society was already as broad and inclusive as any church could ever hope to be.[2] He also described the dedication of a new statue to "St. Daniel [Webster]" on the lawn of the State House—reporting that Heaven had shown disdain for the proceedings by pouring torrential rain on that occasion, driving Edward Everett and his listeners into the nearby Music Hall, of all places. For balance, Clarke reported, he and others were pressing the Commonwealth to commission a statue of abolitionist Horace Mann, who had died in August, for the opposite side of lawn. (Both remain there to this day.)

When he turned to politics, however, Clarke had no jokes. He fretted. By not carrying Pennsylvania in the last national election, Republicans, the party that had arisen from among the antislavery Whigs, had lost the presidency to a mediocrity: James Buchanan of that state. Clarke now worried that in the next election, the antislavery party might settle on "some third rate man" from there or further west. Lincoln of Illinois was not yet a contender. Only after his speech at New York's Cooper Union, in February 1860, did he become even a long shot for the Republican nomination.

Clarke was delighted that his congregant John Albion Andrew had emerged as a major leader in Republican politics in Massachusetts. Andrew had led the successful effort to have Judge Edward Loring removed from the bench for his role in the rendition of Anthony Burns.[3] Andrew had then chaired the state party convention in 1858, but his work in defense of John Brown and of the Secret Six was what really gave him prominence. At an event for Brown's legal defense, both Emerson and Wendell Phillips spoke. Andrew's own words were better than theirs: "I pause not now to consider . . . whether the enterprise of John Brown and his associates in Virginia was wise or foolish, right or wrong; I only know that, whether the enterprise itself was one or the other, *John Brown himself was right.*"[4]

Summoned by the Mason committee of the US Senate, Andrew acquitted himself well, even when badgered by Jefferson Davis of Mississippi. He admitted to giving Brown twenty-five dollars as a personal gift, but denied knowing of all his actions in Kansas or his plans for the raid on Harpers Ferry. He even dared to cite the beating of Charles Sumner and the way it had been "justified, [or] at least winked at throughout the South [as] an act of much greater danger to our liberties and to civil society."[5]

Early in 1860, the Massachusetts Republican Convention overwhelmingly chose Andrew, the defender of the most radical abolitionists, as a delegate to the national convention, giving him 769 votes out of 774. Many expected Senator William Seward of New York to be the nominee for US president, but they found his maneuvering for conservative support a bit distasteful. "We are mainly for Seward," Andrew wrote, "I am so, not for special liking for him."[6] Yet when the national convention met in the Chicago Wigwam, the temporary hall constructed for the occasion, dislike of Seward and distrust of his principal opponent, Edward Bates of Missouri, a onetime slave owner, led to the nomination of Lincoln on the third ballot. Andrew then not only supported Lincoln but also was named to the small delegation sent to Springfield to ask the nominee to accept.

Back in Boston, Andrew addressed a gathering of Mass Bay Republicans at Faneuil Hall. He said that when Lincoln had prevailed, all the delegates exploded in "a peal of human voices, a grand chorus of exultation, the like of which has not been heard on earth since the morning stars first sang together, and the sons of God shouted for joy."[7] "You ask me what Abraham Lincoln is like," he told a crowd still wary of the little-known Westerner. "My eyes were never visited with the vision of a human face, in which more transparent honesty and more benignant kindness were combined with . . . [both] intelligence and firmness." He said that he would gladly trust Lincoln as his own personal attorney, and that "I would trust my country's cause in the care of Abraham Lincoln as its chief magistrate, while the wind blows and the water runs." He then ended in soaring rhetoric. He defined the stakes in the election of 1860 as nothing less than preserving the Union, saving the territories from slavery, and preventing "the opening of the abominable trade in men from Africa to our own shores." He cited the words of a forgotten New England hero of the "second American War of Independence," the War of 1812, who, when asked if he could capture an enemy battery, replied, "We will try, sir!" Republicans now needed to capture the swing states of Pennsylvania, Indiana, and New Jersey. He then ended, "And the heart of patriotism, the impulse of country's love, the hope and heart of American youth and American age, respond, with one long and loud resounding voice, 'By the help of heaven we will try—we will try!'"[8]

With that oration, many Massachusetts Republicans began to talk about John Albion Andrew as the next governor. One barrier was the incumbent, Nathaniel P. Banks, also a Republican, but no antislavery man. The legislature had tried to open military service to men of color. They had sent the bill to Banks as part of a larger package of statutory revisions. Banks had vetoed the whole to block black men from serving in the militia. Then in his third one-year term, Banks had secretly accepted a lucrative post as president of the Illinois Central Railroad, as of January 1, 1861. He wanted Congressman Henry Dawes of western Massachusetts, another conservative Republican on matters of race, to succeed him. Hoping to block Andrew, he kept everyone thinking that he might claim a fourth term until just days before the August Republican convention. His plan did not succeed. Banks declared that Andrew's "John Brown sympathies and speeches, his Garrisonian affiliations, his negro-training predilections and all that sort of extreme anti-slaveryism with which his record abounds will be . . . [used] to harm Lincoln," but Andrew easily outpolled Dawes, 723 to 327.

That November, Lincoln and Andrew both emerged victorious in four-way elections. Democrats divided between a Southern ticket led by John Breckinridge of Kentucky and a Northern ticket headed by Douglas of Illinois. The "Constitutional Unionists," largely former Whigs, supported John Bell of Tennessee and Edward Everett of Massachusetts on a platform of compromise. Republicans in 1860 ran not only against any extension of slavery but also for freedom of immigration, the full rights of immigrants as citizens, and redistribution of national wealth to the poor through a Homestead Act, and for an infrastructure investment in a transcontinental railroad from the Atlantic to the Pacific.

In the North, many conservatives seemed desperate to reach compromise with the South.

Lemuel Shaw resigned as chief justice of Massachusetts in order to lead thirty-four prominent citizens of the Commonwealth in proposing repeal of the Personal Liberty Law that had granted fugitive slaves a hearing before his court. These and all other proposed compromises, including a package put forth by Senator Crittenden of Kentucky, Henry Clay's successor, were futile. South Carolina wasted little time after Lincoln's election. It passed its Ordinance of Secession on December 20. Governor-elect Andrew, despite high blood pressure and a bleeding nose, went to Washington to consult with other Republicans. Their consensus was that the secession of other states, and a war to preserve the Union, was inevitable. As Andrew took office in January 1861, two months before Lincoln did, he ended his inaugural address by quoting a Democrat—President Andrew Jackson—who had responded to South Carolina's attempts to nullify federal law by declaring, "The Federal Union, it must be preserved!" He also ordered a one-hundred-gun salute to the Union fired in every town of the Commonwealth on January 8, at noon.[9]

Not all abolitionists agreed. Wendell Phillips, filling Parker's pulpit in the Music Hall one Sunday a month, preached disunion. During the Fort Sumter crisis of April 1861, he favored letting the South go, telling an audience in New Bedford: "A large body of people, sufficient to make a nation, have come to the conclusion that they will have a government of a certain form. Who denies them the right? Standing with the principles of '76 behind us, who can deny them the right? . . . I maintain on the principles of '76 that Abraham Lincoln has no right to a soldier in Fort Sumter. . . . You can never make such a war popular. . . . The North never will endorse such a war."[10]

In late January, when the Anti-Slavery Society met, a gang of proslavery, antiwar rowdies disrupted the meeting with a rather bawdy chant that ended with the refrain, "Tell John Andrew/ John Brown's dead!"[11] Andrew then undertook a symbolic action. Theodore Parker had left, as a gift to the Commonwealth, the two historic muskets he had alluded to in his letter to Fillmore protesting the Fugitive Slave Law: one carried by his grandfather, Captain John Parker, on Lexington's Battle Green in 1776, and one captured that day from a British soldier. Andrew arranged a formal presentation of the weapons before the legislature. Telling their story, he then lifted the captured musket, kissing it. The silence that followed, he wrote Sumner, "was a melting time." As he contemplated the present crisis and "the beautiful heroism of the ancient men and women of Massachusetts," he "sat down, yielding to a perfect tempest of emotion, and wept as I had not done for years."[12]

Sam Howe's response to the firing upon Fort Sumter was to write to Governor Andrew: "Since they will have it so,—in the name of God,—Amen! Now let all the Governors and Chief men of the people see to it that war shall not cease until Emancipation is secure. If I can be of any use, anywhere, in any capacity (save that of spy) command me."[13] Higginson felt similarly. Having resigned as minister of his church in Worcester, he was restless. He walked around local ponds and wrote Thoreau-like essays observing and reflecting on the natural world.[14] These alternated in the *Atlantic Monthly* with essays on what John Brown had not understood about earlier slave rebellions, such as those of Denmark Vesey and Nat Turner.[15] "Longing for the tonic of war," he also saw that "[w]e cannot transform the world except very slowly . . . Nature . . . does her work almost as imperceptibly as we," and that "a policy of emancipation will be reached by stages so as to unite public sentiment."[16] When war did come, his reaction was to write, "I think the world is growing better all the time."[17]

When Union forces then liberated some of the Sea Islands of South Carolina below Charleston, Higginson began to worry over any "general & indiscriminate arming of slaves." He had read too much history. Unprepared insurrectionists often suffered more than did their oppressors. Yet he did want to go to war. After early battles in Virginia defeated the Union, he gained Andrew's permission to raise a regiment of Massachusetts volunteers. Both saw how few abolitionists, often thought of as pacifists, had taken early roles in the Union Army. He asked Clarke to serve as chaplain, writing, "I think that the army is becoming a power so formidable that [it] is essential to the safety of nation that a high tone of character should prevail in it."[18]

Yet since he was a minister himself, with no military background, his recruitment efforts faltered, even as he realized that his desire to go to war also stood in conflict with his duties as a husband. He felt a "powerlessness to stir, because of Mary, while I am not clear whether it is conscience or weakness."[19] His wife, Mary Channing Higginson, was an invalid. At first he told her he would go only if drafted. Then he arranged for Mary's niece, Margaret Fuller Channing, child of Ellery and Ellen Fuller Channing, to live with Mary and care for her. He then became an officer in the Fifty-first Massachusetts Volunteers.

Andrew responded to the crisis of war much as Lincoln did, recruiting a "team of rivals" to focus on the Union, not emancipation.[20] As head of the militia, he appointed a rival with military experience whom he had defeated for governor: Benjamin Butler, who had run as an ally of the pro-slavery Southern Democrat John C. Breckinridge of Kentucky, Buchanan's vice president. When Lincoln prevailed, there were few troops protecting Washington, where president-elect Lincoln wondered aloud if there really was a "North" beyond Maryland. He desperately needed the slave-owning "Border States"—Maryland, Delaware, Kentucky, Missouri—to remain in the Union. He himself had almost had to be smuggled into Washington through Baltimore, protected by Pinkerton guards. Heading down to help protect him, the Sixth Massachusetts Regiment suffered a brutal attack in Baltimore by pro-slavery mobs. Andrew had the bodies of those killed, the first casualties of the conflict, brought home and buried with full honors. In Boston, Soldiers Committees formed, helping to recruit and outfit soldiers and to organize volunteers.

Among the Disciples, Caroline Healey Dall chaired the church's Soldiers Committee. Clarke offered a site for a training camp: Brook Farm. He had purchased that property in 1856, hoping to gather there not a commune, but rather a cooperative of progressive families living in separate family houses. Although a few friends showed some interest, no one had followed through. Clarke then built a house in Jamaica Plain, near the home of his friend and congregant George Bond, and close to the horse cars going into Boston. Clarke renamed Brook Farm as "Camp Andrew." The Second Massachusetts Regiment, including the sons of some leading abolitionists, trained there. Clarke called them "the best crop" that Brook Farm had ever produced, but it was also the last on that site. Training soon shifted to Camp Meigs in Readville, closer to the rail line to Boston.

In the first months of the Civil War, especially after the defeat at Bull Run, Andrew aptly described the Union Army as "a congregation of town-meetings without a leader."[21] He withheld his own strong preference for immediate emancipation in order to support Lincoln and to build consensus around preserving the Union. Yet when General John C. Fremont, commanding the Army of the West in Missouri, declared the emancipation of all slaves within his jurisdiction, Andrew supported him—while Lincoln felt compelled to countermand the order. His feeling: emancipation? Not yet. The time was not yet ripe.

Governor Andrew did not agree. Later that year, in the autumn of 1861, he and his wife Eliza, Dr. Howe and his wife, Julia, and their minister, James Freeman Clarke, all went together to Washington. Howe was now on the new US Sanitary Commission, appointed by Lincoln and Congress. That group, chaired by Clarke's colleague in New York, Henry Whitney Bellows, inspected camps, guided health care, provided relief, and channeled the humanitarian support offered by the civilian population, largely raised by patriotic churchwomen and their clergy. Andrew rather enjoyed taking part in this "ladies' expedition." It included sightseeing, a brief meeting with Lincoln, and reviewing elements of the army protecting the capital. They heard William Henry Channing, then the Unitarian minister in Washington, on Sunday. The next day, they visited the First Massachusetts Artillery, headed by Colonel William Batchelder Greene, the West Point graduate and Unitarian minister who had married Anna Blake Shaw.

Greene persuaded a reluctant Julia Ward Howe to deliver a brief speech to his soldiers. With her husband elsewhere, Julia made her first public address. The men applauded her speech. Andrew called her "the heroine of the day." It would not be her last public utterance on the war. On yet another day, they attended a review of Union troops outside Alexandria. When the Union cavalry had to respond to prevent nearby Confederates from cutting off some advance guards, the review ended, and soldiers crowded the roads. Clarke and Julia Howe rode in a carriage back to Washington together, "through the Virginia woods, Wisconsin and Pennsylvania regiments marching by our side singing "John Brown's Body" while the moonlight glittered on their bayonets."[22] A chant against abolitionist Brown had met a Methodist camp song. The lyrics now asserted that although "John Brown's body lies moldering in his grave/ His soul is marching on." The men cheered. Then Clarke, sensing that to her the rousing song might be painful, suggested, "Mrs. Howe, why do you not write some *good* words for that stirring tune?"[23]

She said she had often wished to do so, but had not yet found the time or the inspiration. That night, at the Willard Hotel, she slept soundly, but awoke just before dawn with the first stanza of the "Battle Hymn of the Republic" rising in her: "Mine eyes have seen the glory of the coming of the Lord." She then forced herself to write more in the oncoming dawn, while her youngest child slept near her. Then she returned to bed and to sleep, thinking, "I like this better than most things that I have written."[24] The *Atlantic Monthly* published the full poem in February 1862. It gradually became the anthem of the Union cause and one of the most evocative of all American hymns. Often heard as expressing militarism or triumphalism, Howe's "Battle Hymn," if read closely, builds on the John Brown story, casting it as one of submission to a divinely ordained mission of redemption from the collective sin of slavery—through emancipation.

Like Lincoln, John Albion Andrew had tried to stay quiet about emancipation to focus on saving the Union. Then General David Hunter, commander in the Sea Islands, issued an order that freed the slaves not only in his direct control but also in Georgia and Florida. Andrew received a request from the War Department for three more regiments from Massachusetts. He replied, "[I]f the President will sustain General Hunter, recognize that *all* men, even black men, as legally capable of that loyalty the black are waiting to manifest, and let them fight, with God and human nature on their side, the roads will swarm if need be with the multitudes whom New England would pour out obedient to your call."[25] Lincoln again countermanded the order. Abolitionists were again disappointed, but soon helped the freed slaves of the Sea Islands in other ways: by setting up schools and sending teachers. Edward Everett Hale led the New England Educational Commission overseeing the project, with Clarke assisting. Edward Hooper, one of the most devoted of the Disciples, went as a teacher. Later, so did women such as Louisa May Alcott, who had worshipped with Parker's congregation in the late 1850s. The Disciples also joined in sponsoring the Whitney School for freedmen, set up separately from the commission.

During the summer of 1862, the abolitionist campaign for emancipation gained ground. That July, Congress passed, and Lincoln signed, a Second Confiscation Act, allowing the army to organize freed slaves to support the Union. On Sunday, August 10, Andrew spoke before an audience of eight thousand at a Methodist camp meeting on Martha's Vineyard. Later he called it the best speech of his life. He said that he had never believed that the war could end without slavery also ending; that since Lincoln had canceled Hunter's emancipation there had been no more Union victories, the blessing of God having been withdrawn. When he said he had faith that "the appointed hour has nearly come," Methodists shouted amen. Back in his office, Andrew next asked a well-connected Massachusetts Republican leader to go to Washington to lobby Lincoln. When he balked, Andrew said, "You believe in prayer, don't you?" Andrew had them both on their knees, uttering such a fervent prayer to end slavery that the man later repeated it both in New York City and to Lincoln.[26]

On August 20, Greeley's *New York Tribune* carried an editorial in the form of an open letter to Lincoln called "The Prayer of Twenty Millions," demanding emancipation now. Lincoln wrote back, "[I]f I could save the Union without freeing any slave I would do it, and if I could save it by freeing all the slaves I would do it; and if I could save it by freeing some and leaving others alone, I would also do that." Politically savvy, Lincoln knew he could use his power as commander in chief to free the slaves in the rebel states, but that it must not appear as an act of desperation. Only after the costly Union victory at Antietam did he sign a first emancipation proclamation: within all the rebellious states, unless they returned to the Union, he would declare all slaves free as of January 1, 1863. Within the Sea Islands, the Union military governor, General Rufus Saxton, then began to recruit freed slaves for a black regiment, the First South Carolina Volunteers. Needing a white colonel, he heeded the advice of his chaplain and wrote to Higginson, then a captain in the Fifty-first Massachusetts Volunteers. That letter "took his breath away."[27]

As he later said, "I had been abolitionist too long and had known and loved John Brown too well, not to feel a thrill of joy at last on finding myself in the position where he only wished to be." His success in guiding a thousand truly disadvantaged former slaves into "a state of training and morale equal to that of any white regiment of similar experience" became the theme of articles he published in the *Atlantic Monthly* and later collected as *Army Life in a Black Regiment.*[28] Higginson not only rigorously disciplined his troops but also listened to them, becoming one of the first whites to truly appreciate and transcribe the antebellum slave songs known as "spirituals." He also led them into danger, foraging and temporarily capturing the town of Jacksonville, Florida. On one occasion, his black soldiers clearly saved his life. John Albion Andrew by then had written to his friend Lewis Hayden: "Every race has fought for Liberty and its own progress. The colored race will create its own future by its own brains, hearts, and hands. If Southern slavery should fall by the crushing of the Rebellion, and colored men should have no hand and play no conspicuous part in the task, the result would leave . . . the freedmen . . . neither strangers, nor citizens, but 'contrabands,' who had lost their masters but not found a country."[29]

Kansas was by now also raising a regiment of free black soldiers, but Andrew wanted one from Massachusetts to honor the Commonwealth's revolutionary heritage. He succeeded, although recruitment both of officers and of enlisted men proved to be a challenge. Under War Department orders, the officers had to be white. Recruiting experienced white officers truly committed to antiracism would be very difficult. Governor Andrew wrote to Francis Gould Shaw, Parker's onetime neighbor in West Roxbury, asking him to persuade his son Robert, then a lieutenant in the Second Massachusetts Infantry, to lead the new black regiment. Young Shaw was only twenty-five, but already battle-tested several times, including at Antietam. Moreover, he came from a family well known for its staunch abolitionism. Andrew closed his plea saying, "I don't want the offer to go begging; and if this offer is refused I wd. prefer its being kept reasonably private." Robert did in fact decline at first. He both felt attached to comrades in the Second and doubtful of his ability, at his young age, and with his privilege, to transform a thousand black men into an effective fighting force.

Like most white abolitionists, he was also not entirely free from his own race prejudices. His mother wrote him, "[T]he task is arduous . . . but it is God's work." Shaw then reconsidered and accepted. It was also a way of vindicating a friend. An officer in his regiment, R. Morris Copeland, a member of the Disciples, had gone to Secretary of War Edwin M. Stanton to advocate for black regiments. Shaw had gone with him. When Stanton refused, Copeland wrote a letter of protest to a Boston paper. Stanton then had him discharged as insubordinate.[30]

Andrew also knew that recruiting enough black enlisted volunteers in Massachusetts would be no easy task. The 1860 census showed only 1,973 black men of military age in the whole Commonwealth.[31] A regiment needed a thousand men: ten companies of a hundred each. Free blacks in New Bedford provided one company; in Boston, with Hayden helping, another. Somehow a much wider effort seemed imperative. Andrew turned to George Luther Stearns, the wealthy businessman among the Secret Six. He agreed to work with Frederick Douglass in recruiting beyond the Bay State. It helped that so many now joined with Mrs. Howe in seeing the Union cause in redemptive terms. Sarah Sturgis Shaw wrote to her son, the newly made colonel, "I believe this time to be the fulfillment of the Prophecies, & that we are beholding the Second Advent of Christ."[32]

On New Year's Day 1863, elite Boston celebrated the Emancipation Proclamation with a Jubilee Concert at the Music Hall. Emerson recited his new "Boston Hymn." It too cast the freeing of the slaves as part of a God-driven and historic process of democratization.[33] That led to a speech by Wendell Phillips, Handel's "Hallelujah Chorus," Beethoven's Fifth Symphony, and then Mendelssohn's "Hymn of Praise." Meanwhile, at the nearby Tremont Temple, home of Boston's first desegregated church, a less elite, biracial crowd heard the proclamation read aloud. Clarke then spoke.[34] Douglass closed by leading them in singing "Blow Ye the Trumpet, Blow!," John Brown's favorite hymn and sung at his funeral.[35]

Later that night, George and Mary Stearns held a party at their estate, the Evergreens, in Medford. The caterer was Boston African American entrepreneur Joshua B. Smith. Guests were the leading (white) antislavery advocates of the Boston area: Franklin Sanborn, Garrison, Wendell Phillips, Bronson Alcott, Samuel Sewall, Samuel Longfellow, and others. Some had missed the Music Hall event, so Emerson again read his "Boston

Hymn." As young Franklin Stearns later recalled, Phillips then unveiled a white marble bust of John Brown commissioned by his parents, with a brief speech "so graceful, exquisite and timely, that it seemed to him like another poem." Julia Ward Howe then recited, in a "weird, penetrating voice," her "Battle Hymn of the Republic."[36] With the war still far from concluded, abolitionists, pacifists and militants alike, could at last unite, in the midst of war, in celebrating emancipation.

In organizing recruitment for the Fifty-Fourth Massachusetts Volunteers, Stearns had acted as the well-organized business leader he was. He went first to Rochester, to partner with Frederick Douglass, whose two sons both enlisted. He traveled on to Buffalo and Toronto, then into the Midwest. African American leaders in Ohio, New York, Pennsylvania, and elsewhere helped to find recruits from fifteen Northern states, four Border states, five Confederate states, Canada, and the West Indies.[37] In two months, Stearns had overfilled the rolls of the Fifty-Fourth. He then asked Andrew for permission to form a fifty-fifth regiment, soon granted. The Disciples donated over a thousand dollars to this recruitment effort.[38] The church made other gifts to help to outfit and equip the black troops.

For one congregation to have so much to do with instigating, recruiting, and outfitting a military regiment may seem to offend the ideals of church/ state separation, not to mention the Christian goal of peace, but to the Disciples, the effort had a transcendent, redemptive purpose. Others seemed to agree. Soon the five hundred seats in their modest building on Indiana Place were overflowing on Sundays with worshippers inspired by their support for black emancipation and an end to slavery.

Andrew had said that he wanted officers for the Fifty-Fourth "in whom the men put faith" and "who would put faith in the men." One such was young Luis Fenollosa Emilio. Like Shaw, he stood only five-feet-five inches and was blue-eyed but darker in complexion. Born in Salem, he was the son of a Spanish music teacher. Seven years younger than his colonel, he had lied about his age to join the Twenty-Second Massachusetts at only sixteen; yet the next year, leading in a battle on North Carolina's Roanoke Island, he had distinguished himself. Andrew tracked events involving Massachusetts men closely. In February 1863, he wrote to Emilio's superiors. He wanted him sent north to become a lieutenant in the Fifty-Fourth. Before training camp ended, Shaw made eighteen-year-old Emilio captain of Company E.

On the morning of May 28, 1863, over a thousand members of the Fifty-fourth Massachusetts Volunteers, now in crisp new uniforms, carrying rifles, knapsacks, and bedrolls, led by young Colonel Shaw on horseback, marched before the State House in Boston. This is the scene captured in the bas relief monument by Augustus Saint-Gaudens that has stood opposite the Massachusetts State House since it was dedicated in 1897.[39] They paused briefly in front of 44 Beacon Street, the Boston home of Shaw's parents, where Shaw lifted his sword in tribute to his parents and to his bride, Annie Haggerty Shaw, who had become his wife three weeks before. He then led his troops past a reviewing stand filled with dignitaries, including Andrew, Stearns, Garrison, Douglass, and others. With the band playing the John Brown song, they continued to the waterfront, past the Old State House and ground "moistened by the blood of Crispus Attucks." They then boarded ship, headed ultimately for the Sea Islands. As they passed through New York City, a white reporter described the men of the Fifty-Fourth: "Every one of these recruits can read and write. They certainly bear an excellent appearance; they were evidently conscious of their dignity as soldiers, and marched better than white recruits generally do who have been under training for so short a time. They did not seem to heed the curious scrutiny of the crowds of men and boys which gathered round them; and their martial bearing forbade any symptoms of disrespect."[40]

The fate of the Fifty-Fourth, now quite well known, does not bear repetition here in detail. The 1989 film *Glory*, with Matthew Broderick and Denzel Washington, rendered its outlines. The US Army tried to pay the black enlisted men at the rate of laborers, not that of white troops. The men of the Fifty-Fourth refused the lower pay. Andrew and Shaw intervened and prevailed. Then, on July 28, 1863, the Fifty-Fourth led an assault against Fort Wagner, a stronghold on the approach to Charleston. One racist Union general decided it would be good to put them "in the advance, [since] we may as well get rid of them."[41] Two hundred seventy-two members of the regiment were captured, wounded, or killed, including Colonel

Shaw and nearly all the officers. Shaw's parents received an anonymous letter dated three days later:

> I regret to inform you that Col. Shaw is killed. The 54th Mass., of which he was Col., fought so bravely that Gen. Gilmore put them in a white Brigade. When the attack was to be made on Fort Wagner, the Gen. selected his best troops, and among the rest, the 54th. The black soldiers marched side by side with their white comrades in arms to the assault. (Tell it with pride to the world.) The parapet is 30 feet high. Col. Shaw was the first man to mount that high parapet. He waved his sword and shouted ["]come on boys," and then he fell dead. He died well. Neither Greece nor Rome can excell [*sic*] his heroism.[42]

The victors returned the bodies of some white officers, but threw Shaw's in a mass grave along with twenty of his black troops, intending this to be an insult. His father wrote to the regimental surgeon, "We would not have his body removed from where it lies surrounded by his brave and devoted soldiers . . . We can imagine no holier place than that in which he lies, among his brave and devoted followers, nor wish for him better company.—what a body-guard he has!" Captain Emilio, who entered the battle as the regiment's youngest officer, emerged as acting commander and lived to be its historian. In 1891, he published *A Brave Black Regiment: The History of the 54th Massachusetts*. He was not Melville's Ishmael, however, alone left to tell the tale. His fellow survivors helped with a second edition, complete with an appendix on the mistreatment of black soldiers who had become prisoners. Emancipation came only at a high, sacrificial cost. The wisest had always suspected that something of the kind might be required.

Thomas Starr King
(1824–1864)

CHAPTER XII

Organization

In which Transcendentalist disciples
prove themselves not individualists,
but institutional organizers,
mobilizing massive humanitarian relief during the Civil War,
then trying to transcend denominationalism to create
"The Liberal Church of America."

SOME PORTRAYALS OF THE TRANSCENDENTALISTS see them as individualistic eccentrics; those in Concord, even as precursors of some Bloomsbury set of rather sexually louche intellectuals.[1] While such interpretations may have some prurient appeal, the historical record seems to differ. Far from being individualistic or libertine, the Transcendentalists and their disciples were true descendants of their Puritan forebears. Long before thinking of their own pleasure, they thought of what they could do, not alone but in spiritual alliance with others, to improve the society around them for the generations yet to come.

Historian and sociologist E. Digby Baltzell of the University of Pennsylvania showed their cultural inheritance in his classic 1979 study, *Puritan Boston and Quaker Philadelphia*.[2] Having coined the term "WASP," White Anglo-Saxon Protestant, he examined the history of two elite WASP subgroups. What he found was a New England elite that had a sense of noblesse oblige, requiring them to organize for the common good, while Philadelphia's Quaker culture was negative toward authority and therefore less inclined to civic responsibility. Around Boston, a reformed (and ever reforming) religious establishment shaped a civic culture marked by voluntary associations, philanthropy, charitable institutions, and causes. When

America won its independence, Philadelphia was larger than Boston, yet its record in those areas was weaker. Baltzell, himself a Quaker, blamed the antiestablishment and sectarian nature of his own tradition. Egalitarian Friends might say "thee" and "thou" to everyone, but they often resisted the Commonwealth rather than seeking to improve it. They not only refused to do military service; many also declined public service of any form. He offers a long list of Philadelphia lawyers who declined appointment to the US Supreme Court.

In New England, the Transcendentalists of Concord (Emerson, Thoreau, and Alcott) were the most Quakerlike and individualistic. In Boston itself, however, most Transcendentalists demonstrated and nurtured a greater sense of discipleship aimed at service to the common good. To be sure, some unattractive paternalism and arrogance came along with Boston's culture of philanthropy, education, and reform. Clarke's Harvard classmate Oliver Wendell Holmes had his tongue firmly in his cheek in calling Boston the "hub of the solar system," if not of the universe. Living in the "Athens of America," the self-declared "Autocrat of the Breakfast Table" also coined the term "Boston Brahmin." In an 1860 *Atlantic Monthly* piece, Holmes described a caste of high-minded clergy, lawyers, merchants, and physicians like himself. His son, Oliver Wendell Holmes Jr., thrice wounded in Civil War, lost his father's faith on the battlefield, but then became a lawyer, judge, and a long-serving member of the US Supreme Court. Meanwhile the term "Philadelphia lawyer" evolved from meaning "skilled in legal minutiae" to have overtones of being self-serving.

Emerson admired the inward spirituality of the Quakers and, like them, preferred to do without any outward sacraments, obligations to the state, or to the poor.[3] Thoreau had French-Huguenot and Scottish-Quaker ancestry, his civil disobedience in line with both. Baltzell ended his study with the observation that New England Calvinism has been more influential in the development of American culture as a whole, but since the 1960s it has been moving toward the more antinomian individualism preferred by Quakers and Concord. One could argue that this is perhaps more an effect of capitalist consumerism. Whatever the cause, he proved prophetic about the turn that American civic culture had taken: "Since then incivility and barbarism have steadily increased . . . [and] in our era of victim political correctness, moreover, we seem to be stranded between more or less extreme populist ideologies on both the left and the right."[4]

However controversial *that* analysis may feel, it seems clear that most Transcendentalists in their own time were often aiming to try to transcend polarities and—except around moral imperatives like ending slavery—to organize, to both reform and heal, rather than to polarize or to divide. Some carried that mission beyond Boston. Clarke had tried to do so during his years in Louisville. His colleague in St. Louis, William Greenleaf Eliot, was also a Unitarian evangelist to the West. Descended from the first Puritan evangelist to, and defender of, Native Americans, John Eliot, this "conservative radical" was just as devoutly determined to change the world for the better. Clarke felt so close to him that he named his second son Eliot. Now remembered chiefly as grandfather to poet T. S. Eliot, or as the founder of Washington University in St. Louis, he also helped to organize virtually every other local effort for public health, social welfare, education, and antislavery.[5] He was forever bringing home to his long-suffering wife Abigail Adams Cranch Eliot yet another orphan to house, widow to console, or fund-raising tea to hold.[6] In addition to these duties, she bore him fourteen children. Three died as infants, two as toddlers, two more before they were ten. When the eldest daughter, Abby's namesake and helper, died at seventeen, Eliot reminded her of his family's motto: *Tace et Face* (roughly, "Keep Silent and Work"), lest Calvinists accuse Unitarians of not knowing how to accept the will of God. He traveled as a liberal evangelist up and down the Mississippi Valley, from Minneapolis to Mobile, encouraging emigrant New Englanders to organize—first, in Unitarian churches and, then, in other associations to serve the common good and human rights. Antislavery work, of course, was a challenge in Missouri. In the one book that Eliot found time to write, one scene reveals why. He was in his upstairs study, overseeing a neighbor's yard, when, as he wrote:

> I was startled by a terrible scream, and, going to the window, saw under an open shed a young mulatto woman tied up to the joist by her thumbs, so that her feet scarcely touched the ground, stripped from her shoulders

to her hips, and a [white] man standing by her with cowhide whips in hand. He had paused for a moment from his scourging to see if she would "give in." I opened the window to call out to him. He told me to "shut up and mind my own business." But he feared publicity just enough to untie the victim and stop his brutality for a time.[7]

Eliot went straight to the grand jury and had his neighbor indicted. The trial jury then found that the offense of the black girl, that is, her unwillingness to submit to the wishes of her master, somehow offset the potential penalty in law against the perpetrator. Eliot then continued to set up institutions all around St. Louis to help protect abused women, black orphans, the blind, and other neglected persons. Nearly all well-meaning civic institutions in pre–Civil War St. Louis, from the public schools to Washington University (which the founders wanted to call Eliot University, and of which he became the first chancellor), were founded with his involvement. As the danger of secession emerged, he was an urban catalyst opposing rural slaveholding Missouri leaving the Union. When war broke out, he led the organization of the Western Sanitary Commission to deal with health issues on the neglected front in the Mississippi Valley. After the war, Emerson visited and met Eliot, later calling him "the Saint of the West."[8] He should have included Abigail. Their son Thomas Lamb Eliot later took the same spirit to Portland, Oregon, founding a Unitarian church there, Reed College, and much else.[9]

Yet as devoted to local good works as they often were—to what Channing had called "practical Christianity"—Unitarians were slow to organize a denominational structure to support new churches and mission projects. They had only reluctantly formed the American Unitarian Association (AUA) in 1825, as much for mutual self-defense against Calvinist opponents as for mission work. It was then not even an association of congregations, but rather of individuals—clergy and committed lay leaders—raising funds for tracts, evangelists, and new congregations. Its officers were honorary volunteers. The only paid staff consisted of a single minister serving part-time as the secretary of the AUA, assisted by a clerk. Clergy seeking new pastorates and churches seeking new pastors might write the secretary for assistance, but most searches were haphazard and informal. Projects such as setting up a seminary west of the Appalachians to educate new ministers to serve in the West depended more on local initiative than on denominational support.

Clarke understood this. When his brother-in-law, Frederic, funded by his father, Harm Jan Huidekoper, began a theological school in Meadville, Pennsylvania, the AUA helped but little.[10] Other support came from the Christian Connexion, another religious group wary of sectarianism and eager to promote the restoration of nondoctrinal discipleship on the frontier. When the faculty became largely Unitarian, employing historical-critical thinking to biblical texts, more biblically literalistic Connectionists dropped away. The school's energetic Unitarian president Rufus Stebbins then made the Unitarian identity of Meadville Theological School still clearer. When Clarke lectured there on "ethnic religions" in 1849–1850, a key question was whether Unitarians could bridge the gap between biblical authority and Transcendentalists who, like Parker, saw following Jesus as just one religious path among many. Clarke was uniquely qualified to try to do so. As a friend to Parker and other Transcendentalist ministers, he shared many of their spiritual and reformist goals. His method, however, involved making more use of Christian practice. Like his book on forgiveness, a second, *The Christian Doctrine of Prayer* (1854), marked the way.[11]

He was not the first Transcendentalist to explore prayer. As a young would-be minister, Emerson based his trial sermon on the text, "Pray without ceasing" [I Thess. 5:17]—the shortest verse in the Bible except for "Jesus wept" [John 11:35].[12] Working that summer of 1826 on his uncle's farm, alongside an illiterate but pious farmhand, Waldo confessed that he did not think it humanly possible to do what scripture enjoined. His companion assured him that of course it was: every thought we have, he said, includes some hope or wish, and that is a form of prayer. Moreover, our inner thoughts are all wishes shaping who we will become. In that sense, at least, God answers all prayers. Emerson then took that rather Buddhist insight (not yet seen as such) and developed a classic three-point sermon, one that won him approbation and was repeated some twenty times more. His final point was this: therefore, be careful what you pray for!

Clarke applied a similar lens to the practice of prayer, both personal and communal. He distinguished first between "the Prayer of Faith" and the "Prayer of Form," and then between the responses of the God of Law as explored by science and the God of Freedom and Love as revealed by Jesus, and between superficial and deeper levels of religious feeling. The surface level, he said, as a child of Puritanism, is that of mere ethical duty. Deeper still lies a sense of underlying gratitude, of dependency, and of one's own spiritual need, which permits the inflow of unmerited, trans- forming grace. Far too often, he admitted, the most devout have also been guilty of both bigotry and unworthy forms of prayer—such as those ask- ing for revenge on enemies or oppressors. He had no desire for those. Yet when it came to helping to organize growing personal powers, cooperation, and philanthropy toward good ends, he recommended much deeper reflec- tion and prayer: "Let us not merely say, *To work is to pray*," he said, "but [also] *Pray that we may work*."[13]

Perhaps Clarke should have been more careful for what he prayed. When the American Unitarian Association met in Boston in May 1859, he delivered the opening address. Rufus Stebbins had proposed reorganizing: no more do-nothing honorary presidents, vice presidents, and the like, but rather a focus of all resources on the mission field. Clarke knew that many attending were themselves present or former honorary officers, so he had not spoken on that aspect of Stebbins's proposal. He simply called for more coordinated effort. The next day, pastoral and civic duties caused him to miss the vote on the Stebbins proposals and the election of new officers. He came home to learn that, while the AUA had rejected reorganization, he was now its new secretary. He felt tempted to refuse the office: he had not agreed to the nomination, nor did he need the money. He and Anna were comfortable. Yet when he consulted colleagues and congregants such as Mrs. Dall, all urged him to apply his gifts for organizing others to the AUA. He then set three conditions. First, that he remain as pastor of the Disciples. Second, that he take no salary, only reimbursement of expenses. Third, that he have one Sunday a month to stay in Boston, to preach for the Disciples, and to be with his family. Those accepted, Clarke took up the role. Wisely, he shared the placement of ministers with his colleague in New York, Henry Whitney Bellows.[14]

That year they worked to counsel Thomas Starr King, a gifted young preacher and lecturer, on his next pastorate. Coming from a working-class, Universalist background, self-taught and eloquent, Starr King had never been to college. At age twenty, he had followed his own father as pastor of the Universalist church in Charlestown, Massachusetts. Three years

*Henry Whitney Bellows
(1814–1882)*

later, this bold, well-spoken young man introduced himself to Bellows in New York. The latter was impressed enough to invite him to preach the next week. He then tried to recruit him as his Unitarian colleague in New York. That failed when leaders of the second Unitarian congregation in the city there were unwilling to have a minister without a college degree.[15] Starr King then accepted a call to the troubled Hollis Street Church in Boston, where the temperance preaching of John Pierpont had alienated the wealthy. Starr King, the Universalist, did so well in promoting reconciliation that Harvard soon gave him an honorary MA. Parker referred to him as "the best preacher in Boston." Theologically, Starr King was influenced by the writings of British Unitarian James Martineau, who, like Clarke and Bellows, joined Transcendentalist philosophy with respect for church tradition. He became part of a short-lived group called the "Town and Country Club," which tried to bridge the gap between Transcendentalists and reformers in Boston and in Concord. Starr King thus became part of a second generation of Transcendentalists still practicing spiritual friendship, yet not immune to worldly or political concerns.

By 1859, Starr King felt frustrated. His Hollis Street salary was three thousand dollars, but one-third of that went to support his widowed mother and a disabled brother. The rest was simply not enough to support his family in a manner appropriate to his professional position. Lecturing added to his income somewhat. He jocularly said that he would speak anywhere for "F.A.M.E.—Fifty dollars And My Expenses." After another financial panic struck in 1857, however, he often had to settle for less. His lectures, on "Substance and Show," "Sights and Insights," "The Ideal and the Real," "Existence and Life," on "Socrates," or on "Webster and the Constitution," were given with humor and verve and were very popular. Yet he had also exhausted himself on the lecture circuit. He began seeking, as gifted ministers are wont to do, a field of wider influence and a higher salary. Several churches in the East and Midwest offered to pay him well, but the greatest need in the denomination was for a preacher/organizer to lead the Unitarians in San Francisco. He agreed to go, at least on a trial basis.

Before he and his family sailed from New York, Bellows arranged an elaborate breakfast at the Fifth Avenue Hotel attended by three hundred prominent Unitarians. William Cullen Bryant presided. Frederic Henry Hedge sent a message: "King is with you for a parting word, and your fraternal benediction on his way. Happy soul! himself a benediction wherever he goes, benignly dispensing the graces of his life wherever he carries the wisdom of his word."[16] Starr King's ministry on the Pacific Coast would last only four years, and he would die there, prematurely. Yet he would also help to transform the attitude of his fellow followers of liberal faith toward their own potential as effective organizers of collective collaboration.

Bellows had spoken at Harvard in 1859 about the sorry state of the Unitarian movement. The site was the chapel in Harvard's Divinity Hall, where, twenty-one years before, and on the same occasion, Emerson gave his Divinity School Address. This message was quite different. Emerson had urged the newly graduating ministers "to go alone; to refuse the good models . . . and dare to love God without mediator or veil." Bellows, by contrast, in "The Suspense of Faith: A Discourse on the State of the Church," said that Unitarian "ministers, churches, charities, public gatherings, manifestations of all sorts, were never so numerous and popular as at present." Yet he also diagnosed "an undeniable chill in the missionary zeal, an undeniable apathy in the denominational life of the body; with general prosperity, in short, there is despondency, self-questioning, and anxiety." What remedy did he propose? Here he contradicted Emerson. He said that the Holy Spirit, making for holiness and wholeness, communicates itself more reliably through the historic Church, rather "than through private persons."[17]

This was a clear rebuke to the more radical individualists within the denomination. He did not directly speak of it, but he hated that a third Unitarian church in New York had formed without his collegial blessing. Its minister was Octavius Brooks Frothingham, a child of Puritan Boston and a spiritual rebel against that heritage. He had grown up under a ministerial father who often hid his real skepticism under a safe formality of tradition. The son was more like Parker in his radical theology and oratory. His flock met in a rented hall, just blocks from the church Bellows led, and was pointedly less traditional. Bellows also fretted, without saying so, over the growing number of Unitarians leaving to join the Episcopal Church. Many of the privileged were hearing the call "Friend, go up higher" (Luke 14:10) and seeking a more traditional and high church liturgy.

This included gifted clergy such as Frederic Dan Huntington, onetime minister of the South Congregational (Unitarian) Church in Boston. He had become Plummer Professor of Christian Morals at Harvard in 1855, but while Bellows was speaking at Divinity Hall, this prominent Unitarian was in the process of resigning that post and applying for holy orders as an Episcopalian.[18] Numerous Unitarian laypeople were making the same change. Bellows tried to be clear that "if I speak in the language of a Churchman, it is not as an Episcopalian, much less one aiming at the re-establishment of a hierarchy." Nor did he accuse the defectors of trying to avoid Unitarian preaching on controversial topics. He simply said that the Unitarian pendulum of faith had swung too far in the direction of Protestant individualism. They needed to become again what Channing had hoped for, "catholic Christians" building a new church universal—one in which "the needed but painful experience of Protestantism shall have taught us how to maintain a dignified, symbolic, and mystic church-organization without the aid of the State, or the authority of the Pope." Some reacted as though he himself wanted to be a new sort of pope. That was far from his intention. The model he had in mind was that of Clarke and the Disciples. In Britain,

Martineau, using the same philosophical shift that characterized Transcendentalism, had led Unitarians away from dry rationalism and toward a faith that used Anglican forms of worship without the Trinity or creed. As the controversy over his address continued, Bellows had to write "A Sequel to the Suspense of Faith," assuring his own congregation that he had no intention of introducing prayer book worship, and that he remained a staunch Unitarian, devoted to strengthening all of its institutions.

Antioch College was one such. Located on the site of a short-lived utopian community at Yellow Springs, Ohio, it had begun, like Meadville Theological School, as a joint project of Unitarians and Connectionists. Like Oberlin College—better funded, more orthodox, further north in Ohio—Antioch was open to both men and women of any race. Bellows chaired its board of trustees. As Unitarian Horace Mann became its president, Connectionist support fell away, while his abolitionism threatened financial support from wealthy but conservative Unitarians. The mission of Antioch was noble, but its financial condition was fragile, especially after the Panic of 1857. Mann told its 1859 graduates, in a sentence that later became the college motto: "Be ashamed to die until you have won some victory for humanity." That very fall, having done much for free public education, antislavery, and co-education, Mann died of typhoid. Antioch seniors, including Olympia Brown—later one of the first regularly ordained woman ministers in America—begged Dr. Bellows to come to Yellow Springs as president of Antioch. He had more in mind, however. He hoped to lead Harvard, and he recruited in his stead a Unitarian minister and educator, Thomas Hill, who had married a Bellows cousin. In an ironic turn of events, when the war forced Antioch College to close temporarily in 1862, the presidency at Harvard became vacant, and Hill was available while Bellows was not. He had taken on leading the US Sanitary Commission and soon found it a more demanding role, especially when added to his pastoral duties, than leading any college. While professedly entirely nonsectarian, the Sanitary Commission's success derived almost entirely from a network of spiritual friendships between Unitarians and other liberal religionists.

On the Sunday after the attack upon Fort Sumter, Bellows preached a stirring sermon in support of the Union. A group of Unitarian women who wanted to help support the army asked him to meet with them that Thursday. Dr. Elizabeth Blackwell, an English-born Unitarian and the first woman to be a doctor of medicine in the United States, presided. She and a male colleague described the unhealthy conditions already threatening soldiers in training camps on nearby Staten Island. Present were the leading women in the congregation Bellows led. They included Frances Fairchild Bryant, spouse of the poet/editor of the *New York Post*, William Cullen Bryant. He had led the effort to create Central Park and introduced Lincoln at his Cooper Union address. Unitarian philanthropist Peter Cooper, whose wife Sarah also attended, had endowed that tuition-free institution. Louisa Lee Schuyler, the daughter of another wealthy, prominent family was also present. It was resolved to hold a meeting of all concerned women at the Cooper Union. They asked Bellows to help them to organize the program. He recruited Vice President Hannibal Hamlin of Maine, a fellow Unitarian, to preside. Four thousand women filled the Great Hall. Bellows prepared resolutions for a Women's Central Association of Relief. The goal was to coordinate the many local efforts for relief then developing. Bellows and Dr. Blackwell were to lead a committee of three women and three men to guide the organization. Louisa Lee Schuyler became corresponding secretary, with an office at Cooper Union. Bellows was sent to Washington to lobby Lincoln, his cabinet, and the military to establish a sanitary commission.

Within two months, Congress had authorized the commission, with Bellows as president and Sam Howe among its eight commissioners. At the same time, Dorothea Dix became the superintendent of nurses for the United States Army, the first woman ever to hold an executive post in the federal government. To head the staff of the commission, Bellows recruited Frederick Law Olmsted. Now remembered chiefly as a pioneer in urban design and landscape architecture, Olmsted had shown his organizational gifts in implementing the plan for Central Park under the commission headed by Bryant. He had also earned credibility as an abolitionist by traveling through the South between 1852 and 1857, reporting for the *New York Times* on the realities of slavery in the cotton kingdom.[19] Organizing the many efforts needed to keep soldiers from dying of disease required his knowledge of drainage, journalism, politics, and logistics. Fund-raising and organization fell to Bellow's network of liberal ministers and their people.

Persuading everyone to stay in one big tent was difficult. Some orthodox Protestants, rejecting Unitarian leadership, set up a rival, but far smaller Christian Sanitary Commission. In St. Louis, Eliot led a separate Western Sanitary Commission to serve the Mississippi Valley, a theater of the war that felt neglected and misunderstood in the East. Mary Livermore, the wife of a Universalist minister in Chicago, organized a Sanitary Fair that raised over seventy thousand dollars for the commission and became a model for similar efforts in other cities. Like other women who took leadership roles during the war, she was inspired to a more public career, later becoming America's "Queen of the Platform" with lectures such as "What Shall We Do with Our Daughters?" on women's rights and education. "As the war went on with all its horrors," said Bellows's daughter Anna, "the desire to save suffering increased, enthusiasm and zeal rose high. Hospitals, ambulances, doctors, surgeons, and nurses were needed to supplement those already on the battle-field."[20] At her father's church, as at the Disciples and other Unitarian churches, the Sunday school served on weekdays as a place where women gathered to prepare bandages, clothing, medicine, and other necessities for soldiers, both wounded and well.

No one did more for success of the US Sanitary Commission than Thomas Starr King. When he arrived in California in April 1860, most voters there were Southern sympathizers. They held the governorship and a majority in the legislature. A moderate Democrat, US Senator David Broderick had opposed expanding slavery, but died in a duel with a pro-slavery member of the state Supreme Court. That fall, because of the four-way presidential race, the opposition split so that Lincoln won the state's four electoral votes with less than one-third of Californians voting for him. Starr King not only served the San Francisco Unitarians, but worked to save California for the Union. His friends soon included the leading Republicans in the Golden State, including Jessie Benton Fremont, whose husband had been the Republican presidential candidate in 1856, and Leland Stanford, later the first Republican governor of California. Starr King traveled up and down the state, lecturing on patriotic themes and making the case for the Union and humanitarian relief. He wrote back to Bellows, "At home, among you big fellows, I wasn't much. Here they seem to think I am somebody. Nothing like the right setting."[21]

His San Francisco congregation grew so large that it required a larger church building, seating over fifteen hundred. It rose in the very heart of the city, on Union Square, which he had helped to name. His fund-raising ability was extraordinary. Early on, he astonished Bellows by telegraphing a bank draft for a hundred thousand dollars—more than had been raised to that point in all the rest of the country—saying more would be coming shortly. Over one-third of all the money for humanitarian relief during the war came from California, through his efforts. Visiting mining camps and frontier towns that had their own sanitary problems, the minister-organizer exhausted himself. In early March 1864, having preached in his newly dedicated church only seven times, Starr King succumbed to diphtheria and died at thirty-nine. He was mourned across the state, and his statue for many years was one of two that represented California in the US Capitol's Statuary Hall.[22]

Many stories could attempt to describe the work of the Sanitary Commission, but one seems especially appropriate here. The turning point of the Civil War came in July 1863, with one of its bloodiest battles at Gettysburg, Pennsylvania. On July 4, James Freeman Clarke learned that his wife's nephew, Major Henry Huidekoper, was missing in action there. His father had died a year before. The Clarkes felt called to act in loco parentis. They immediately took an evening train to Baltimore. There was a Sanitary Commission train going to the scene of the carnage the next night. Clarke took it alone, leaving Anna behind and riding in an "arctic" car carrying ice-packed fruits, vegetables, and meat for the ailing soldiers. There was only one track. The seventy-five-mile journey took seventeen hours. After diligent searching, he found Henry. Of four hundred men he had led, two hundred sixty were casualties. He himself had three wounds. Surgeons had amputated his arm below the elbow. His uncle spoke as a surrogate father and pastor, until he felt Henry needed more rest than consolation.

Then he turned to a wounded Confederate soldier, lying nearby, his arm out as if trying to say, "Help me!" Clarke later wrote, "[I]n the inhumanity that is war, they are mere 'rebels.' But each had a home, a mother or father, a wife, and children. The children will ask the mother, 'Where is papa?' She will answer, 'He has gone to Pennsylvania with General Lee, but he will come back and bring us something.' Poor desolate homes, North and South. Long will they look in vain for those dear to them as ours to us, who lie undistinguished, cumbering the bloody field."[23] The Sanitary Commission was so efficient in providing auxiliary nurses at Gettysburg that the War Department thereafter attached a nursing unit from the commission to every army corps. It became "the largest, most powerful, and most highly organized philanthropic activity that had ever been seen in America."[24]

This success in leading such an enormous humanitarian effort then inspired Unitarian leaders like Clarke and Bellows to feel more confidence in their collective capacity to organize for "joint action" of the kind they had been urging their colleagues to undertake even before war. Clarke had served only two years as part-time AUA secretary, so as not to neglect the Disciples. Yet he had corresponded with nearly every Unitarian church and minister, just as Bellows had through the Sanitary Commission. When Starr King suddenly died, in 1864, San Francisco Unitarians begged Bellows to come to them, if only for a time. He arranged a leave of absence from his New York church, All Souls, persuading Horatio Stebbins, the minister in Portland, Maine, to supply his pulpit and then to prepare for a call to San Francisco. In his six months in San Francisco, Bellows persuaded them to invite Stebbins. Then he returned to the East and to a greater challenge: to gather all religious liberals into a more effective national church body.

After his return from California, Bellows went to Boston in December 1864 for a special meeting of the American Unitarian Association. He emphasized the prospects for Unitarianism on the West Coast, the need for a stronger commitment to joint action, and the evidence that it was possible. He knew that the division between traditionalists and radicals was still a real issue. Hedge had written to him, complaining about the latter group. No matter how he felt about his post-Christian colleague Frothingham,

Bellows's reply is both sympathetic to that wing of the Unitarian movement and insightful concerning the challenges ahead. As he wrote to Hedge,

> The real life in our body is in the *heretical* wing. If we cut *it* off, there is nothing to move with. My theological instincts and my Christian feelings are outraged by the *Rationalism* of our young men—but as my whole practical nature & working instincts are equally outraged by the paralytic imbecility of our sounder & more Christian wing, I am not willing to *rely* on *that* for the future . . . We must solve our difficulties by ignoring our theological differences, & finding *in work*, a way out of our heresy & our deadness.[25]

Bellows's address in Boston was a success. Clarke was his ally, although both doubted that the rifts between institutionalists and radicals could ever heal entirely. The AUA promised to raise a hundred thousand dollars for joint work in the year ahead. Bellows proposed a convention in New York in April 1865. Edward Everett Hale, who had succeeded Huntington at the South Church in Boston and come to prominence with his 1863 story, "The Man without a Country," written to support the Union cause, proposed that Bellows chair the planning, since his vision and hope clearly transcended merely organizing Unitarians. What he really wanted, as he told his son, was "the Liberal Christian Church of America." It would transcend mere sectarianism, and "while allowing the fresh air of intellectual liberty to blow in at the doors, & present light of science and experience to shine in at its windows, would be, nevertheless, eminently Christian, worshipful & tender, humane & devout, tolerant yet earnest; in short a Church in which the openly avowed Creed should be in congruity with men's opinions on other subjects."[26] On February 1, 1865, a notice went out to all Unitarian congregations inviting them to send their pastor and two lay delegates to New York on April 5, "to hold a convention for a more thorough organization of the Liberal Church of America." Bellows also solicited a list of Universalist ministers most likely to be interested in helping to form a broader liberal church. Getting just the Unitarians to embrace his vision, however, proved difficult enough. When he met with fifty Boston-area ministers, a lengthy discussion of the proposed convention ensued. The elders were wary, the younger clergy, more enthusiastic, but the divisions were also theological. To his son, Bellows wrote that he found four factions to deal with:

> First, "*the elder men*, old-fashioned Unitarians, very ethical in their humor, preaching the doctrine of self-culture & personal righteous-ness," led by Ezra Stiles Gannett, "spiteful toward the transcen-dental or radical wing, and pretty jealous of anything which don't originate in Boston."
> Second, "a pretty large section of Radicals—transcendental in their philosophy, unhistorical in their faith—men like Frothingham, [Samuel] Longfellow, [William James] Potter of New Bedford, a strong body of young men just out of Divinity Studies—who re-ally think Xity [Christianity] only one among a great many other religions . . . thinking some test may be applied, some creed slipped around them . . . but . . . willing to co-operate on some platform of *Work* which has no doctrine in it."
> Third, a "*small section* of Evangelicals—who really believe that Jesus Christ was a strictly miraculous person & a savior indeed, & are dis-posed to deny any fellowship with the looser & more liberal party."
> Fourth, "another set of *Broad Church men*, like J. F. Clarke, Dr. Hedge, E. E. Hale—& numerous others—who recognize the elements of truth in all the other sections, & believe in the possibility of weld-ing them together." He then added, "With this party I belong & am working."[27]

Planning was thorough. Getting some Boston churches led by "elder men" to send lay delegates, even without attending themselves, required rebellions by the younger lay members. In the end, three-quarters of all Unitarian churches in the United States sent over six hundred delegates. The Universalists send two observers. Governor Andrew of Massachu-setts presided. His pastor gave the opening sermon. Clarke had vetted his address with both Hale and Bellows, who approved of its inclusive tone. All three organizers felt that Unitarianism had become what Channing had never wanted it to be: namely, too sectarian; and that it would take their best efforts to make it broader. The "Liberal Church of America" would have no common creed (asking, "What do we all believe in common?") but rather ask a more basic covenantal question: "What hopes do we share? How shall we support one another in order to fulfill those hopes?" The Unitarians promised, inclusively, to aim to "build up the Kingdom of God, and promote the reign of the Gospel."

Sadly, Universalists showed little interest in the effort. Tired of losing their best leaders, such as Starr King, to the Unitarians, they needed to reorganize around their own tradition. Therefore the gathered Unitarians became "the National Conference of Unitarian Churches." That sectarian label then drove Frothingham and other Free Church radicals to decline to join. His church dropped the name Unitarian to become the "Independent Liberal Church."

Despite their commitment to individual conscience and the New England tradition of localized, congregational polity, Unitarians had now created an association not of individuals, but rather of churches. This was due entirely to the organizational gifts and spiritual friendships of ministers like Bellows, Clarke, Hedge, Hale, and lay leaders like John Albion Andrew. All considered themselves disciples of Jesus and felt that they followed him— but by seeing religion not as a matter of creeds or scriptural proof-texting, but rather one of shared spiritual and moral insight about the imperatives of the time. They denied that religion can ever properly be an entirely private matter, since it will always require, to fulfill its hope and ideals, what a later Unitarian theologian described as "the power of organization, and the organization of power."[28] Like every other organism, their collective work would go through further stages of evolution, preparing for other moments of catalyzing ecumenical and interfaith cooperation in America and in the wider world.

PART FOUR

Spirit

Your spirit will live on, you know.
Your spirit is others in you; you in others.

BORIS PASTERNAK, *Dr. Zhivago*

William James Potter
(1829–1893)

CHAPTER XIII

Evolution and Differentiation

In which Transcendentalists welcome Darwin's theory,
yet divide once more over inclusion and church reform.
Women's rights advocates also divide over giving
black men the vote before women;
and a woman poet, widowed, becomes an activist.

MOST ACCOUNTS OF THE TRANSCENDENTALISTS end well before or with the Civil War. This overlooks the many ways in which they continued to have influence, not only as writers but also as mentors, activists, organizers, and spiritual leaders. They did not disappear; they merely evolved. Yet they also divided, since that is how evolution works: through differentiation.

Charles Darwin's book *On the Origin of Species by Means of Natural Selection*, published in 1859, reached America at the end of that year. Among the first to give it a positive reception were Transcendentalists. On January 2, 1860, Franklin Sanborn, the Concord schoolmaster who had been among the Secret Six, composed a letter to his co-conspirator Theodore Parker, then in Italy trying vainly to recover from tuberculosis.[1] The night before, Sanborn had hosted a dinner. The guest of honor was New York reformer Charles Loring Brace, founder of the Children's Aid Society. Invited by Bronson Alcott to speak in Concord, he discussed help for orphaned, abandoned, and runaway children. His "orphan trains" placed many with adoptive families in the West.[2] After the lecture, Sanborn wrote, "Mr Alcott and Mr Thoreau dined with him here." The four discussed John Brown as a martyr, a recent letter from Parker, and Brace's enthusiasm for Darwin as demonstrating "that one race can be derived from another." Sanborn ended, "But you no doubt know the book."[3]

Parker probably knew only reviews of Darwin, but in his reply, he almost claimed to have been a Darwinian before Darwin.⁴ Many Transcendentalists had embraced evolutionary thinking, at least in the broad sense, long before he described the process of natural selection. Emerson's epigraph for *Nature*, for example, he derived from Plotinus: "And striving to be man, the worm/ Mounts through all the spires of form." Darwin's theory would come to divide people. Alcott, for example, would never fully accept natural selection. He thought the process described to be mechanistic, lacking in transcendent spirit. Thoreau, on the other hand, embraced the idea. He obtained Darwin's book from the Concord library and, in the final seasons of his own life, applied it to observing the flora and fauna of New England, seeing transcendence *within* the natural process. Sanborn saw it in social-political terms: as scientific evidence against the racist idea of separate origins for each of the races. Brace understood evolution as showing that environment can influence adaptation, confirmation of his own experiences in working for children's welfare. He called it a social "theory of the moral and mental development of mankind . . . a law of progress."⁵

Darwin became a topic in many Boston drawing rooms, clubs, societies, and lectures otherwise then focused on John Brown and the struggle over slavery. Thomas Wentworth Higginson lectured in Concord three weeks later, on the theme of "Barbarism and Civilization." He began by quoting *The Voyage of the Beagle*, about an encounter with the indigenous inhabitants of Tierra del Fuego.⁶ Some thought them a separate species; Darwin did not. Higginson pronounced those who consider dark-skinned peoples as sub-human as the true barbarians, and America's present struggle as between civilization and the barbarism of slavery: "a moral evil more formidable, a barrier denser and darker, a Dismal Swamp of inhumanity, a barbarism upon the soil, before which civilization has thus far been compelled to pause."⁷ Sanborn, of course, felt similarly, but was not present. Having barely escaped arrest for his part in the Secret Six, he had fled temporarily to Quebec. Emerson was also away, lecturing, but wrote to Lydian asking her to obtain a copy of Darwin's book so that he could read for himself.

That spring, the *Atlantic Monthly* published a three-part review of *Origin of Species*, by Asa Gray, who, as Harvard's professor of botany, received some copies directly from Darwin.[8] He read the book before Christmas, arranged for an American edition, then gave a copy to Brace, a cousin of his wife and frequent visitor, who had it with him when he went to speak in Concord. In his review, Gray acknowledged that some thought Darwin "atheistical," since natural selection did not require divine intervention. Neither did Newton's theory of gravitation, he pointed out, yet no person of faith seemed to feel that gravity abolished the presence of God in the universe. He also asked how any "scientific man" could say that a material tie between all humans could be "inconsistent with the idea of their being intellectually connected with one another through the Deity."[9] The scientist he had in mind was his Harvard colleague Louis Agassiz, the Swiss-born professor of zoology and geology, who opposed Darwin's theory. He held that each race had a separate origin.

Agassiz had married into the Boston elite, where many preferred his version. He spoke against Darwin at the Boston Society for Natural History. The more traditional religious press took his side, of course, while in the *New York Tribune*, George Ripley reviewed the book favorably. Among religious voices, the Transcendentalists and their disciples were by far the most receptive. Some younger Transcendentalist ministers praised Darwin and his theory in print and from the pulpit. One even came to Concord that summer to discuss the matter with Emerson and Alcott.

Moncure Daniel Conway was born in Virginia, but while studying at Harvard for the ministry, he became both a Transcendentalist and an abolitionist. When Starr King declined the pulpit in Cincinnati to go to California, Conway accepted. "Now comes Darwin," he preached, "and establishes the fact that Nature is all miracle, but without the special [miracles] desired," and "that by perfect laws the lower species were trained to the next higher."[10] Conway also tried to revive the *Dial* and in that publication carried two reviews of Darwin—his, enthusiastic, and another, more skeptical—just as Emerson was open to natural selection, and Alcott less so. He wrote, "In the year (1836) when Darwin abandoned theology to study nature, Emerson, having also abandoned theology, published his first book, 'Nature,' whose theme is Evolution."[11] In the *Dial*, he also urged supporters of religion to see that it, too, must evolve: "It must everywhere sum up all the preceding formations, and lose none of their contributions, as the animal generations are summed up in the forehead of man."[12]

Another Transcendentalist who embraced Darwinism in 1860 was the young minister of the Unitarian Church in New Bedford, Massachusetts, William James Potter.[13] Like many in his flock, he was a Quaker by birth. The local Friends Meeting had disowned some for marrying non-Quakers or for holding modernist views. Others such as Potter had simply departed, finding the Friends upholding an older consensus that his own generation simply could no longer accept. Having left Harvard without a degree to complete his studies in Germany, he was only thirty when he preached his first sermon in New Bedford, yet adroit enough to choose as his theme "Apostolic Succession." Some of those in his care called themselves "Channing Unitarians." These included Congressman Thomas Dawes Eliot, the brother of William Greenleaf Eliot, the Unitarian traditionalist minister in St. Louis.[14] Others had once invited Emerson to the pulpit. Although many Unitarians—including Channing, Emerson, and Parker—spoke of a return to the religion *of* Jesus, rather than creeds *about* him, Potter saw that religion, like life or science itself, evolves stage by stage, and must forever continue to do so.[15] A true apostle, he said, is one who has both received and *lives* an authentic word of truth, "whether in limits or out of the limits of ecclesiastical lines." He then also redefined "the true Broad Church, real Catholic Church" as espoused by Channing and by his followers, as forever breaking "over the partition lines of sect" to join "in one spiritual fellowship the true and holy souls of all nations, ages, and religions."

His true radicalism was to use Christian language and ideals to call for a form of spiritual fellowship broader than Christianity itself. Convinced that sectarian institutions could only hold back spiritual progress, he then warned that he would emphasize the prophetic role of ministry, rather than the pastoral or priestly aspect:

> I do not come before you to help build up a sect, or to fill up your pews, or to perform merely the priestly office in your homes. I come to speak to you whatever of truth may by God's grace be shown to me. I ask

only that you may listen by the same grace . . . I believe that the mission of [this church] is . . . to liberalize and spiritualize [all] religious sects, to make all society religious and all life worship; and all ecclesiastical organizations, forms, rituals, ministers, missions, houses of worship, the very Church itself, are nothing, and worse than nothing, if they do not effect this.[16]

During the war, Potter was prophet enough to see that New Bedford's prosperity, earlier based on whaling, was now dying, ended by petroleum. He urged his people of wealth to avoid both nostalgia and panic: to be civic-minded, and rather than seek higher returns at a distance, to reinvest in new local industries. Many did so. He also promoted generosity to liberal charities both local and distant—Antioch College, the New York Children's Aid Society, and education for young women in India.

One congregant had helped to recruit and outfit a local company of free black soldiers that as "Morgan's Guards" joined the Fifty-Fourth Massachusetts Volunteers as Company C.[17] When Potter himself received a draft notice, some parishioners assumed that he would not want to serve and offered to pay for a substitute. He declined, preaching about why he hated violence but supported the Union and a peace based on justice. The sermon reached Secretary of War Stanton, who had it printed and distributed widely. Potter served for a time as chaplain at an army convalescent camp near Washington, but found the work too pastoral and passive, and then became an active agent for the Sanitary Commission. Yet as Bellows and Clarke built on that network of Unitarian colleagues to try to form a stronger liberal denomination, Potter balked. The National Conference of Unitarian Churches, hailing "the Lord Jesus Christ" in the preamble to its bylaws, was too sectarian for him, since it did not aim to join in "fellowship with the true and holy souls of all nations, ages, and religions."

As the war ended, progressive activists were evolving, differentiating, and even dividing in every key area of their work: church reform, women's rights, and antiracism. When the Thirteenth Amendment to the US Constitution passed, ending slavery, some white abolitionists followed Garrison in declaring victory and their work over. The *Liberator* ceased publication.

Transcendentalists as different as Higginson and Clarke saw that the struggle for racial justice was being betrayed under Andrew Johnson, but much of the public in the North was war-weary and eager for an early reconciliation with the South. Women's rights advocates also divided, over Fourteenth and Fifteenth Amendments to the Constitution that introduced the word "male" for the first time and then guaranteed the right to vote regardless of "race, color, or previous condition of servitude"—but not regardless of gender. Horace Greeley had declared, "This is the negro's hour," and supported the amendments; but women led by Susan B. Anthony and Elizabeth Cady Stanton did not.[18] The latter even descended into racist rants against giving black men the vote before white women had it. An organizational split divided the women's rights movement for an entire generation.

Unitarian Transcendentalists also divided organizationally, differing again over issues of inclusion and church reform. The more pragmatic had organized the National Conference of Unitarian Churches. The most radical rejected it. In 1866, at its second annual meeting of the conference, they provoked what they called "the Battle of Syracuse."[19] With that staunch abolitionist Samuel J. May as the host minister and Potter's parishioner Congressman Eliot presiding, delegates divided over revising the statement of purpose adopted just the year before. The proposed new wording spoke of "the universal diffusion of love, righteousness, and truth" with "perfect freedom of thought" and "practical Christian work, based rather on unity of spirit than on uniformity of belief"—all of which was quite acceptable to nearly everyone.

Becoming the National Conference of Unitarian *and Independent Churches*, however, and dropping the preamble reference to the Lord Jesus Christ, raised ecclesiastical problems. Clarke realized that more conservative Unitarian Christians would focus on nothing but that. This would include his friend Eliot in St. Louis, whose brother was presiding. It could also shut down relations with other liberal Christian bodies, such as the Universalists. If the conference acceded to Parker's radical disciples, the broader Christian world might shun the Unitarians just as they had once shunned Parker. He decided to speak out against the changes, which then failed, by a margin of roughly two to one.

What emerged was the National Conference of Unitarian *and Other Liberal Christian Churches*. This was still too sectarian for Potter and others wanting a global basis for religious fellowship. Caroline Dall's childhood pastor, Cyrus Bartol, hosted a meeting in Boston of ministers upset with the Syracuse decision. Some led churches that called themselves "Free" or "Independent." Others, like himself and Potter, led Unitarian congregations. Those present resolved to form a new Free Religious Association. Potter went so far as to refer to the FRA as "a spiritual anti-slavery society."[20] Emerson became its first member and agreed to speak at its first annual convention. Potter became its secretary, overseeing a small office in Boston. Simply to maintain collegial friendship, Clarke would sometimes meet him there. He had never broken with Parker, nor would he break with those feeling, as Jesus had put it, that "in my Father's house, there are many mansions. If it were not so, I would have told you." (John 14:2)

The FRA never became an organization of congregations, like the National Conference. Its eclectic membership—Transcendentalist Unitarians, freethinkers, Quakers, liberal Jews, spiritualists, and others—probably never exceeded more than five hundred individuals.[21] Bartol decided against joining, and Emerson soon lost interest. As with the first Transcendentalists, no two Free Religionists seemed to think alike. Some still based their sense of spiritual and moral truth on transcendent intuition. Others wanted a more scientific basis. The FRA journal, the *Index*, bore endorsements both from Darwin and from Max Mueller, then teaching comparative religion at Oxford.[22] One way to join the two impulses was to search for the common ideals in the world's religions. Lydia Maria Child's now forgotten work, *The Progress of Religious Ideas, Through Successive Ages*, in three volumes (1854, 1855) provided some inspiration.[23] Moncure Conway used it for his multifaith *Sacred Anthology: A Book of Ethnical Scriptures.*[24] In New York City, the first president of the FRA, Octavius Brooks Frothingham, used multifaith readings at his Independent Liberal Church to differentiate it from the nearby Unitarian Church of All Souls, where Bellows always took his texts from the Bible.

Clarke also stepped into this debate. Having studied "ethnic religions" for many years while maintaining his own liberal Christian identity, he hoped again to be a moderating voice. He could do so quite safely. His Church of the Disciples in Boston had grown quite markedly. After Governor John Albion Andrew escorted Mrs. Lincoln to worship there one Sunday, Clarke often preached to overflow congregations. His friend Parker had died in Florence in May 1860. While his society at the Music Hall went on, without his presence, it lost some of its adherents. Some came over to Clarke, but the Indiana Place church could hold only five hundred people. The Disciples now needed a larger building, and they found a site for one still in the South End. The new building would seat fifteen hundred. Clarke now had an honorary DD from Harvard. He was serving on both its board of overseers and on the Massachusetts board of education. On the latter, he advocated for the education of poor children. On the former, for the admission of women, and for the Divinity School to open itself to the study of comparative religion.

Starting in 1867, Clarke began teaching at the Divinity School part-time. His course on "The Great Religions of the World" was innovative not only in its topic but also in its method. Rather than simply lecture, he assigned student teams to research each tradition and report. Discussion focused on appreciation of what each faith had to teach or offer about the human condition, rather than on simply refuting its ideas. The *Atlantic Monthly* in 1869 then carried six articles by him: on ethnic and "catholic" (universalizing) forms of faith, Chinese philosophies, Hinduism, Buddhism, Zoroastrianism, and Egyptian religion. The positive response was almost overwhelming. In an era of Western imperialism and colonialism, and of missionary Christianity, no doubt some readers merely wanted to read about the various errors of the "heathen." Other Transcendentalists, however, focused on truly learning from other faiths. It prompted Lydia Maria Child to write an essay on "The Intermingling of Religions," and Higginson to lecture on "The Sympathy of Religions."[25]

Yet Clarke's approach to religious evolution was different from theirs. His work was careful not to minimize differences or conflicts between the varied forms of faith. Asked to give the Lowell Lectures for 1871, Clarke published them as *Ten Great Religions: An Essay in Comparative Theology*. Eventually expanded into two volumes, his treatment went through twenty-two editions and stayed in print for over half a century.[26] To counter the disparagement of non-Christian faiths behind nineteenth-century missionizing and imperialism, he said his goal was "to show that all the religions of the earth are providential, and that all tend to benefit mankind." Religion also does and must evolve, Clarke wrote. History shows that. It may begin in a sense of the spirit everywhere. Then it evolves into spiritual powers we name as being here or there, gods and goddesses: various forms of polytheism. Then again into a sense of one omnipresent reality or divinity. Finally, into contests among those who claim to know the ways of the one only true divine reality. How then how does this resolve? Not easily, he suggested.

In comparison to his contemporaries, Clarke tried to be both more scientific and cautious about religious evolution. His radical friends in the FRA wanted to leap ahead to easy unity. Higginson, for example, in an essay adapted from his own lecture, insisted on commonalities. "There is a sympathy in religions," he declared. "[E]very step in knowledge brings out the sympathy between them. They all show the same aim."[27] Both Potter and Francis Ellingwood Abbott, an FRA exponent of relying on science, rather than mere intuition, said that Higginson's essay needed another piece called the "Antagonisms of Religions."[28] Yet his optimism inspired Transcendentalist sympathizers in the Midwest to organize a Parliament of the World's Religions at the time of the Chicago World's Fair of 1893.

Tolerance and openness to the faith of others would become more and more important as technology, commerce, and migration seemed to shrink the globe and intermingle its people. Child's essay on the "Intermingling of Religions" even described an "Eclectic Church, which shall gather forms of holy aspiration from all ages and nations, and set them on high in their immortal beauty, with the sunlight of heaven to glorify them all."[29] Yet some Free Religionists—and Clarke—worried that a "unification of religions" could mask a drive to conformity rather than creativity. On the other hand, should mere individualism prevail, with as many religions on the planet as there are persons, what becomes of the evolutionary role of religions in helping all of us to overcome our egocentrism and tribalism?

Through all this, Clarke's work stayed centered on pastoring a wide variety of friends, often with a broad spectrum of opinions. Within his own flock, he supported brilliant, high-strung Caroline Dall, even during a misguided relationship with a younger Unitarian minister. Just before the war, she published three lectures given under the title *Woman's Right to Labor, or, Low Wages and Hard Work*.[30] Peabody predictably disliked her tone, not to mention the indelicacy of considering the women driven to prostitution. Susan B. Anthony disliked the focus: it was not on women's suffrage. Elizabeth Cady Stanton, however, embraced the broader agenda. She invited Dell to address an 1864 women's rights meeting in New York. In doing so, however, she stunned Dall by suggesting she organize women in Boston to fight the reelection of Lincoln, since he had not made emancipation and equal rights his war aim from the start. Dall demurred. Like her pastor, she had become more pragmatic in her approach. During the war, she headed both the Disciples' Sunday school and its Soldiers Committee. Her son Willie hoped for an appointment to the Naval Academy. When he failed to get one, he wanted to enlist in the army. At Caroline's behest, Clarke talked him out of doing so. With his father off in India, his mother simply could not stand it if he, too, were to go away forever. Instead, he became a naturalist and an early explorer of the newly acquired Alaska territory.

Another longtime friend who had become rather difficult was Nathaniel Hawthorne. After years in England as a consul appointed by Democrats in the White House, he and his family had returned to America and were once again living in Concord. Yet he avoided Alcott, his near neighbor, and Hawthorne's politics appalled many abolitionists. When he died in May 1864, his wife and daughter asked Clarke to conduct the funeral. After all, he had officiated when Hawthorne married Sophia Peabody in 1842. In his eulogy, Clarke made this defense: "I know of no other thinker or writer who had so much sympathy with the dark shadow, that shadow which the theologian calls sin, as our friend. He seemed to be the friend of all sinners, in his writings."[31] This was not only right about Hawthorne, but about Clarke as well. Unlike some Transcendentalist idealists, he did not minimize the reality of human sin and evil.

A month later, like every other preacher in the country, he had had to respond on Easter Sunday to the death of President Lincoln, murdered on that Good Friday. He saw in it another "consequence of a system [slavery] that produces contempt for human nature."[32] He recalled how Union soldiers had found in a Confederate medical school the body of John Brown's son, skinned, under a sign that declared, "thus always with abolitionists."[33] The Sanitary Commission had also found Southern soldiers using the skulls of Union soldiers as tent decorations. The issue now was how to stop the cycle of revenge and recrimination. Not by being harsh. Nor yet by an easy forgiveness, either. To the postwar challenge of Reconstruction, Clarke advocated a balanced approach. He was opposed to hanging Confederate leaders as traitors. Yet he also wanted Southern plantations divided among former slaves as compensation.[34] The promise of "forty acres and a mule," however, were soon betrayed. This is not the place to recount the politics and tragic failures of the Reconstruction Era. Suffice it to say this: racism had not ended with the abolition of slavery; it had simply evolved.

A month later, Clarke faced another difficult death. His seemingly indomitable mother, Rebecca, seventy-five, had taken rooms in the very house in Boston where she herself had taken in boarders, and where James came to try to tell her of his father's death. She died there, on May 25, 1865. For him, it was like the breaking of a link in the great chain of being, that idea that he, like Emerson, associated with evolution. Once penniless, always parsimonious, by borrowing and saving to invest wisely, Rebecca left an estate valued at sixty-five thousand dollars. It was enough to sustain her daughter Sarah and some charities, especially the home for aging women of color that she had started. Clarke led her funeral at the new, larger Church of the Disciples, in the South End, decorated as it had been for Lincoln's death. Women of color helped by Rebecca knelt at her coffin and kissed his mother's face.[35]

American women's rights advocates, sadly, had a more difficult time with issues of race. The eleventh National Women's Rights Convention in 1866 voted to become the American Equal Rights Association, promoting the voting rights of all, white and black, male and female. Yet when a hard-fought campaign for state-based female suffrage failed in Kansas, and the Fifteenth Amendment emerged, Lucy Stone led the New England Woman Suffrage Association in asking the Republican Party to "drop its watchword of 'Manhood Suffrage.'" Her husband, Henry Blackwell, wrote an open letter to Southern legislatures saying that if both blacks and white women had the vote, "political supremacy of your white race will remain unchanged." Stone debated with Frederick Douglass, but accepted that "Woman must wait for the Negro."

Stanton and Anthony simply refused. In 1869, the Equal Rights Association divided. Stone and others formed the American Woman Suffrage Association (AWSA), focused on winning female suffrage, state by state if necessary, and by including and persuading males. Anthony, Stanton, and their allies formed the National Woman Suffrage Association (NWSA), led by women only, its agenda now including not only a women's suffrage amendment but also equal pay and divorce reform.[36]

The divide soon took on tabloid tones. In 1871, NWSA supporter Victoria Woodhull became the first woman to testify before Congress. She got there because she and her sister, backed by Cornelius Vanderbilt, were the first women brokers on Wall Street. They were also advocates, based on sad personal experience, of a woman's right to divorce and control over her own sexual life. She asked Congress to rule that the first clause of the Fourteenth Amendment, which did *not* use the word "male," implicitly gave equal rights to *all* citizens, including women. It did not do so. Attacked as an advocate of "free love," Woodhull, using gossip transmitted by Elizabeth Cady Stanton, then revealed that the famous Brooklyn preacher, Henry Ward Beecher, president of the AWSA, was involved in an adulterous affair with a parishioner whose husband supported Stanton. Beecher somehow escaped any real consequences. The women in this conflict did not.

When Susan B. Anthony dared to cast a ballot in 1872 she suffered arrest for doing so. Since she admitted having voted, the judge told the jury to return a verdict of guilty. She replied: "You have trampled underfoot every vital principle of our government. My natural rights, my civil rights, my political rights, my judicial rights, are all alike ignored." When he then imposed a hundred dollar fine, Anthony replied, "I shall never pay a dollar of your unjust penalty." She never did. She also did not go to prison, because from there she could have filed an appeal.

In this fight, no one lost out to history so as much as Boston-based feminists from Margaret Fuller through Caroline Healey Dall to Lucy Stone. In 1876, Stanton, Anthony, and Matilda Joslyn Gage began work on their *History of Woman Suffrage*. Envisioned originally as a modest treatise, it evolved into a six-volume work of over 5,700 pages. Stone declined to assist. Fuller and Dall had no significant place in the narrative. This was entirely unfair to them and to other Boston-centered Transcendentalists who were pioneers in the struggle for women's rights. The history even tried to erase any emancipationist or abolitionist perspective on the Civil War. It developed what historian Lisa Tetrault has called, in her book of the same name, "The Myth of Seneca Falls" as the origin of the women's rights movement, with Stanton at the very center.

Fuller had died. Dall was difficult. She at times embarrassed other women in Boston. Blackballed from membership in the New England Women's Club in 1870, she then asked her longtime male ally Higginson to try to help her understand it. He replied, "I can't help it, Mrs. Dall, . . . [that] you're such an *intensely* unpopular person!"[37] Yet the eventual success of the women's suffrage movement owed as much to New Englanders like Lucy Stone and her convert Julia Ward Howe as it did to New Yorkers.

Another Disciple, Julia Ward Howe, played a pivotal role. She had become almost *too* popular, thanks to the success of her "Battle Hymn of the Republic." This deepened her battle with her chauvinist husband, the dashing "Chev." In 1863, five-year-old Samuel Gridley Howe Jr. developed diphtheria. His father returned from his Sanitary Commission work just in time to have the boy die in his arms. Clarke conducted the funeral. Chev said he was too grief-stricken even to attend. So Clarke rode alone with Julia in a carriage to Mount Auburn Cemetery, just as he had the evening before she wrote the "Battle Hymn of the Republic." Near the gate, she opened the little casket, took the boy's cold hand in her own, and bade him farewell.[38]

His father poured himself back into building his own reputation as reformer and hero; Julia, into six lectures on practical ethics. The third, "Moral Triangulation, or The Third Party," is a meditation on divorce and secession. She asked a rhetorical question: "If North and South agree to set aside their bonds of union, and to become two republics, why should they not do it?" Yet in marriage, as in politics, she advocated preserving the union. Barred by Chev from ever lecturing for a fee, Julia instead read them at home, before an invited group, with him absent. She also recited her "Battle Hymn" at the dedication in Boston of a new statue of John Brown. Large audiences in Washington, with Lincoln himself present, heard her recite it there as well. When she told Chev that she meant to lecture in New York, Philadelphia, and Washington, but donate the earnings to his Sanitary Commission, his reaction made her write in her journal, "Some illusions left me today, giving place to unwholesome facts." What this meant about him is not clear.[39] A few days later, however, she spoke on "Duality of Character" at the Indiana Place church, before "quite a full audience." It was the first time she wore the white-lace cap that later became her trademark.[40] It was as though she had declared herself a widow, with her husband still living.

Her growing reputation earned her an invitation to read a poem at the seventieth birthday of William Cullen Bryant in New York. On the train, she sat next to Dr. Oliver Wendell Holmes. She was the only woman on the program. News reports spoke of her voice, saying she was "received with much applause." Yet Chev continued to oppose her public speaking, and their oldest daughters took their father's side. Julia wrote an essay called "Polarity," saying that the roles of women and men were not innate, but the product of social factors. Only if women had a chance at self-development equal to those accorded men, could the true complementarity of the sexes evolve. This idea guided her activism for the rest of her life, but did no real good at home.

On their wedding anniversary in 1865, she said that she would be preaching that evening at the Charlestown Women's Prison. Her daughters objected. Chev, as she told her journal, "attacked me with the utmost vehemence and temper, calling my undertaking a mere courting of public-ity." She relented, but then added, "I have been married twenty-two years today. In the course of this time, I have never known my husband to ap-prove any act of mine which I myself valued. Books—poems—essays—everything has been contemptible or contraband in his eyes, because it was not *his* way of doing things."[41]

Yet she was still not yet ready to join the public movement for women's rights. The Civil War had both ended slavery and helped many women to find "a new scope for their activities, and developed abilities hitherto unsus-pected by themselves."[42] Magnanimously, she also realized that what Chev needed was a new challenge for himself. He hoped to head an American mission to Greece, where Crete required humanitarian relief after wresting its freedom from the Turks. She went with him to Washington to support his sense of mission, although she had no desire to follow him. Relieved herself when the post went to a younger man, she then helped him to raise relief funds for Crete. She and two daughters then went with him on a seven-month trip to Europe to deliver this help, via England and Rome. On that journey, they met a young Greek man who became Chev's assistant, married their eldest daughter, and succeeded him at the Blind School. Re-turning in October 1867, Julia wrote a book about the trip, not once naming her husband.

Late that month, John Albion Andrew suddenly died of a stroke, at only forty-nine. Boston's black community joined in mourning their staunch ally, the abolitionist governor. They kept vigil at his home, gathered around the Indiana Place church during the funeral, and then trailed the hearse to Mount Auburn Cemetery. Julia even wrote a poem for the memorial ser-vice. Chev forbade her to read it in public. Then, without consulting his wife, he rented out both their townhouse and country home, driving them back to living in stark quarters at the Blind School. Julia was incensed. She poured herself into public life, joining the Radical Club, which included Emerson, Higginson, Peabody, Bartol, and others. When Chev learned that she was to be a delegate at the 1868 National Conference of Unitar-ians and Other Liberal Christian Churches in New York and then to attend a women's rights meeting in Boston, he rather overplayed his hand. He wrote a letter so full of projection, manipulation, and narcissism that she found it not only painful to read but also easy to resist.[43]

She went to the women's meeting in Boston's Horticulture Hall half-expecting the tone to be as hysterical as Chev and others had sometimes caricatured the women's movement. Yet there, along with the women leaders, was her own minister, James Freeman Clarke; Chev's colleague in the Secret Six, Thomas Wentworth Higginson; Wendell Phillips and William Lloyd Garrison. Lucy Stone rose to speak. Insistent on keeping her own name, rather than taking that of her husband, Lucy had long been for Julia "the object of one of my imaginary dislikes." Yet as she spoke, Julia found her "sweet-faced and silver-voiced, the very embodiment of Goethe's 'eternal feminine,'" and voicing opinions that "harmonized with my own aspirations." She could now see more fully the connection between antislavery and the rights of women. When asked to speak herself, she said only, "I am with you."[44] The next day, she became the new president of the New England Woman Suffrage Association.

In the split among suffragists, Julia stood with Stone and served the American Woman Suffrage Association, as its foreign corresponding secretary. This made use of her European contacts and language skills. As a speaker on women's rights, she was somewhat less adept. Caroline Dall rarely forgot the class divides among the women she addressed. Julia often did. She once spoke to a group of working-class women in rural Vermont as if they suffered the ennui afflicting women of far greater privilege. She did see, however, how traditional religion helped to oppress women. "I felt how much the masculine administration of religious doctrine had overridden us women, and I felt how partial and one-sided a view of these matters had been inculcated by men, and handed down by man-revering mothers," she later told her daughters. "We need to have the womanly side of religion represented."[45]

Perhaps only as a member of the Disciples, where lay preaching by both lay men and women had been a principle from the first, and with a pastor like Clarke, could Julia have realized that she, too, was also a minister. She then organized women preachers, ordained or nonordained, as president of the world's first Women's Ministerial Association.

Julia had come to recognize that during the first two-thirds of her life she had identified leadership with the masculine principle that she had romanticized in Chev. Now she needed support from other women who also needed to find their voice on spiritual and public matters. Religious and reflective, she also saw that her "Battle Hymn" had romanticized bloodshed. During the Franco-Prussian War of 1870, she repented by asking women on both sides of the Atlantic to rise up and initiate an international Mother's Day for Peace:

Arise, then, women of this day! All women who have hearts, whether our baptism be of water or of tears! Say firmly: We will not have great questions decided by irrelevant agencies. Our husbands shall not come home to us, reeking with carnage, for caresses and applause. Our sons shall not be taken from us to unlearn all that we have been able to teach them of charity, mercy and patience. We, women of one country, will be too tender of those of another country, to allow our sons to be trained to injure theirs. From the bosom of the devastated earth a voice goes up with our own. It says: Disarm, disarm! The sword of murder is not the balance of justice. Blood does not wipe out dishonor, nor violence vindicate possession.[46]

For the author of the "Battle Hymn," this was quite an evolution. Her eldest daughters, having taken their father's side in their parents' struggle, married and left in 1870 and 1871. When Chev died, in 1876, she felt a liberation. At the funeral, Clarke did not criticize the deceased, although as Julia's friend, pastor, and confidant, he probably knew more than was entirely conducive to public edification. He simply read a poem that Whittier had written about Dr. Howe, called "The Hero," which described him as a "knight of a better era/without reproach or fear," but also of an age long transcended.

Transcendentalists expanded the influence of their circle in many different ways: through spiritual friendship, mentoring, public speaking, writing, and organizing. During her later years, Julia Ward Howe used them all to become a hero herself in the long struggle for women's rights. She urged spiritual friendship among women through the growing movement of women's clubs. She spoke publicly. She published more. She stayed in the Disciples to mentor younger women. Her friend Thomas Wentworth Higginson saw "a new brightness to her face, a new cordiality in her manner."[47] He himself was trying to mentor a shy young poet named Emily Dickinson.

Their spiritual friendship definitely changed them both.

Thomas Wentworth Higginson and his
daughter Margaret on a tricycle, Cambridge, 1885

CHAPTER XIV

Circumference and Expansion

*In which a spiritual friendship between an activist and a poet enlarges both;
Transcendentalist disciples widen the circumference of the original circle,
and in remembering one another, expand their spiritual influence.*

THE FRIENDSHIP OF EMILY DICKINSON and Thomas Wentworth Higginson developed in the most nonmaterial, spiritual way possible: by correspondence. Only twice during the twenty-four years that they wrote to one another did they meet face-to-face. Yet their spiritual friendship surely transformed them both.

Like Emerson, Higginson had never truly wanted to be a minister. In fact, he had once dropped out of Harvard Divinity School. Two considerations had brought him back. One was Mary Channing. He had met her at the Church of the Disciples when he was only twenty. Like Margaret Fuller at the same age, she was witty, insightful, and often challenging. Churches, on the other hand, did not enough challenge society, he already felt. When James Freeman Clarke succeeded in getting over 170 Unitarian ministers to sign a petition to Congress asking for an end to slavery, he began to feel that perhaps the ministry could be a relevant profession for him after all. He also knew that before he could ask Dr. Walter Channing for his daughter's hand in marriage, he would have to have a clear plan for earning a living. He then returned to finish his degree, be ordained, and marry. Yet neither ministry nor marriage had gone quite as he had hoped.

He still loved his wife dearly, but she gradually had become almost a complete invalid. The term was not yet in use, but Mary Channing Higginson may have suffered multiple sclerosis. Her symptoms certainly seem compatible with that modern diagnosis. She also had a fear of ever going through childbirth. When she was fifteen, she had been present when her stepmother, Barbara Higginson Channing, delivered a stillborn child and then died herself, despite the expert intervention of Dr. Channing, the leading obstetrician in Boston. The physical side of his marriage to Mary may well have been a factor in Higginson's adult restlessness and risk taking. The spiritual side had only helped to make him a bold advocate for abolition, women's rights and education. His essay in the *Atlantic Monthy*, "Ought Women to Learn the Alphabet?" (February 1859) was protest dripping with sarcasm.

After the John Brown affair, he resigned as minister of the Free Church in Worcester, and began to write more for the magazine. He did a series of essays on slave insurrections that Brown had not studied closely enough. Those alternated with Thoreau-like essays of observations of the natural world as he paced the perimeter of ponds. Politically, he felt conflicted about secession. Part of him favored disunion and agreed with Garrison: "Let the South go." The stronger part wanted to see the conflict purge the nation of the sin of slavery. He proposed that a battalion led by John Brown Jr. go to the Mason-Dixon Line, since he could not leave Mary to go himself. Another part of him wanted to repeat what Emerson had done: after leaving the pastoral ministry, reinvent himself as a writer, lecturer, and public intellectual. That winter, he unconsciously emulated Emerson's address "The American Scholar," with an essay of encouragement to other aspiring writers. Both came from minister-writers preaching to themselves in the guise of speaking to others.

Higginson's "Letter to a Young Contributor," appeared in the *Atlantic Monthy* in January 1862. "There may be years of crowded passion in a word," he wrote, "and half a life in a sentence. . . . A single word may be a window from which one may perceive all the kingdoms of the earth." Like Emerson, he valued the terse over the smooth. "Charge your style with life," he wrote.[1] Most responses, as he had feared, were deadly dull and tedious. Then on an April morning, he stopped at the post office on his way back from the local gym. As an advocate for physical fitness and for women, he had been observing a women's exercise group. Opening a letter postmarked Amherst, he read, "Are you too deeply occupied to say if my

Verse is alive?" Enclosed he found four short, striking poems that astonished him. "Poetry torn up by the roots," he later called them.[2] The note was unsigned. The author identified herself with a card in another enclosed envelope: Emily Dickinson. He wrote back immediately.

Higginson was then thirty-eight. Emily was then thirty-one. His father had once served as the treasurer of Harvard. Her father was a lawyer and the treasurer of Amherst College—an institution created by Calvinists as an alternative to liberal Harvard. That coincidence, however, went unmentioned. So did the fact that Emily, like Mary Higginson, had an undiagnosed illness. Recent biographers, tracing prescriptions and medical appointments, suggest that it was probably a form of epilepsy.[3] Spasms, sometimes triggered by stress or by sudden light, and the stigma attached to "the falling sickness," led her to withdrawn habits and writing mostly by night. Seeking encouragement from an older, male Transcendentalist made sense, given her own spiritual journey.

Her Calvinist father sent her to Miss Mary Lyon's Female Seminary at Mount Holyoke. There, the converted went to one side, while those still hoping for salvation moved to the other. Emily stood still, declining to dissemble, declaring herself a "no hoper."[4] Back at home, a law clerk working for her father, Benjamin Franklin Newton, a Unitarian nine years her senior, introduced her to a new interpretation of life. He became her "gentle, yet grave Preceptor, teaching me what to read, what authors to admire, what was grand or beautiful in nature, and that sublime lesson, a faith in things unseen, and a life again, nobler, and much more blessed."[5] He gave her a volume of Emerson's poems, models of terse, lively verse. But he then died, while still young, in Worcester, in 1853.

The only other man with whom she had shared more than a few poems was Sam Bowles, editor of the *Springfield Republican* and a frequent visitor to the Dickinson homestead, a hub of spiritual, moral, and political influence in the region. He often stayed with Emily's brother Austin and his wife, Susan, at The Evergreens, just across the street. Like both his siblings, Austin was both outwardly conventional and inwardly seething. He succeeded his father as the "squire" of Amherst and treasurer, but then betrayed Susan by starting an affair with Mabel Loomis Todd, wife of the college astronomer. Emily was incensed. She had a spiritual friendship with Susan. Her younger sister and housemate, Vinnie (Lavinia), meanwhile abetted the adultery.

Emily wrote Higginson shortly after Bowles left on a long trip to Europe. Although Higginson's letters to Emily are now lost (Vinnie burned them after Emily died), we can reconstruct some of their content from her responses. The correspondence went on for twenty-four years. Although he initially suggested some changes to the poems that she referred to as "surgery," she found it "not so painful as I supposed." The few questions he posed, she answered. She read Keats, the Brownings, Ruskin, Thomas Browne, and Revelations—adding, "I had a terror since September I could tell to none; and so I sing, as the boy does of the burying ground, because I am afraid . . . [W]hen a little girl, I had a friend who taught me Immortality; but venturing too near, himself, he never returned. Soon after my tutor died . . . Then I found one more, but he was not contented I be his scholar, so he left the land." Of her family, she said, "I have a brother and sister; my mother does not care for thought, and father, too busy with his briefs to notice what we do . . . buys me many books, but begs me not to read them, because he fears they joggle the mind. They are religious, except me, and address an eclipse, every morning, whom they call their 'Father.'" She signed herself, "Your friend, E. Dickinson."[6]

She enclosed three more poems. Higginson must have praised them. "Your letter gave no Drunkenness," she replied, "because I tasted Rum before . . . yet I have had few pleasures so deep as your opinion," adding, "You think my gait 'spasmodic'—I am in danger—Sir . . . You think me 'uncontrolled,'" she then added. "The 'hand you stretch me in the Dark,' I put in mine." He must have asked about publishing. "'To publish,'" she replied, was "as foreign to my thought as Firmament to Fin," and yet, "if fame belonged to me, I could not escape her." She alluded to his *Atlantic* essay "Gymnastics," in which he said that, if practiced "thoroughly and patiently," one might "attain evolutions more complicated, and, if you wish, more perilous."[7] She asked, "Would you have time to be the 'friend' you should think I need? I have a little shape—it would not crowd your Desk." This time she sent no poems. "But, will you be my Preceptor, Mr.

Higginson?"⁸ When he continued the correspondence, she then sent more poems to both set the hook and then reel him in, including, "Dare you see a Soul at the 'White Heat'?" and "Success—is counted sweetest." He now wanted to meet her, but she only made excuses. Their correspondence continued even as he went off to war.

Leaving Mary in the care of her niece, Margaret Fuller Channing, Higginson went to the Sea Islands of Georgia and South Carolina, as a colonel of a regiment of freed slaves, and there did perhaps his best writing about that experience and about of the spirituals that he heard there. Nearly half of the eighteen hundred poems Dickinson left to us also date from those war years, 1862–1865, or else she sent them to Higginson later. Some have noted that she said nothing about slavery. Or war. True. She did not know that reality firsthand; but she also no longer wrote just about nature. She wrote about death—and transcendence. This also helped Higginson, who after the war needed a new life.

When he returned, Mary persuaded him to move to Newport, Rhode Island, the ancestral home of the Channing family. He tried to like it there. He even wrote his only novel there, set in the old town.⁹ It had no real popular success, but Emily said that she liked it. She encouraged him as much as he did her. He kept trying to meet her, asking her to come to Boston, perhaps to attend a meeting of the Radical Club with Julia Ward Howe. "I do not cross my father's ground," she replied. That was not strictly true. She had relatives in Cambridge and consulted an eye doctor in Boston, but she went there with Vinnie without ever seeing her "Preceptor." Not only did she "tell the Truth, but tell it slant," about both bodily problems and her feelings, the letters and poems she sent him often read like riddles only half-revealing her soul. Yet what she liked in him most was his directness.

"That it is true, Master," she wrote, "is the Power of all you write."¹⁰ Seduced by her indirectness, he finally went far out of his way to pay her a visit in Amherst, in October 1870. Her conversation in the flesh—as intense, allusive, elusive, and demanding as any he had ever engaged in—left him with a sense of his energy being drained. He concluded that he was glad they did not live nearer one another. Yet Emily kept asking him to visit again. He did when he came to lecture in Amherst on women's suffrage, in December 1873. "Each time we seem to come together as old & tried friends," he wrote, "and I certainly feel that I have known you long & well through the beautiful thoughts and words which you have sent me. I hope you will not cease to trust me and turn to me; and I will try to speak the truth to you, and with love."[11]

When her father died the next year, she teased him that as a clergyman, he surely owed her a condolence call. She also knew why he could not, however, with his other "friend" so ill. Occasionally Emily sent Mary notes, flowers, or a poem, and condolences when her own father died in 1876. Then Mary herself died.

More acquainted with grief than he, Emily counseled Higginson to be gentle with himself. "The Wilderness is new—to you," she wrote to him. "Master, let me lead you."[12] In another letter: "Danger is not at first, for then we are unconscious, but in the after—slower—Days. Do not try to be saved—but let Redemption find you—as it certainly will—Love is it's [sic] own rescue, for we—at our supremest, are but it's [sic] trembling Emblems." She also advised against stoicism. "To be human is more than to be divine," she added, "for when Christ was divine, he was uncontented til he had been human."[13] He implied he might again visit her in Amherst. Instead, he traveled. He first went to the South, to revisit his fight for black emancipation and to bemoan the culture of white supremacy that had spoiled Reconstruction. Then to Europe. Emily read of his travels in the *Republican*.[14] Meanwhile, she became intimate with another older, recent widower: Judge Otis Lord, a friend of her father.

When Higginson returned home, he was fifty-eight. He surprised his friends by also finding a new love. Mary Thatcher (Minnie), thirty-five, was "refined & dainty in all her ways," he told another woman.[15] As an assertive advocate of the rights of women, Higginson had somehow chosen a very traditional, conventional woman to be his wife. Yet he took her to Harpers Ferry for their honeymoon to recall his own activism. They then moved to Cambridge, where he had grown up. He reentered politics, speaking widely on behalf of women's issues. When their first child, Louisa, died seven weeks after birth, Dickinson replied with her poem "The Face in Evanescence lain/ Is more distinct than our's." When a second child, Margaret, came, she sent another, with the blessing, "Her Travels daily be/ By routes of ecstasy."[16]

They now corresponded less often, but she continued to send poems, although she was more often ill than entirely well. She died in May 1886. Higginson went to Amherst for the funeral, which took place, not in the church, but in the parlor of her lifelong home. A minister prayed, another read scripture, and then Higginson read a poem he knew to have been a favorite of hers: Emily Bronte's "Last Lines," which begins, "No coward soul is mine,/ No trembler in the world's storm-tossed sphere;/ I see Heaven's glories shine."[17]

Many of the Transcendentalists and their disciples could identify with those last lines. They were now dying. Yet not without cultivating successors to carry on their ideas and ideals.

James Freeman Clarke
(1810–1888)

CHAPTER XV

Succession

In which the Transcendentalists pass
the torch from generation to generation.

WHILE HIGGINSON HAD LEFT THE MINISTRY, Clarke had not. He dedicated
the third meetinghouse of the Disciples on February 28, 1869.[1] They had
not built just for themselves. Fifty teachers led a Sunday school for over
four hundred children, mostly poor. Two-thirds came from nonmember
families. Public forums drew three hundred to four hundred. A series of
presentations called "What Is Being Done in Boston?" discussed varied social problems. Another carried the title, "The True Universal Church," and
included speakers from Roman Catholic, Episcopalian, Methodist, Baptist,
Universalist, Quaker, and Free Religion perspectives. On many Sundays, a
third of those present might be visitors, drawn more by Clarke's reputation
or writings than by anything else. Every year he seemed to produce either
a new book or a new edition of one that he had previously published. Seeing the mission of the inclusive church to be "irenic, not polemic," he tried
to find common ground even with those with whom he could not agree.
Clarke sought to summarize the stance of liberal religion. As he said in
Orthodoxy: Its Truths and Errors (1866):

> The Protestant Reformation has its Principle and its Method. Its Princi-
> ple is Salvation by Faith, not by Sacraments. Its Method is Private Judg-
> ment, not Church Authority. But private judgment generates authority;
> authority, first legitimate, that of knowledge, grows into the illegitimate
> authority of prescription, calling itself Orthodoxy. Then Private Judg-
> ment comes forth again to criticize and reform. It thus becomes the duty

of each individual to judge the Church; and out of innumerable individual judgments the insight of the Church is kept living and progressive. We contribute one such private judgment; not, we trust, in conceit, but in the hope of provoking other minds to further examinations.[2]

As a Transcendentalist, Clarke applied similar methods derived from German idealists like Hegel to the reexamination of all intellectual history, setting up polarities only to take a synthesizing yet progressive position. For example, contrasting naturalism and supernaturalism, he defended naturalism, but then also the role of religion in challenging humans to rise *above* their nature. Materialism and religious literalism he treated in a similar fashion. In *Steps of Belief; or, Rational Christianity Maintained Against Atheism, Free Religion, and Romanism* (1870), he used the Transcendentalist premise of an intuitive soul centering all consciousness and morality.[3] Such thinking, once anathema in Boston, had now become widely accepted. Starting in 1873, Clarke's sermons from the previous Sunday appeared weekly in the *Boston Saturday Evening Gazette*.[4] These applied religious principles to ongoing social ills of the day. As technology and population growth accelerated, Clarke emphasized spiritual and moral imperatives.

Boston itself was growing in circumference. Thanks to immigration, by 1870 the city now had over 250,000 people, an increase of 40 percent in one decade, absorbing the adjacent towns. The postwar economy was booming, but political corruption seemed more pervasive. Many seemed to interpret Darwin as an apologist for the "survival of the fittest," rationalizing away the need to care for the vulnerable and to provide greater equality of opportunity for all. Clarke himself felt just a bit vulnerable economically, not as secure as he had hoped to be by his mid-sixties. He had finally sold Brook Farm, a terrible investment. Through his brothers, he had invested in Chicago properties. The Great Chicago Fire of 1871 destroyed them all. Boston itself, the next year, had its own Great Fire, burning sixty-five acres of the downtown. Yet his new church had survived, as had his own house in Boston's Jamaica Plain neighborhood. He turned down chances to work less and to earn more in Cambridge or in New York. His three young adult children were doing well.[5] He himself had become an amateur astronomer, intrigued by what science was slowly revealing about cosmic as well as evolutionary progress.

Postwar politics, however, appalled him. Republican politicians maintained power by using Northern rancor against the South for their personal profit. He wanted two more amendments to the US Constitution: one requiring each state to provide free, nonsectarian schools; and another, equal rights for all, making accepting both a condition for any rebel state's readmission to the Union. In 1874, he traveled to the South. He continued to preach about the need for progress at all levels—religious, scientific, intellectual, and moral—before true social progress, toward what Dr. Martin Luther King Jr. would later call the "Beloved Community," might yet emerge. Thinkers like Clarke—Transcendentalists and their disciples—later often stood accused of a naïve faith in human progress. This is unjust.

Clarke never considered such progress as inevitable. He merely prayed that it *might* be possible—and then held out that hope to others, showing them ways to moral and spiritual growth, leading toward greater political justice, one step at a time. His book *Common Sense in Religion* (1874) is a fine example.[6] It patiently leads the reader through polarities of thought prevalent back then and still common now. The very term "common sense," of course, had many layers of allusion: Paine's call for revolution in America but also the Scottish "common sense" philosophers against whom he and the earliest Transcendentalists had rebelled. Not to mention, "in theology, that part of Christian truth . . . taken up into the average mind of Christendom." The problem with some common sense, he suggested, was that it does always deal with the ultimate mystery: Why is there this great evolving something, rather than nothing? And what is our place in it? He also tried to show that Christian teaching and moral altruism in all traditions accord with any form of common sense that cares for the quality of human life in the future.

In 1875, around his sixty-fifth birthday, Clarke received two honors, from both church and state. The Disciples commissioned a painting of him by William Morris Hunt, the preeminent portraitist in Boston and his daughter's teacher. The mayor and city council then asked him to deliver an oration in the Music Hall, on July 5. Clarke referred to it as a "preparatory lecture," of the kind once given in New England churches to prepare a community for a coming celebration of communion; in this case, the centenary the coming year of the Declaration of Independence.[7] He now felt more elegiac than prophetic, however. Most of his mentors and friends had died. His *Memorial and Biographical Sketches* appeared in 1878. There were chapters in tribute to his grandfather and to Dr. Channing. Others were sermons occasioned by the death of friends like John Albion Andrew, Walter Channing, Charles Sumner, and Sam Howe. Yet he took care to remember newer and younger harbingers of hope and progress, such as Susan Dimock, MD.

Born in the South, she began medical studies at Harvard, thanks to Walter Channing. Dimock learned quickly and attended rounds attentively, but male students and other teachers treated her so badly that she had to withdraw to finish her studies in Zurich. Returning to Boston, she then served as resident physician at the New England Hospital for Women and Children, succeeding Walter Channing as its chief obstetrician and gynecologist. In 1875, along with two female friends, she boarded the S.S. *Schiller*, bound for Plymouth, England. In heavy fog, the ship hit a submerged ledge off the Scilly Islands. Three hundred thirty-six people lost their lives, including Dimock, who was then only twenty-eight.[8]

Clarke led not only her memorial service but also the funeral for Sam Howe on January 13, 1876. Present was Laura Bridgman, sent to Howe as a deaf-blind child, whom he had both taught and exploited to become famous.[9] As her pastor, however, he focused on his widow, Julia. The last five years had been deeply difficult. Having failed at a diplomatic appointment to Greece, Sam took a rather imperialistic assignment: to obtain a US naval base in Santo Domingo (the Dominican Republic). Julia accompanied him there. He then invested her inheritance there, speculatively, as he tried to get the US to annex the whole country. Even his closest friend, Charles Sumner, opposed this. As Julia's inheritance was lost, she tried to maintain her sanity by preaching in a small African Caribbean church that seemed open to hearing a woman speak the gospel truth. Her determination to remain a disciple of Jesus had helped her endure her husband's derision of her suffrage work, his resentment of her "subordinating domestic duties to supposed public ones," and an irritability that only grew as he aged.[10]

Although he at times begged her forgiveness—for telling her to "go to hell," for example—and she then gave it, he also said other women, and not she, were "not only sensual, but lustful, & that men are attracted, rather than shocked by this trait." Before he died, however, they had a talk that "reached the bottom of these years of estrangement, in wh[ich] there has been fault & wrong on both sides." She "solemnly swore to him never to allude to any thing in the past which, coming up lately, has given us both pain." She then had her bed moved into his room, so that they could have "the comfort of being near each other in the dark & silent hours." When he died, she put her bridal veil on his bed. Her farewell poem read,

> *A mother and grandmother, / A widow, long a wife,*
> *I recognize the childhood / That follows me through life.*
> *Oh! Take me yet, dear Master / Where thy disciples stand;*
> *And set me down before them, / With thy instructing hand.*
> *Show them the faulty record, / The willful brow and face,*
> *And tell them this offender / Is conquered by thy grace.*[11]

At the funeral, Clarke tried to be as kind as he could about Dr. Howe, saying,

In him were united the qualities of Sir Lancelot and the Good Samaritan. He was not a saint, in any sense of the word . . . he had his faults, no doubt; he was far from perfect. Perhaps his strong will sometimes made him despotic; his determination may have made him intolerant of the tendencies of minds different from his own. According to the common definition he was not a religious man, for he made little profession [of faith], and cared little for ceremonial worship. But according to the definition of Jesus, he may be called a citizen of Heaven: "Not everyone that saith unto me, Lord, Lord, shall enter into the kingdom of Heaven; but he that *doeth* the will of my Father, who is in Heaven." But even if I were able to point out his defects, I should not care to do so, for to look at faults seldom does us good.[12]

The day after the funeral, Julia wrote in her journal, "Began my new life today." Sam had not made it easy. His will gave everything to the children, assuming that Julia still had income of her own, despite his having lost much of her capital. Letters from women turned up in his papers. Their son-in-law refused to show some to Julia and burned them. She herself threw a private letter from Sumner into the toilet. Yet she had to behave properly, not only through the funeral Clarke led but also through a public memorial at the Music Hall. She was desperate to get away. Once having earned enough from lectures to pay her debts, she took her youngest daughter on a two-year trip to Europe—coming home even more heavily in debt. Fortunately, her brother was now both wealthy and generous to her. In April 1880, he set Julia up at 241 Beacon Street, with the capacity to live as the grande dame that, at an energetic sixty, she had now become.[13]

That month, the Disciples marked Clarke's seventieth birthday with a party more lavish than those they had given for him when he had turned fifty and sixty. He, and Julia, and other speakers sat on the chancel. Oliver Wendell Holmes read a long poem. It began with these lines:

> I bring the simplest pledge of love,
> Friend of my earlier days;
> Mine is the hand without the glove,
> The heart-beat, not the phrase.
> How few still breathe this mortal air
> We called by schoolboy names!
> You still, whatever robe you wear,
> To me are always James.
> That name the kind apostle bore
> Who shames the sullen creeds,
> Not trusting less, but loving more,
> And showing faith by deeds.[14]

Musical interludes by a Schubert Quartet broke up tributes, letters, poems, and hymns. William Henry Channing, in Boston from his Unitarian pastorate in Liverpool, told stories of Clarke as a boy at Boston Latin, calling him the most "utterly fearless, entirely conscientious, and the most faithful man" he ever knew. Julia handed him flowers, ending her own poem for him by calling him "leader, brother, friend, and chief."[15]

Edward Everett Hale, his Boston colleague, then also the chaplain of the US Senate, sent a letter proclaiming him the "metropolitan" (or archbishop) of Boston's Unitarian clergy: "And a first-rate metropolitan he is. He is so radical, that the most radical of us takes shelter behind him; and he is so conservative, that the most hard-shelled conservative of us takes comfort in his wisdom. He is a reformer so audacious that, in our little reforms, we are sure of his encouragement; and the same time he knows the past so thoroughly, that he teaches us how to respect it." Clarke then gave thanks for his friendships, especially that with Margaret Fuller:

> I bless God for the friendships of my life. It is a great thing to have had for friends such men as Theodore Parker and Charles Sumner; a great thing to have known somewhat intimately Dr. Channing, Henry Ware, Ralph Waldo Emerson, Father Taylor, Ephraim Peabody, James Walker, Francis Greenwood. Nor can I ever forget the influence which came to me from that noble and wonderful woman Margaret Fuller. From her I learned the possibilities of intellectual achievement, the power of progress in us all which is the mighty moral force of the soul. She did for me what she did for so many others—aroused me to see the value of life, and how to live for a great end. She was my intimate friend during several years, and the mental and moral stimulus which I received from her, it would be idle to attempt to describe.[16]

Julia that evening began to plan her own biography of Fuller, whose memoir by male friends she felt lacked a woman's perspective.[17] Higginson later also wrote a Fuller bio, emphasizing not her marital status but rather her social vision.[18] Clarke's new book that year was *Self-Culture: Physical,*

Intellectual, Moral and Spiritual (1880). The very theme went back to Dr. Channing. Clarke referred to it as "the duty to grow." His introduction, "Beginnings of Culture, in Childhood—Natural and Artificial Methods in the Education of Children," endorsed the mission of his friend Elizabeth Peabody: kindergarten and preschool education for children of all economic backgrounds. He also made it clear how her reform work connected to other Transcendentalist themes:

> How does Mother Nature teach? She takes on herself the most difficult part of all the course, and she does her work thoroughly. Hers is the real Primary School. She says, "I will take the little child who knows nothing, and I will teach him to know the use of his own body, the nature of the world about him, and the articulate language of his country." And she does it. The little thing learns to see, hear, touch, taste, walk; to jump, run, climb, hold objects, know what is hard and soft, heavy and light, round and square; to know wood, stone, earth, water, air; to distinguish between things far and distant, sounds remote and close by. Finally, she teaches him to speak a language.[19]

The original Transcendentalists had rebelled against teaching based in dead languages and a focus on the past, not on nature in the present. Clarke continued on those themes.

> Now, how does the dear mother do all this? What is her method?
> FIRST,—She mixes nine parts of pleasure and one of pain, nine of hope and one of fear in her system. We [too often] do the opposite . . .
> Nature trains while she teaches, she disciplines the powers while she imparts information to the intellect. We are too analytic; teach only the memory—she teaches all the primary faculties at the same time . . .
> I do not propose that boys and girls should spend their time [all] in play. But I propose to use the principle involved in play in acquiring knowledge.[20]

Just as his grandfather Freeman had let him have free run of both the outdoors and his library, he maintained a sense of playfulness even with his own children, grandchildren, friends, and congregants. In his last years, he was often retrospective but never nostalgic. There is a difference, he knew, between learning from the past and trying to replicate it.

This, too, was a central legacy of the Transcendentalists.

John Muir
(1838–1914)

Application

In which the Transcendentalists and their disciples
transfer their influence and ideas to our time.

AS WE HAVE SEEN IN THE STRUCTURE OF THIS NARRATIVE, the Transcendentalists began in the fire of rebellion against injustice. They passed through the waters of death toward their hope for human liberation. They came down to earth, as organizers, in the mud and conflagration of Civil War. They then wanted to pass on their spirit, as we all do, as best they could.

Similarly, in a traditional New England sermon, there were typically four distinct parts: first an introduction, then an explication (often of the biblical text), followed by interpretation or explanation, and, finally, an application to the spiritual/moral needs of those present and beyond. The Transcendentalists have relevance for us still. Not merely as writers but also as prophetic activists who went before us—loving nature, fighting racism, seeking equal rights regardless of gender or sexual differences, yearning for greater economic equity and equality of opportunity.

When Emerson died in 1882, Clarke gave the memorial address. The First Parish in Concord had to reinforce the beams under the sanctuary and gallery to hold the overflow crowd. Clark knew that during his last decade, the Sage of Concord, suffering dementia, had also needed support: his daughter Ellen to be his secretary, his son Edward to turn from medicine to turning the pages of lectures for him, and daughter Edith's husband to oversee his finances. He said nothing of this. Instead, he expressed what all shared:

> I cannot speak of a sense of loss in the death of Emerson. His life appears like something complete. His work was done: we have it; the

world will keep it. In a few weeks he would have entered his 80th year; with increasing infirmities, he could give nothing more to the world and derive nothing more from it. For himself, to die is to gain. As he once said, "There is hope of a world in which we may see things but once and then pass on to something new." Yet . . . to have lived in his time and country, and to have shared his life, is an honor and a blessing: most of all if we have caught his confidence in our own near relation to the Eternal Powers.[1]

Clarke in his own last years tried to use his remaining powers fully, engaged with moral and political issues. He preached and worked against the Chinese Exclusion Act, then pending in Congress. He published a memoir called *Anti-Slavery Days: A Sketch of the Struggle Which Ended in the Abolition of Slavery in the United States.* Designed for a generation beginning to forget there had been principled purposes behind the Civil War, it was a mass-market paperback, priced at twenty cents.[2] He also applied his principles to electoral politics, almost as a surrogate for his friend and fellow Disciple, John Albion Andrew.

For the Unitarian Sunday School Society, he published *A Manual of Unitarian Belief,* with a series of questions for discussion. He asked his readers to steer between dogmatism and credulity on the one hand, and skepticism and nihilism on the other, seeking a transcendent goal: the kingdom of God, a beloved community of equals—already present, for those with eyes to see, ears to hear, and hearts to understand.[3] Kept in print for over forty years and more than twenty revised editions, the manual mirrored his formula of the Five Points of Liberal Theology as a spiritual response to the Five Points of Calvinism, then known by the mnemonic TULIP. Rather than *Total* depravity, he declared all humans to be the children of a loving, forgiving God. Rather than the *Unconditional* election of a few, he saw an equal brother- and sisterhood of all God's children. Rather than *Limited* atonement, he spoke of the ability of all to join as disciples in serving the common good. Rather than salvation only for the elect through *Irresistible* grace, he spoke of salvation not by faith, nor works, but rather by character. Finally, rather than *Perseverance* only of the saints, he spoke of spiritual progress in this life and any yet to come. Unitarian churches for the next forty years then taught "The Fatherhood of God; the Brotherhood of Man; the Leadership of Jesus; Salvation by Character; and the Continuity of Human Development in All Worlds, or the Progress of Mankind, onward and upward forever."[4]

Such a terse formula, of course, soon inspired parody. Some said it left out Unitarian belief in "the neighborhood of Boston." The last clause, reduced to its final phrases, seemed like just so much foolish optimism. Yet for Clarke, it affirmed, as did the Universalists, a faith in an ultimate harmony of all souls with the divine. Accused of optimism, he replied, "It may be that my temperament is too sanguine, and that in reading the gospel I love to dwell more on its hopes and promises than on its threats and warnings. But let us consider this a little and ask, '*which is the truest and wisest view of life, that which hopes or that which desponds?*'"[5]

His wife began urging him to write a memoir.[6] Otherwise, she warned, Mrs. Dall would write his life for him. He began one. But having known so many Transcendentalists so intimately and done so many memorial addresses, Clarke knew how difficult it is to tell the full story of any individual, friendship, or group of friends. There is something—perhaps one might call it, as Emerson did, "the Soul of the Whole"—that perpetually remains transcendent and elusive. Then, in 1888, as his own health was failing, he struggled to complete a final series of sermons: on the Lord's Prayer. The answer to that prayer, he said, comes only when the meaning of each of its phrases is both understood spiritually and then lived inwardly. On May 18, he was so weak that he had to have someone else read his penultimate sermon, while he listened. Two weeks later, he could not even get to church to hear his sermon, "Deliver Us from Evil," read to the Disciples. Finally, on June 8, surrounded by his family, he died so peacefully they scarcely knew when he breathed his last.[7]

One of the youngest of the original Transcendentalists was gone. Fuller had died in 1850, Thoreau in 1862, Ripley in 1880, Emerson in 1882. Alcott had died just months before. Hedge lived another two years. Peabody lived on to try to tell her version of the whole story, until 1894. More importantly, they all left successors, directly or indirectly. Consider these few scenes:

In 1871 Emerson visited California. His wealthy son-in-law, William Forbes, arranged for a private railway car to take him there. The sixty-eight-year-old sage was serene but starting to experience dementia. When he spoke in what had been Starr King's church in San Francisco, it was not apparent.[8] Yet as he visited Yosemite Valley, near a mountain named for Starr King, who had fought to protect its beauty, the fatigue that had prompted the trip became more visible. Like many others, John Muir, who made popular Thoreau's insight that "in wildness is the preservation of the world," had been reading Emerson from his youth. Mentored as a naturalist by Unitarians on the faculty of the university in his native Wisconsin, Muir received the visit of the author of *Nature* as a spiritual laying-on of hands. He spent a whole day showing the Sage of Concord the many varieties of Western Sierra pines, but he could see that his hero was not what he once had been. He wanted Emerson to stay, to camp out with him, but other members of the party would not hear of it. They were forced to part near the Mariposa Grove.

"Emerson lingered in the rear," Muir wrote, "and when he reached the top of the ridge, after all the rest of the party were over and out of sight, he turned his horse, took off his hat and waved me a last good-bye."[9] The giver of that benediction later told a friend of Muir's, "He is more wonderful than Thoreau."[10] He tried to entice Muir to Harvard, to join Gray and Agassiz. "I never for a moment thought of giving up God's big show for a mere profship!" wrote Muir.[11] Although Muir was best known for cofounding the Sierra Club, his biographer accurately describes his mission as nothing less than "saving the American soul from total surrender to materialism."[12]

By then, Emerson again had influence at Harvard. Given an honorary degree, like Clarke, he was also an overseer. Before the trip, he had given a series of university lectures on "The Natural History of Intellect."[13] As with his final book *The Conduct of Life*, released in 1860, there was less idealism, more on science and pragmatism. "I like not the man who is thinking how to be good," said this older, tempered Emerson, "but the man thinking how to accomplish his work." Recent scholars now rightfully place him at the source of the whole pragmatist tradition in American philosophy.[14]

The following year, in January 1872, a group of younger thinkers had gathered in Cambridge as the Metaphysical Club.[15] The name recalled the Transcendentalist circle of decades before. They often met at the Quincy Street home of the James family. The best-known members were William James, son of Emerson's friend Henry James Sr.; his friend and future Supreme Court Justice Oliver Wendell Holmes Jr., son of the "Autocrat of the Breakfast Table"; and Charles Sanders Peirce, son of Benjamin Peirce, Harvard's professor of mathematics. Sometimes called "the father of American pragmatism," Peirce argued for judging the meaning of a belief by the actions and uses to which it gives rise. The Socrates within this group was Chauncey Wright. The son of a traditional Unitarian, once he had read Emerson he had become an agnostic, placing the question of God beyond proof by any kind of science. He had become secretary of the American Academy of Arts and Sciences, a defender of Darwin, mathematician for the *Nautical Almanac*, and a Harvard lecturer on psychology. He loved conversation but also suffered from depression and alcoholism. Wright never married, and died of a stroke in 1875.

William James, who also lived with depression, wrote his essay "The Will to Believe" both out of an experience of having to change his own thinking as well as his behavior in order to transcend toward wholeness, and as his own response to Wright's neutrality about all beliefs. Like Clarke, James had asked himself, quite pragmatically, "which is the truest and wisest view of life, that which hopes or that which desponds?" He then argued, in *The Varieties of Religious Experience*, that a faith born of despondency—a "twice-born" experience—often proves more effective, in the long run, than any "once-born" discovery of one's internal power.[16] Clarke would have agreed. While Margaret had helped him find his own inner strength, only the death of his eight-year-old son, his own near death, and then the spiritual resurrection of the Disciples, both institutionally and individually, had shown him the need for true spiritual regeneration. Where Transcendentalists had earlier counted on spiritual power *within* in order to confront social arrangements of power *over* and in need of reform, they had also gradually learned to exercise their own power *with* others in order to effect real change.

Higginson, once fiercely independent and scornful of compromisers, was now also more willing to try to build ongoing efforts against racism and for women's rights. During his postwar years in Newport, he joined Julia Ward Howe in a later version of the Town and Country Club.[17] While the term "club" has overtones of exclusion, these Transcendentalist disciples, oriented toward goals of inclusion, saw more than ever the need for friendships to sustain their efforts. Howe once entertained the group with a picnic, at which she sang a song, "O So-ci-ety," mocking Beacon Hill pretensions.[18] Both Howe and Higginson supported Lucy Stone and the American Women's Suffrage Association, he serving fourteen years as co-editor and contributor to its weekly *Woman's Journal*. Her work with women's clubs did more to advance the cause of equal suffrage than is usually acknowledged. Both also worked for reconciliation with the NWSA. The rival organizations finally merged in 1890, advancing the cause of suffrage considerably.

When a divide later came among African American leaders, Higginson also tried to be an even-handed ally. At issue was the "Atlanta Compromise," a bargain struck by Booker T. Washington. By accepting white supremacy, blacks were to get limited educational and economic opportunities. W. E. B. Du Bois led the black opposition. Mentored by William James, he was the first African American to earn a Harvard doctorate. Teaching history and economics at Atlanta University, and radicalized by attending the first Pan-African Congress in 1900, he came to prominence by launching the Niagara Movement in 1905, an all-black group challenging lynching and other ongoing violence against people of color.

The aging Higginson felt excluded. Four years later, as Du Bois helped form the National Association for the Advancement of Colored People (NAACP), he did not join the offspring of abolitionists and Transcendentalists in its founding.[19] Yet at Higginson's death, in May 1911, an honor guard of black soldiers played muffled drums. The flag of the First South Carolina Volunteers draped his coffin as it left the First Parish in Cambridge, the church of his boyhood, to his burial at Mount Auburn Cemetery. Garrison's son, then president of the Boston NAACP, noted that Higginson had written asking why his name was not on a committee to welcome the annual NAACP convention to Boston. He added, "I was sorry that I had not given him a last chance."[20]

Within the Unitarian movement after the Civil War, legacy issues also loomed large. Christian traditionalists such as William Greenleaf Eliot fought disciples of Parker's post-Christian form of Transcendentalism in the Western Unitarian Conference. Leading the latter was Jenkin Lloyd Jones. Trained at Meadville, born of Welsh Unitarians in rural Wisconsin, Jones dreamed of taking liberal, non-creedal religion not only to cities or college towns but also to new immigrants in rural areas. In nine years of leading the conference, he traveled 122,370 miles, preached 1,370 times, and doubled the number of churches from 43 to 87.[21] He also supported a remarkable increase in the number of women ministers, especially around Iowa.[22] His journal, *Unity*, declared "Jesus wrote no creed, appointed no bishop, organized no church and taught no trinity . . . Reverence lies not in the acceptance of dogma bequeathed to you, but in the receptive spirit, the truth-seeking attitude . . . [that] religion is a verity best understood when least defined," and "in ethics all religions meet."[23]

Such Midwestern progressive religionists influenced by Transcendentalists organized a Parliament of the World's Religions in conjunction with the Chicago World's Fair of 1893. Jones served as executive secretary. Thousands attended. Swami Vivekananda represented Hinduism. A Buddhist asked how many knew the story of the Buddha. Only five people raised their hands. Another spoke of signs he had observed in America: "No Japanese allowed." "If such be Christian ethics," he said, "we are perfectly satisfied to be heathen."[24] Thanks to Jones, nineteen women addressed the parliament. One was his African American parishioner Fannie B. Williams, whose lecture was on "The Condition of the American Negro." Julia Ward Howe delivered "What Is Religion?" saying, "I think you will all say it is aspiration, the pursuit of the divine in the human. . . . I think nothing is religion which puts one individual absolutely above others, and surely nothing is religion which puts one sex above another. . . . Any religion which sacrifices women to the brutality of men is no religion."[25] This line of thought surely found even more followers in the twentieth century.

Howe's own pastor, and Higginson's first mentor, Clarke, had realized the need for a successor for his own life's work: leading the Disciples, promoting the expansion of liberal religion, and maintaining spiritual friendships transcending differences in theology to promote transcendent, ethical ends. During the time that he was secretary of the American Unitarian Association, just before the Civil War, he spent an evening with a former Baptist minister, Charles Gordon Ames, who had become a Unitarian. The conversation ran late into the night. Clarke was only then nearing fifty; Ames, almost two decades younger. As he later recounted, Ames felt Clarke had truly heard him. Yet he was unprepared when Clarke ended the evening by saying, "I have chosen my successor. I want you to come to the Church of the Disciples when I am through. I do not know about your theology, but I believe you will teach my people religion." Then they sat together in silence.[26]

Ames was just as much of a liberal evangelist as Jones but closer to Clarke in theology. He served congregations in Bloomington, Illinois; Cincinnati; and Albany before becoming a missioner for Starr King's former church in San Francisco, founding new churches in San Jose, Santa Cruz, and Sacramento. In suburban Philadelphia, he then founded a new congregation around a very simple covenant: *"In the freedom of the truth, and in the spirit of Jesus, we unite for the worship of God, and the service of man."* Hundreds of Unitarian churches adopted that formula. As Clarke grew frail, he repeated a hope Ames might succeed him. He couldn't refuse.

In 1889, Julia Ward Howe also went West on a cross-country trip by Pullman car, lecturing in Chicago, Saint Paul, Spokane, Seattle, and Portland. When she reached San Francisco, she spoke at a Decoration Day event at the Opera House. The audience sang the "Battle Hymn of the Republic." She also spoke to the Unitarians in Oakland, across the Bay, on "Women in Ministry." The new Unitarian congregation there was putting up a new and impressive building. The narthex would feature six stained-glass portraits of leaders in liberal religion: Channing, Starr King, Bellows, their founder, his successor, and her own pastor, James Freeman Clarke. Whether Julia had a role in that decision or not is unclear, but she lived long enough to compose yet another poem in his honor, on the centenary of his birth in 1910.

Yet perhaps the most poignant scene I know of a Transcendentalist spiritual friendship forged in the fire of conflagration is this one:

In 1887 Frederick Douglass, by then the most famous African American in the world, was touring Europe. He arranged to take the overnight train from Rome to Florence to arrive on the morning of May 10, the anniversary of the death in that city of his friend Theodore Parker. That evening he wrote to journalist Theodore Stanton, the son of Elizabeth Cady Stanton, who had visited previously and warned him that Parker's plain, brown gravestone felt inadequate. Perhaps it had been all that his widow, Lydia, could afford when her husband died twenty-seven years before. Douglass wrote Stanton that night, "Our first move outward after coffee was to visit the grave of Theodore Parker. . . . I am not an advocate of costly monuments over the decaying bodies of the dead, but . . . the stone at such a man's grave should be a sermon."

Douglass and Stanton then arranged for the most noted sculptor in Rome, William Wetmore Story, an American, to create a new monument. Story was the son of US Supreme Court justice Joseph Story, who in 1839 had ruled in favor of enslaved Africans who had freed themselves aboard the ship *Amistad*. The new gravestone still stands in the Protestant Cemetery in Florence. It features a bas relief medallion of Parker, who sat for a clay bust by Story before he died. It calls him "The Great American Preacher," gives the dates and places of his birth and death, and then adds, "His Name Is Engraved in Marble / His Virtues in the Hearts of Those He / Helped to Free from Slavery / and Superstition."

Those lines were composed by Moncure Daniel Conway, a Unitarian Transcendentalist minister born in Virginia who had both freed his father's slaves and then went on to compose one of the earliest anthologies of spiritual-ethical teachings from a multiplicity of the world's religions. Such insight, now often taken for granted, is our enduring gift from the Transcendentalists.

Theodore Parker monument by William Wetmore Story, Protestant
Cemetery, Florence, Italy. Photograph by Julia Bolton Holloway.

When asked, "What became of the Transcendentalists?" I answer in
this way: the founders died, of course. Yet their disciples passed on their
ideals via spiritual friendships, writings, speeches, and organizations that
continue into the twentieth century, and now beyond. One could speak of
the Anti-Imperialist League that opposed American colonialism during and
after the Spanish-American War. The peace movement that opposed World
War I. The start of the American Civil Liberties Union during that war, by

Unitarian Roger Baldwin, to protect the rights of conscientious objectors, or the many connections to Margaret Sanger's courageous work in founding Planned Parenthood. Behind the Universal Declaration of Human Rights issued by the United Nations after World War II lies an interfaith process grounded in Transcendentalism. I could easily go on.

There is a chance that, having read this far, you may be, in one way or another, a Transcendentalist disciple yourself. If you care about nature as transcending yet nurturing us all, they, too, saw materialistic greed threatening the sustainability of earth as a home for our children and our children's children. If you care about equality, as they did, transcending divisions based on gender, race, religion, class, and wealth. If you consider the affections as well as traditions, as important in moral discernment; if you want religion to offer transcendent ends around which to unite for human survival and flourishing, rather than to require dogmas around which we humans are easily divided, then the Transcendentalists of this narrative are not long ago or far away. They are actually quite *near*. Their hopes live on in all of us who are variously inspired by their prophetic insight, courage, and example.

ACKNOWLEDGMENTS

MY HEAVIEST DEBTS GO TO THE GREAT SCHOLARS who in recent decades have written well-researched individual biographies and other treatments of the Transcendentalists. I think especially of those whom I have had the privilege to meet or correspond with: Robert D. Richardson, Megan Marshall, Philip Gura, Phyllis Cole, David M. Robinson, Helen Deese, Dean Grodzins, Dan McKanan, Cynthia Grant Tucker, Barry Andrews, and Bruce Ronda. Without their work, and that of others such as Brenda Wineapple, David Reynolds, Carolyn Karcher, David Blight, Andrew Delbanco, David Cameron, and those whom I still hope yet to meet, this book would not have been possible. I have simply tried to connect the dots that they have made more vivid.

My debts also extend to those no longer living. The relevance of faith to all attempts to ground social activism in sustaining spirituality came to me during my senior year at Harvard College, when I graduated in History and Literature in 1968. I was a research assistant to Dr. George Hunston Williams, then Hollis Professor of Divinity, helping on a new edition of his magnum opus, *The Radical Reformation*. Meanwhile, he was preaching at the famous draft-card-burning service at the Arlington Street Church— although William Sloane Coffin, Dr. Benjamin Spock, and Michael Ferber got most of the press. That year a classmate in History and Lit was writing her thesis, "Transcendentalism Goes West," about the early ministry of James Freeman Clarke.

As I entered Divinity School, William R. Hutchison, author of *The Transcendentalist Ministers*, became my adviser. There the late Conrad Wright taught me to appreciate not only the radicals but also the institutionalists such as Bellows and Clarke. Later I served with the late Forrest Church as co-minister of the Unitarian Church of All Souls in Manhattan. The Currier print *The Conflagration of the Steamer Lexington* still hangs in the parlor there.

When I became president of the Unitarian Universalist Association (1993–2001), I had the William Morris Hunt portrait of Clarke over the mantle in my office. It was across from a photo of the Reverend Lewis Allen McGee (1893–1979), the only African American Unitarian minister actively serving in 1954, as *Brown v. Board of Education* came down. Both led me to extend my own spiritual friendships across all lines of division. I also had Thomas Starr King's desk in that same room.

I also owe a great debt to the Reverend Rob Hardies, senior minister of All Souls Church (Unitarian) in Washington, DC. Rob first pointed me to the Transcendentalist practice of spiritual friendship, as exemplified in the relationship between James Freeman Clarke and Margaret Fuller, and then shared with me the correspondence between them that he had assembled to try to write a book on that very theme—while also growing an urban, diverse, justice-oriented congregation. As I well know, combining such goals is anything but easy. So if I stole any of his thunder in this book, please forgive me, Rob! There is certainly much more commentary still needed on the theme of spiritual friendship and how it both sustains efforts for social justice and is formed and reformed in such collaboration.

During the ten years that I was privileged to serve as minister of First Parish in Needham, Massachusetts (where the Reverend Henry Appleton Dall and his wife, Caroline, had once served), that congregation allowed me to write and publish three earlier books, ending with *Universalists and Unitarians in America: A People's History* (Boston: Skinner House, 2012). When I retired from serving them, the Unitarian Universalist Church of the Monterey Peninsula, in Carmel, followed by the First Unitarian Universalist Society of San Francisco, also put up with me trying to help them learn from our forebears how to transcend temporary setbacks. Their reactions to my preaching and teaching on these themes helped me to discern what is still relevant from what is only historical.

Meanwhile, I was reading avidly and going east to do more research at the Andover Harvard Theological Library, where Gloria Korsman and the entire library staff were immensely helpful; at the Boston Public Library, with its great collections on the abolitionists; and especially at the Massachusetts Historical Society. The fact that so many nineteenth-century books and even archival collections are now available online made the seven-year labor over this book so much easier.

At Beacon Press, I enjoyed the early support of its great director, Helene Atwan; executive editor Amy Caldwell; and, at the conceptual stage, Will Myers. Three colleagues in the field of liberal religious history kindly read and commented on some early drafts. They were Dr. Dean Grodzins, the leading scholar on the life and work of Theodore Parker; David M. Robinson, Oregon Professor Emeritus at Oregon State University and a scholar of Emerson and Thoreau; and Dr. Dan McKanan, Ralph Waldo Emerson Unitarian Universalist Association Senior Lecturer in Divinity at the Harvard Divinity School. All three helped to save me from multiple errors of fact and then to steer me toward better interpretations. I thank them deeply. The errors that remain are mine only, and not theirs.

For the images included in this book, I must thank not only the institutions and individuals that graciously provided permission for their reproduction here but also my diligent young assistant on this project, Nathan Gandrud, and his counterpart at Beacon Press, Molly Velazquez-Brown. For my late discovery of the role of Frederick Douglass in providing a new monument in Florence for Theodore Parker, I thank the erudite and very welcoming current keeper of the Protestant Cemetery in Florence, Sister Julia Bolton Holloway, PhD.

My most personal debts go to the two women who sustained me through all challenges of this project. Amy Caldwell was both a faithful and a meticulous editor. No author could ever hope for someone more capable than Amy both to shape and pause, and then to complete such a project. Yet closer to home, impatiently waiting for Amy to send me her new edits and suggestions, was my patient wife, Reverend Gwen Langdoc Buehrens. Without them, no book. I bless them both.

I dedicate this volume to my four grandchildren, Isabel Joan Murray, Hannah Rose Murray, Simon Nathaniel Fernandez-Buehrens, and Layla Fernandez-Buehrens. In the next generation, they represent those who will have to transcend differences in origin, gender, race, ethnicity, sexual orientation, ideas, politics, and more, in order to work together for all forms of justice. May the spirit that inspired the Transcendentalists be with them, and with us all!

NOTES

INTRODUCTION

1. David W. Blight, *Frederick Douglass: Prophet of Freedom* (New York: Simon & Schuster, 2018), 279.

2. Sidney E. Mead, *The Nation with the Soul of a Church* (New York: Harper & Row, 1975).

3. E. Brooks Holifield, *Theology in America: Christian Thought from the Age of the Puritans to the Civil War* (New Haven, CT: Yale University Press, 2003), 205.

4. James Luther Adams, "Theological Bases of Social Action," *Journal of Religious Thought* 8, no. 1 (autumn/winter, 1950–51): 6–21.

5. Margaret Fuller, *Woman in the Nineteenth Century and Kindred Papers Relating to the Sphere, Condition and Duties of Woman*, ed. Arthur B. Fuller (Boston: John Jewett & Co., 1855), 172, 116, 194. The last quotation is an extract from a journal not published in Fuller's lifetime.

6. Robert D. Richardson Jr., *Emerson: The Mind on Fire* (Berkeley: University of California Press, 1995), 383, citing multiple passages in Emerson's journal.

7. Julia Ward Howe, *The Hermaphrodite*, ed. Gary Williams (Lincoln: University of Nebraska Press, 2004), using an incomplete manuscript in the Houghton Library, Harvard University.

8. Sarah Helen Whitman, "Emerson's Essays, by a Disciple," *US Magazine and Democratic Review* 16 (June 1845): 600.

9. Jana L. Argersinger and Phyllis Cole, eds., *Toward a Female Genealogy of Transcendentalism* (Athens: University of Georgia Press, 2014).

PROLOGUE: EXPOSITION

1. *Liberator*, January 1, 1831, http://www.accessible-archives.com/collections/the-liberator.

2. Eliza Lee Cabot Follen, *The Life of Charles Follen* (Boston: Thomas H. Webb, 1844), 363.

3. "History of Follen Church," http://follen.org/about/history.

4. T. J. Stiles, *The First Tycoon: The Epic Life of Cornelius Vanderbilt* (New York: Knopf, 2009).

5. *Steamboat Lexington*, "Long Island Shipwrecks," http://www.longislandgenealogy.com/shipwrecks.html#lexington.

6. Cliff McCarthy, "Steamer Lexington Disaster," https://pvhn3.wordpress.com/1800s/steamer-lexington-disaster.

7. "The Wreck of the Hesperus," based on the story of a shipwreck off Cape Ann, Massachusetts, January 6, 1839, was published on January 10, 1840, in the *New World*.

8. *Ruins of the Merchant's Exchange N.Y. After the Destructive Conflagration of Decbr 16 & 17, 1835*, in the *New York Sun*.

9. "Casabianca," by English poet Felicia Dorothea Hemans (1793–1835), first published in 1826, tells of the death of the son of a French admiral aboard his father's ship in the Napoleonic Wars, at the 1798 Battle of the Nile. In America, it became associated with the *Lexington*.

CHAPTER 1: CONVICTION

1. Edmund Spevack, *Charles Follen's Search for Nationality and Freedom: Germany and America, 1796–1840* (Cambridge, MA: Harvard University Press, 1997), 46–85, unsympathetic to Follen's early idealism, calling it "utopian and intolerant."

2. Elizabeth Palmer Peabody, *Reminiscences of Rev. Wm. Ellery Channing, D.D.* (Boston: Roberts Bros., 1880), 214–17.

3. Follen, *Life of Charles Follen*, 112–13.

4. William Ellery Channing to Charles Follen, in William H. Channing, *Memoir of William Ellery Channing* (Boston: Crosby and Nichols, 1850), 3:315.

5. Eliza Lee Cabot Follen, *Sketches of Married Life* (Boston: Hilliard and Gray, 1838).

6. Eliza Lee Cabot Follen, *Poems* (Boston: Crosby, 1839); also at https://www.poetrynook.com/poem/remember-slave.

7. Some blacks thought Walker was poisoned. It is more likely that he died of TB, which also took the life of his daughter. A son, E. G. Walker, born after Walker's death, became a Massachusetts legislator.

8. Kathryn Gin Lum, *Damned Nation: Hell in America from the Revolution to Reconstruction* (New York: Oxford University Press, 2014).

9. W. E. C. to D. Webster, May 14, 1828, cited in Madeleine Hooke Rice, *Federal Street Pastor: The Life of William Ellery Channing* (New York: Bookman Associates, 1961), 158.

10. Follen, *Life of Charles Follen*, 225.

11. W. E. Channing to Charles Follen, July 7, 1834, in W. H. Channing, *Memoir*, 3:159.

12. Speech, January 14, 1811. In Joseph Gales, *The Debates and Proceedings in the Congress of the United States: With an Appendix, Containing Important State Papers and Public Documents, and All the Laws of a Public Nature; with a Copious Index*, Eleventh Congress, Session 3 (Washington, DC: Gales and Seaton, 1853), 526.

13. Follen, *Life of Charles Follen*, 226–29.

14. Patrick Browne, "The Garrison Mob of 1835, Boston," *Historical Digression*, March 1, 2016, https://historicaldigression.com/2016/03/01/the-garrison-mob-of-1835-boston.

15. Wendell Phillips et al., *The Boston Mob of "Gentlemen of Property and Standing": Proceedings of the Anti-Slavery Meeting Held in Stacy Hall, Boston, on the Twentieth Anniversary of the Mob of October 21, 1835* (Boston: R. F. Walcutt, 1855), 14.

16. Harriet Martineau, *Society in America* (1837; Cambridge, UK: Cambridge University Press, 2009).

17. Henry Mayer, *All on Fire: William Lloyd Garrison and the Abolition of Slavery* (New York: St. Martin's, 1998), 201.

18. Harvard's Boylston Professor of Rhetoric and Oratory, 1819–1850, was Edward Tyrell Channing, brother of the eloquent minister. He taught not only Phillips but also Emerson, Thoreau, Clarke, T. W. Higginson, and many others.

19. Follen, *Life of Charles Follen*, 256–67.

20. Harriet Martineau, *Autobiography*, 2 vols., ed. Gaby Weiner (1877; London: Virago, 1983), 2:31.

21. Follen, *Life of Charles Follen*, 255.

22. Harriet Martineau, *Retrospect of Western Travel* (London: Saunders and Otley, 1838).

23. Although quite ill, and having Peabody as his ears at the meetings, Channing attended once. When he returned from New York, Follen also attended at least one meeting.

24. William Ellery Channing, "Unitarian Christianity: Discourse at the Ordination of the Rev. Jared Sparks," *Works* (Boston: James Munroe and Co., 1841), III, 59–104.

25. Follen, *Life of Charles Follen*, 290.

26. Follen, *Life of Charles Follen*, 276.

CHAPTER II: INCLUSION

1. Peabody, *Reminiscences*, 364.

2. William E. Channing, "The Moral Argument Against Calvinism," *Works*, 1:217–42, and "Unitarian Christianity Most Favorable to Piety," *Works*, 3:163–206.

3. W. E. Channing, *Slavery* (Boston: James Munroe & Co., 1835), 135; *Works*, 2:5.

4. Christopher Cameron, *To Plead Our Own Cause: African Americans in Massachusetts and the Making of the Anti-Slavery Movement* (Kent, OH: Kent State University Press, 2014); and Robert Greene II, "William Ellery Channing and Abolitionist Historiography," *Society for U.S. Intellectual History*, February 23, 2014, https://s-usih.org/2014/02/william-ellery -channing-and-abolitionist-historiography.

5. Dan McKanan, *Identifying the Image of God: Radical Christians and Nonviolent Power in the Antebellum United States*, Religion in America (Oxford, UK: Oxford University Press, 2012).

6. William Henry Channing, *The Life of William Ellery Channing, D.D.*, Centennial Memorial Edition (Boston: American Unitarian Association, 1880), 675.

7. Eliza Buckminster Lee, *Memoirs of Rev. Joseph Buckminster, D. D., and of His Son, Rev. Joseph Stevens Buckminster* (Boston: W. Crosby & H. P. Nichols, 1849), 440.

8. Jack Mendelsohn, *Channing, the Reluctant Radical* (Boston: Little Brown, 1971), 22–23.

9. Mendelsohn, *Channing*, 40, 44.

10. This is the familiar wording from the Westminster Shorter Catechism of 1646 but based on Calvin's own catechism of 1560.

11. The classic study of this process is Conrad Wright, *The Beginnings of Unitarianism in America* (Boston: Beacon, 1966).

12. Part IV of Priestley's critique of Calvinism in his *Institutes of Natural and Revealed Religion*, 1772–74; see J. D. Bowers, *Joseph Priestley and English Unitarianism in America* (University Park: Penn State University Press, 2009).

13. Gary Dorrien, *The Making of American Liberal Theology: Imagining Progressive Religion, 1805–1900* (Louisville, KY: Westminster John Knox, 2001), begins with Channing.

14. Peabody, *Reminiscences*, 45–46.

15. Perry Miller called this Channing at his "most Transcendental." The occasion was the ordination of another Channing disciple, Frederick A. Farley, at Providence, Rhode Island. Chenning's sermon was so praised that it was noted in England's eminent *Westminster Review*; see Channing, *Works*, 3:227–56.

16. Elizabeth Peabody to Orestes Brownson, 1840, in *Letters of Elizabeth Palmer Peabody: American Renaissance Woman*, ed. Bruce A. Ronda (Middletown, CT: Wesleyan, 1984), 248.

17. Mendelsohn, *Channing*, 242.

18. *Liberator*, December 19, 1835; December 26, 1835; January 2, 1836; Mendelsohn, *Channing*, 253.

19. James T. Austin, *Remarks on Dr. Channing's "Slavery" by a Citizen of Massachusetts* (Boston: Russell, Shattuck and Co., 1835), 14; John White Chadwick, *William Ellery Channing* (Boston: Houghton, Mifflin, 1903), 277.

20. Charles F. Adams, ed., *Memoirs of John Quincy Adams*, 12 vols. (Philadelphia: J. B. Lippincott, 1874–77), 9:266; Mendelsohn, *Channing*, 254; Rice, *Federal Street Pastor*, 223.

21. W. H. Channing, *Memoir*, 571.

22. W. E. Channing, *Works*, 5:231–60.

23. W. E. Channing, *Works*, 5:240.

24. W. E. Channing, *Works*, 5:249–250.

25. Samuel J. May, *A Discourse on the Life and Character of the Rev. Charles Follen, L.L.D.* (Boston: Henry Devereux, 1840). Marlboro Chapel, built in 1837 for the First Free Congregational Church, was behind the Marlboro Hotel at 229 Washington St.

26. W. E. Channing, *Letter of the Rev. William E. Channing to the Standing Committee of the Proprietors of the Meetinghouse in Federal Street* (Boston: Joseph Dowe, 1840).

27. I capitalize "Transcendentalist" as an inclination, or identity, as they often did, and as one might so designate a group of "like-minded" individuals in politics or theology variously as Arians, Whigs, or Conservatives. I decline to capitalize "circle" or to suggest that those who participate in the meetings of the group from 1836 to 1840 truly constituted a "Club," because membership was variable, nor were there any officers, dues, or minutes.

28. Peabody, *Reminiscences*, 364, quoting Channing, "Likeness to God," *Works*, 4:230–39.

29. Peabody, *Reminiscences*, 371.

30. Channing, "The Church," given before the First Congregational Unitarian of Philadelphia, May 30, 1841, in *Works*, 6:183–226, esp. 211.

CHAPTER III: MUTUAL INSPIRATION

1. Bryan F. Le Beau, *Frederic Henry Hedge: Nineteenth Century American Transcendentalist* (Allison Park, PA: Pickwick, 1985).

2. From a letter from Carlyle to Emerson, quoted by Harold N. Brown, "Hedge, Frederic Henry (1805–1890)," *Harvard Square Library*, http://www.harvardsquarelibrary.org /biographies/frederic-henry-hedge-1805–1890.

3. F. H. Hedge, "Coleridge," *Christian Examiner*, March 1833, https://archive.vcu.edu /english/engweb/transcendentalism/roots/hedgecoleridge.html.

4. Ralph Waldo Emerson to his brother Edward, December 22, 1833, in *The Letters of Ralph Waldo Emerson*, ed. Ralph L. Rusk, 6 vols. (New York: Columbia University Press, 1939–66), 1:401–3.

5. See ch. 27, "A Living Leaping Logos," in Richardson, *Emerson: The Mind on Fire*, 164–69.

6. Charles Crowe, *George Ripley: Transcendentalist and Utopian Socialist* (Athens: University of Georgia Press, 1967).

7. Ezra Ripley (1751–1841), pastor of the First Parish in Concord, married his predecessor's widow and so became R. W. Emerson's step-grandfather; their son Samuel Ripley (1783–1847) was pastor of the First Parish in Waltham and husband to Sarah Alden Bradford Ripley (1793–1867).

8. Unsigned review, "Inaugural Discourse, Delivered Before the University in Cambridge, Massachusetts, Sept. 3, 1831, by Charles Follen, Professor of the German Language and Literature," *Christian Examiner* 11:3 (1831): 373–80.

9. Jeter A. Isely and Elizabeth R. Isely, "A Note on George Ripley and the Beginnings of New England Transcendentalism," *Proceedings of the Unitarian Historical Society* 13:2 (1961): 78.

10. Charles Emerson to Mary Moody Emerson, cited in Ronald A. Bosco and Joel Myerson, *The Emerson Brothers: A Fraternal Biography in Letters* (Oxford, UK: Oxford University Press, 2006), 266.

11. Emerson told this story on himself. Compare the ms. left by his son, Dr. Edward Emerson, called "What I Can Remember About Father," pp. 47–48, cited in Richardson, *Emerson*, 91n5.

12. Philip F. Gura, *American Transcendentalism: A History* (New York: Hill and Wang, 2007).

13. G. Ripley, "Schleiermacher as a Theologian," *Christian Examiner* 20 (March 1836): 1–46.

14. Hedge to Emerson, June 1836; Joel Myerson, "Frederick Henry Hedge and the Failure of Transcendentalism," *Harvard Library Bulletin* 23:4 (October 1975): 396–410.

15. The original first stanza of "Fair Harvard," by Samuel Gilman, reads:

> *Fair Harvard! thy sons to thy Jubilee throng, / And with blessings surrender thee o'er*
> *By these festival rites, from the age that is past, / To the age that is waiting before.*
> *O relic and type of our ancestors' worth / That hast long kept their memory warm,*
> *First flow'r of their wilderness! Star of their night! / Calm rising thro' change*
> *and thro' storm.*

16. Joel Myerson, "A Calendar of Transcendental Club Meetings," *American Literature* 44:2 (May 1972): 198.

17. Ralph Waldo Emerson, *Nature* (Boston: James Munroe & Co., 1836). Rather than an entire second part on "Spirit," he wrote a penultimate chapter with that title and a final chapter, "Prospects," in which he used Orphic sayings of his friend Alcott, beginning with "The foundations of man are not in matter, but in spirit. But the element of spirit is eternity."

18. Emerson to Hedge, July 20, 1836, *The Letters of Ralph Waldo Emerson*, 2:29.

19. *Sartor Resartus* ("The tailor re-tailored") is an 1836 work by Carlyle that purports to be a commentary on the life and thought of a German philosopher, Diogenes Teufelsdröckh ("god-born devil-dung"), author of "Clothes: Their Origin and Influence." It is both an exposition of German idealism and a parody of its extreme in Hegel.

20. Myerson, "A Calendar of Transcendental Club Meetings," 199.

21. Alcott may not have been a minister, nor college-educated, but his wife, Abigail May Alcott (1800–1877), was the sister of the Unitarian minister Samuel Joseph May (1797–1871), then an agent for the Anti-Slavery Society. Elizabeth Peabody had lived with them while assisting Alcott at the Temple School without pay. See Madelon Bedell, *The Alcotts: Biography of a Family* (New York: Clarkson Potter, 1980), 120.

22. M. Matter, "De l'Influence des Moeurs sur les Lois, et de l'Influence des Lois sur les Moeurs," *Christian Examiner and General Review* 20:3 (June 1836): 160.

23. Meyerson, "A Calendar of Transcendental Club Meetings," 201, using Alcott's journal, assumes Brownson lived in Boston. In fact, the Brownsons lived in nearby Chelsea, commuting by ferry. See Arthur Schlesinger Jr., *Orestes A. Brownson: A Pilgrim's Progress* (Boston: Little, Brown, 1939), 41–42.

24. Crowe, *George Ripley*, 79.

25. Orestes A. Brownson, *New Views of Christianity, Society and the Church* (Boston: James Monroe, 1836).

26. The Norton-Ripley exchange on miracles appeared in the Unitarian *Christian Register* (November 1836), 21: 182. Ripley had been the acting editor.

27. David M. Robinson, "'Partakers of the Divine Nature': Ripley's Discourses and the Transcendental *Annus Mirabilis*," *Religions* 9:1 (2018): 12; https://doi.org/10.3390/rel9010012.

28. John Matteson, *Eden's Outcasts: The Story of Louisa May Alcott and Her Father* (New York: Norton, 2007), 83–85.

29. Alasdair Roberts, *America's First Great Depression: Economic Crisis and Political Disorder After the Panic of 1837* (Ithaca, NY: Cornell University Press, 2012).

30. Clarke had also hosted in late summer. Myerson places that meeting, and this one, presumably, "at J.F. Clarke's house, Boston," but this seems an error. Clarke's mother and sister then lived in Newton. See Arthur S. Bolster Jr., *James Freeman Clarke: Disciple to Advancing Truth* (Boston: Beacon, 1954), 108.

31. Carolyn L. Karcher, *The First Woman in the Republic: A Cultural Biography of Lydia Maria Child* (Durham, NC: Duke University Press, 1994); Deborah Pickman Clifford, *Crusader for Freedom: A Life of Lydia Maria Child* (Boston: Beacon, 1992).

PART TWO: WATER

1. Richard Brown, "Disease in the Victorian City: Extended Version," *Looking at History* (blog), November 18, 2010, http://richardjohnbr.blogspot.com/2010/11/disease-in-victorian-city-extended.html.

CHAPTER IV: DISSOLUTION OF THE PASTORAL RELATION

1. For the role of church councils in the Standing Order churches of Massachusetts, see Conrad Wright, "Institutional Reconstruction in the Unitarian Controversy," in *American Unitarianism: 1805–1865*, ed. Conrad Edick Wright (Boston: Massachusetts Historical Society and Northeastern University Press, 1983), 3–29.

2. Channing, "Charge at the Ordination of the Rev. John Sullivan Dwight, May 20, 1840," in *Works*, 5:295–317, as cited in Rice, *Federal Street Pastor*, 263.

3. Crowe, *George Ripley*, 120–21.

4. Channing, "Self-Culture," *Works*, 2:354.

5. Channing, "Remarks on Associations," *Works*, 1:239–332.

6. Albert Brisbane, *A Concise Exposition of the Doctrine of Association: Or, Plan for a Reorganization of Society* (New York: J. S. Redfield, 1844), 2.

7. George Ripley, *A Letter Addressed to the Congregational Church in Purchase Street, by Its Pastor* (Boston: Freeman and Bolles, 1840).

8. Myerson, "A Calendar," 197–207.

9. E. P. Peabody to John S. Dwight, September 20, 1840, in *Letters of Elizabeth Palmer Peabody*, 245–47.

10. Carol Johnson, "The Journals of Theodore Parker: July–December 1840," PhD diss., University of South Carolina, 1980, cited in Sterling Delano, *Brook Farm: The Dark Side of Utopia* (Cambridge, MA: Belknap Press of Harvard, 2004), 25n16.

11. Emerson to E. P. Peabody, September 8, 1840, in *The Letters of Ralph Waldo Emerson*, 2:329–330.

12. E. P. Peabody to John S. Dwight, September 20, 1840, in *Letters of Elizabeth Palmer Peabody*, 245–47.

13. W. E. Channing to Elizabeth Peabody, September 1840, in Peabody, *Reminiscences*, 414.

14. W. E. Channing, "Emancipation," in *Works*, 6:5–89.

15. Channing, "Emancipation," 6:86.

16. Dorothy C. Wilson, *Stranger and Traveler: The Story of Dorothea Dix, American Reformer* (Boston: Little, Brown, 1975).

17. Dorothea L. Dix, *Memorial to the Legislature of Massachusetts, 1843*, http://www .archive.org/stream/memorialtolegisloodixd#page/n4/mode/1up.

18. David Gollaher, *Voice for the Mad: The Life of Dorothea Dix* (New York: Free Press, 1995).

19. W. E. Channing, "The Present Age," in *Works*, 6:163–82.

20. W. E. Channing, "The Church," in *Works*, 6:183–230. The text came from the last verses of the Sermon on the Mount: "Not everyone that saith unto me, Lord, Lord, shall enter into the kingdom of heaven." (Matt. 7:21)

21. He told his son, William Francis Channing, that he was "more and more disposed" to regard Jesus as "simply human," although divinely anointed. W. F. Channing to T. W. Higginson, January 24, 1879; Higginson, "Two New England Heretics," *Independent* (May 1902): 1235.

22. Channing, *Works*, 6:375–420.

23. Channing, *Works*, 6:420.

24. Chadwick, *William Ellery Channing*, 420–21.

CHAPTER V: AFFECTION AND VOCATION

1. Bolster, *James Freeman Clarke*.

2. James Freeman Clarke, "Journal of Understanding," ms., Andover Harvard Theological Library, James Freeman Clarke papers.

3. Charles Capper, *Margaret Fuller: An American Romantic Life: The Private Years* (Oxford, UK: Oxford University Press, 1992), 30.

4. The oldest Fuller son, Eugene, was five years Margaret's junior, followed by William Henry, Arthur, Richard, and Lloyd. There was a sixth son, Edward, who died as an infant in 1829.

5. Megan Marshall, *Margaret Fuller: A New American Life* (Boston: Houghton Mifflin, 2013), 53.

6. Marshall, *Margaret Fuller*, 58.

7. James joined his aunt Maria Hull Campbell in writing a defense of his grandfather, *Revolutionary Services and Civil Life of General William Hull* (New York: D. Appleton, 1848).

8. J. F. Clarke, *What God Gives, He Gives Forever* (Boston: Geo. Ellis, 1892), 17.

9. J. F. Clarke, *Self-Culture: Physical, Intellectual, Moral and Spiritual; A Course of Lectures* (Boston: J. R. Osgood, 1880), 11. Compare Shakespeare, *As You Like It*, act II, sc. 1.

10. Edwin Palmer Hoyt, *The Improper Bostonian: Dr. Oliver Wendell Holmes* (New York: Morrow, 1979).

11. O. B. Frothingham, *Memoir of William Henry Channing* (Boston: Houghton Mifflin, 1886), https://archive.org/details/memoirwilliamheoofrotgoog.

12. *Memoirs of Margaret Fuller Ossoli*, 2 vols., ed. R. W. Emerson, J. F. Clarke, and W. H. Channing (Boston: Phillips, Sampson, 1852), 1:139–42; Marshall, *Margaret Fuller*, 65.

13. *Letters of Margaret Fuller*, 6 vols., ed. Robert N. Huspeth (Ithaca, NY: Cornell University Press, 1983–94), I:347.

14. Marshall, *Margaret Fuller*, 77.

15. James Freeman Clarke to Margaret Fuller, August 12, 1833, in *Letters of James Freeman Clarke to Margaret Fuller*, ed. John W. Thomas (Hamburg: Cram, de Gruyter & Co., 1957), 56–57.

16. M. Fuller to J. F. Clarke, August 30, 1833, *Letters of Margaret Fuller*, I:215.

17. May 4, 1834, in *Letters of James Freeman Clarke to Margaret Fuller*, 77.

18. Robert D. Habich, *Transcendentalism and the Western Messenger: A History of the Magazine and Its Contributors, 1835–1841* (London: Associated University Presses, 1985).

19. Bolster, *James Freeman Clarke*, 108–11.

20. Channing, *Works*, 2:181–254.

21. Channing, "Remarks on the Slavery Question, in a Letter to Jonathan Phillips, Esq., 1839," in *Works*, 5:5–105.

22. Cynthia Grant Tucker, *No Silent Witness: The Eliot Parsonage Women and Their Unitarian World* (Oxford, UK: Oxford University Press, 2010).

23. Nina Moore Tiffany and Francis Tiffany, *Harm Jan Huidekoper* (Cambridge, MA: Riverside, 1904). Another agent of the Holland Land Company who became wealthy was James Brisbane of Batavia, New York, father of Albert Brisbane, the American apostle of Fourier's socialist utopianism.

24. Fuller to Clarke, summer 1839, *Letters of Margaret Fuller*, II:314–15.

25. Rebecca and Sarah Clarke came to the wedding and accompanied the couple to Niagara Falls.

26. Bolster, *James Freeman Clarke*, 143.

27. Ripley, *A Letter Addressed to the Congregational Church in Purchase Street*, 10.

28. Matt. 5:17.

29. The phrase "elective affinities" came from Goethe. It had overtones of affectional attractions that could transcend conventional marriage.

30. The word "liturgy" comes from the Greek: *leitos* = people; and *ourgos* = work.

31. Ralph Waldo Emerson, Journal, November 1841, *Emerson in His Journals*, ed. Joel Porte (Cambridge, MA: Harvard University Press, 1982), 294–95.

32. Caroline Dall, *Margaret and Her Friends, or Ten Conversations with Margaret Fuller upon the Mythology of the Greeks and Its Expression in Art* (Boston: Roberts Brothers, 1895), 46.

33. Caroline Dall, March 23, 1841, *Selected Journals of Carolyn Healey Dall*, ed. Helen R. Deese, 2 vols. (Boston: Massachusetts Historical Society, 2006–13), 1:67–69.

34. Dall, *Journals*, April 4 and May 9, 1841; Tuesday, March 23, 1841, 1:71, 78–79.

CHAPTER VI: DIVISION BECAUSE OF INCLUSION

1. Delano, *Brook Farm*, 19.

2. Dean Grodzins, *American Heretic: Theodore Parker and Transcendentalism* (Chapel Hill: University of North Carolina Press, 2002).

3. Delano, *Brook Farm*, 21.

4. 2 Corinthians 6:17 KJV.

5. R. W. Emerson, "Lecture on the Times: Read at the Masonic Temple, Boston, Dec. 2, 1841," in *Nature, Addresses, and Lectures* (Boston: Houghton Mifflin, 1898), 245–76.

6. "O ye hypocrites, ye can discern the face of the sky; but can ye not discern the signs of the times?" Matthew 16:3 KJV. Carlyle's essay, "The Signs of the Times," *Edinburgh Review* 49 (1829): 441, deeply influenced Emerson.

7. Roberts, *America's First Great Depression*.

8. Ronald G. Shafer, *The Carnival Campaign: How the Rollicking 1840 Campaign of "Tippecanoe and Tyler, Too!" Changed Presidential Campaigns Forever* (Chicago: Chicago Review, 2016).

9. Jesus said, in his Sermon on the Mount, "But I say unto you: That ye resist not evil, but whosoever shall smite thee on the right cheek, turn to him the other also" [Matt. 5:39 KJV]

10. Nell Irvin Painter, *Sojourner Truth: A Life, a Symbol* (New York: Norton, 1996).

11. Louisa May Alcott, "Transcendentalist Wild Oats: A Chapter from an Unwritten Romance," *Independent* 25:1307 (December 1873): 1569–71, and often reprinted.

12. Grodzins, *American Heretic*, 226.

13. Edward K. Spann, *Hopedale: From Commune to Company Town, 1840–1920* (Columbus: Ohio State University Press, 1992).

14. Adin Ballou, *Practical Christianity: An Epitome of Practical Christian Socialism* (New York: Fowlers and Wells, 1854), outlines his "Eight Principles of Theological Truth, and Eight Principles of Social Order." More influential was his *Christian Non-Resistance* (1846), read by Leo Tolstoy, Mohandas Gandhi, and Martin Luther King Jr.

15. R. W. Emerson, *An Address Delivered Before the Senior Class in Divinity College, Cambridge* (Boston: James Munroe and Co., 1838).

16. Grodzins, *American Heretic*, 42.

17. Grodzins, *American Heretic*, 181.

18. Grodzins, *American Heretic*, 184.

19. Grodzins, *American Heretic*, 91–95.

20. Grodzins, *American Heretic*, 317.

21. Frances Power Cobbe, ed., *The Collected Works of Theodore Parker*, 14 vols. (London: Trubner & Co., 1866–72), 8:1–30.

22. Grodzins, *American Heretic*, 246.

23. Stephan Papa, *The Last Man Jailed for Blasphemy* (Columbus, OH: Trillium, 1998).

24. Mark 13:31; Luke 21:33; Matthew 24:35.

25. Elizabeth Peabody to J. S. Dwight, June 10, 1841, in *Letters of Elizabeth Palmer Peabody*, 251–55.

26. T. Parker to Church of the Disciples, May 29, 1841, Massachusetts Historical Society; Grodzins, *American Heretic*, 296–7.

27. Peabody to Dwight, in *Letters of Elizabeth Palmer Peabody*, 251–55.

28. William Larned, S. E. Brackett, Charles L. Thayer, and Charles Ellis to Theodore Parker, June 21, 1841, Massachusetts Historical Society; Grodzins, *American Heretic*, 264. At least Brackett was a member of the Disciples.

29. Peabody to Clarke, in *Letters*, 257.

30. Peabody to Clarke, in *Letters*, 269.

31. "Mr. Parker and the Unitarians," *Boston Quarterly Review* 5, no. 2 (April 1842): 198–220.

32. Grodzins, *American Heretic*, 271.

33. Theodore Parker, *Critical and Miscellaneous Writings* (Boston: James Munroe, 1843), cited in Grodzins, *American Heretic*, 275.

34. Theodore Parker, "The Hollis Street Council," *Dial* 3:2 (October 1842): 221.

35. Emerson to Theodore Parker, cited by Grodzins, *American Heretic*, 348.

36. Grodzins, *American Heretic*, 362.

37. Grodzins, *American Heretic*, 371.

38. Grodzins, *American Heretic*, 374.

39. Bolster, *James Freeman Clarke*, 154.

40. Bolster, *James Freeman Clarke*, 155.

41. Delano, *Brook Farm*, 192.

42. Delano, *Brook Farm*, 192.

CHAPTER VII: UNEQUAL UNION, OR MARRIAGE
IN THE NINETEENTH CENTURY

1. Channing, *Works*, IV, 217.

2. Jonathan Messerli, *Horace Mann: A Biography* (New York: Knopf, 1971), 179, citing a letter of Elizabeth Peabody to Mary Peabody, April 4/5, 1834, ms. at the New York Public Library.

3. James R. Mellow, *Nathaniel Hawthorne in His Times* (Boston: Houghton Mifflin, 1980), 65.

4. Megan Marshall, *The Peabody Sisters: Three Women Who Ignited American Romanticism* (Boston: Houghton Mifflin, 2006), 352.

5. Mellow, *Nathaniel Hawthorne*, 28

6. Marshall, *The Peabody Sisters*, 362.

7. Edwin Haviland Miller, *Salem Is My Dwelling Place: A Life of Nathaniel Hawthorne* (Iowa City: University of Iowa Press, 1991), 228.

8. Grodzins, *American Heretic*, 177.

9. Grodzins, *American Heretic*, 180.

10. Grodzins, *American Heretic*, 321.

11. Grodzins, *American Heretic*, 327.

12. Theodore Parker, *Lessons from the World of Matter and the World of Man*, ed. Rufus Leighton (Boston: American Unitarian Association, 1865), 191–93.

13. Marshall, *Margaret Fuller*, 18.

14. Marshall, *The Peabody Sisters*, 340–41.

15. Matteson, *Eden's Outcasts*, 97.

16. Emerson, "Experience," *Essays: Second Series* (1844), many reprints.

17. Ralph Waldo Emerson, "Friendship," *Essays: First Series* (1842), 173–93 (Boston: Houghton Mifflin, 1898), 190.

18. Marshall, *Margaret Fuller*, 193.

19. *Emerson in His Journals*, 392–93.

20. Frederick T. McGill Jr., *Channing of Concord: A Life of William Ellery Channing II* (New Brunswick, NJ: Rutgers University Press, 1967).

21. Marshall, *Margaret Fuller*, 200.

22. Matteson, *Eden's Outcasts*, 270.

23. Martha L. Berg and Alice De V. Perry, "Stories Unfolded: William Hull Clarke and His Tracing of Margaret Fuller's 1844 Summer Journal," *Massachusetts Historical Review* 16 (2014): 122–48.

24. Herman Melville, *Mardi: and a Voyage Thither* (New York: Harper & Brothers, 1849).

25. McGill, *Channing of Concord*, 56.

26. Frothingham, *Memoir of William Henry Channing*, 166.

27. Marshall, *Margaret Fuller*, 213.

28. Marshall, *Margaret Fuller*, 214–15.

29. Marshall, *Margaret Fuller*, 215.

30. Berg and Perry, "Stories Unfolded," 129–30.

31. Marshall, *Margaret Fuller*, 215.

32. Margaret Fuller, "The Great Lawsuit," *Dial* IV (July 1843), https://archive.vcu.edu/english/engweb/transcendentalism/authors/fuller/debate.html.

33. Margaret Fuller to Clarke, August 14, 1845; *Letters of Margaret Fuller*, II:359.

34. Another founding member of the Church of the New Jerusalem was Parker's neighbor in West Roxbury, Francis George Shaw. See also Emerson's essay, "Swedenborg; or, The Mystic."

35. Letter 13 in Lydia Maria Child, *Letters from New York, Second Series* (New York: C. S. Francis, 1845), 125–30; see Argersinger and Cole, eds., *Toward a Female Genealogy of Transcendentalism*, 1–3.

36. R. W. Emerson, "The Transcendentalist: A Lecture Read in the Masonic Temple, January, 1842," in *Nature, Addresses, and Lectures* (Boston: Houghton Mifflin, 1898), 309–39.

CHAPTER VIII: TRIBULATION AND SEPARATION

1. Bolster, *James Freeman Clarke*, 162.

2. Grodzins, *American Heretic*, 457.

3. Bolster, *James Freeman Clarke*, 173–74.

4. *Liberator*, May 1, 1846. Albert J. Von Frank, in *The Trials of Anthony Burns: Freedom and Slavery in Emerson's Boston* (Cambridge, MA: Harvard University Press, 1998), 43, places the wedding in 1844 and calls Catherine Mason "a white Catholic girl," without citing a source. Garrison, present at the wedding, referred to the couple as "identified in complexion with a race long . . . kept in the galling chains of slavery."

5. Finding him depressive, given to drink, and difficult to live with, she considered leaving him. Afraid that he would kill himself, she remained. Their eldest son died of a self-inflicted gunshot wound at eighteen.

6. *Daughter of Boston: The Extraordinary Diary of a Nineteenth-Century Woman, Caroline Healey Dall*, ed. Helen R. Deese (Boston: Beacon Press, 2005), 223.

7. *Selected Journals of Caroline Healey Dall*, ed. Helen R. Deese (Boston: Massachusetts Historical Society, 2006), I:183.

8. Caroline Healey Dall, *Essays and Sketches* (Boston: S. G. Simpkins, 1849).

9. Amy Greenberg, *A Wicked War: Polk, Clay, Lincoln, and the 1846 U.S. Invasion of Mexico* (New York: Vintage Random House, 2012), 76.

10. Dean Grodzins, "'Of All, by All, for All': Theodore Parker, Transcendentalism and the Gettysburg Address," in *The Gettysburg Address: Perspectives on Lincoln's Greatest Speech*, ed. Sean Conant (Oxford, UK: Oxford University Press, 2015, 88–102.

11. In April 1847, the Massachusetts legislature called for an end to the Mexican War, "without further attempt to dismember the territory of . . . a sister republic." Lincoln himself was present in Lexington, Kentucky, when Clay made his famous speech against a war in which

his own son had died, saying, "I would rather be right than President." Greenberg, *A Wicked War*, 229–34.

12. Bolster, *James Freeman Clarke*, 165–67.

13. Bolster, *James Freeman Clarke*, 179.

14. Marshall, *Margaret Fuller*, 334.

15. James Freeman Clarke, *Autobiography, Diary, and Correspondence*, ed. Edward Everett Hale (Boston: Houghton Mifflin, 1891), 173.

16. Bolster, *James Freeman Clarke*, 184.

17. Marshall, *Margaret Fuller*, 373.

18. Marshall, *Margaret Fuller*, 356.

19. Marshall, *Margaret Fuller*, 374

20. *Memoirs of Margaret Fuller Ossoli*, 2:349.

21. *Emerson in His Journals*, 413–14.

22. Marshall, *Margaret Fuller*, 386.

23. *Selected Journals of Carolyn Healey Dall*, 1:308.

24. Lisa Tetrault, *The Myth of Seneca Falls: Memory and the Women's Suffrage Movement, 1848–1898* (Chapel Hill: University of North Carolina Press, 2014).

25. Tetrault, *The Myth of Seneca Falls*, 1:331.

26. *Emerson in His Journals*, 410–11.

27. *Selected Journals of Carolyn Healey Dall*, 1:398.

CHAPTER IX: COLLABORATION

1. Joel Strangis, *Lewis Hayden and the War Against Slavery* (North Haven, CT: Linnet Books, 1999).

2. Cameron, *To Plead Our Own Cause*.

3. Hayden was among the first to urge Andrew to run for governor of Massachusetts. On Thanksgiving Day 1862, Andrew came to the Hayden house for a turkey dinner. He gave Hayden a job in the secretary of state's office. After the war, and the death of John Andrew, Hayden served a term in the Massachusetts legislature.

4. Garrison to Sydney Howard Gray, March 31, 1846; *The Letters of William Lloyd Garrison*, ed. Walter M. Merrill, 6 vols. (Cambridge, MA: Belknap Press of Harvard, 1971–81), 3:334–35.

5. *Liberator*, August 7, 1846, cited in Strangis, *Lewis Hayden*, 45.

6. Strangis, *Lewis Hayden*, 47.

7. Strangis, *Lewis Hayden*, 56.

8. Porte, *Emerson in His Journals*, July–October 1851, 428–29.

9. Strangis, *Lewis Hayden*, 61.

10. Strangis, *Lewis Hayden*, 63.

11. Dean Grodzins, "'Constitution or No Constitution, Law or No Law': The Boston Vigilance Committees, 1841–1861," in *Massachusetts and the Civil War: The Commonwealth and National Disunion*, ed. Matthew Mason, Katheryn P. Viens, and Conrad Edick Wright (Amherst: University of Massachusetts Press, 2015), 47–73.

12. Henry Steele Commager, *Theodore Parker* (Boston: Beacon, 1947), 216.

13. Parker to President Fillmore, November 21, 1850, Theodore Parker Papers, Andover-Harvard Library, bMS 101/18; John Weiss, *The Life and Correspondence of Theodore Parker*, 2 vols. (Boston: Appleton, 1863–64), 2:100–102.

14. Fillmore to Webster, October 23, 1850, *Millard Fillmore Papers*, ed. Frank Severance, Publications of the Buffalo Historical Society 10 (Buffalo, NY: Buffalo Historical Society), 1:334–335, https://archive.org/details/millardfillmore01fillgoog.

15. Porte, *Emerson in His Journals*, April 1850, 412.

16. Stephen Kendrick and Paul Kendrick, *Sarah's Long Walk: The Free Blacks of Boston and How Their Struggle for Equality Changed America* (Boston: Beacon, 2005).

17. *Reports of Cases Argued before the Supreme Judicial Court of Massachusetts*, ed. Luther S. Cushing (Boston: Little, Brown, and Co., 1852), 209.

18. Gary Collison, *Shadrach Minkins: From Fugitive Slave to Citizen* (Cambridge, MA: Harvard University Press, 1997).

19. John Andrew to J. F. Clarke, March 5, 1851, reprinted in J. F. Clarke, *Anti-Slavery Days: A Sketch of the Struggle Which Ended in the Abolition of Slavery in the United States* (New York: John W. Lovell, 1883), 171–72, where the date is misprinted as 1857.

20. Collison, *Shadrach Minkins*, 195.

21. Albert Réville, *The Life and Writings of Theodore Parker* (London: British and Foreign Unitarian Association, 1877).

22. This prefigured the refusal of so-called "sanctuary" states and cities in the 2000s to cooperate with federal efforts to deport undocumented immigrants from Latin America.

23. T. W. Higginson, *Cheerful Yesterdays* (Boston: Houghton Mifflin, 1898), 140; Strangis, *Lewis Hayden*, 80.

24. Von Frank, *The Trials of Anthony Burns*, 27–28.

25. Von Frank, *The Trials of Anthony* Burns, 29.

26. Matteson, *Eden's Outcasts*, 181.

27. J. F. Clarke, *The Christian Doctrine of Forgiveness of Sin* (Boston: Crosby & Nichols, 1852), https://catalog.hathitrust.org/Record/011600483; and *Eleven Weeks in Europe* (Boston: Ticknor, Reed & Fields, 1852), https://catalog.hathitrust.org/Record/008643691.

28. Clarke, *Autobiography, Diary, and Correspondence*, 193–94.

29. I owe this interpretation to Julia Bolton Holloway, custodian of the Swiss Protestant Cemetery in Florence, where Browning lies buried near the grave of Theodore Parker.

30. Clarke, *Autobiography, Diary, and Correspondence*, 200.

CHAPTER X: RENDITION AND INSURRECTION

1. Von Frank, *The Trials of Anthony Burns*, 15.

2. Clarke, *Autobiography, Diary, and Correspondence*, 233.

3. Von Frank, *The Trials of Anthony Burns*, 52–61.

4. Von Frank, *The Trials of Anthony Burns*, 69.

5. Bolster, *James Freeman Clarke*, 235–37; Clarke, *Autobiography, Diary, and Correspondence*, 233.

6. Von Frank, *The Trials of Anthony Burns*, 207.

7. Von Frank, *The Trials of Anthony Burns*, 271.

8. Bobbie Groth, *The Incredible Story of Ephraim Nute* (Boston: Skinner House, 2011).

9. T. W. Higginson, "A Ride Through Kansas," in *The Magnificent Activist: The Writings of Thomas Wentworth Higginson*, ed. Howard N. Meyer (Boston: Da Capo, 2000), 88–89.

10. David S. Reynolds, *John Brown, Abolitionist: The Man Who Killed Slavery, Sparked the Civil War, and Seeded Human Rights* (New York: Vintage Books, 2005).

11. Charles Sumner, "The Crime Against Kansas: The Apologies for the Crime, the True Remedy," speech, May 18, 1856, http://eweb.furman.edu/ffibenson/docs/sumnerksh2.htm.

12. Clarke, *Anti-Slavery Days*, 153–54.

13. James W. Trent Jr., *The Manliest Man: Samuel G. Howe and the Contours of Nineteenth Century Reform* (Amherst: University of Massachusetts Press, 2012).

14. Reynolds, *John Brown, Abolitionist*, 162.

15. Clarke, *Anti-Slavery Days*, 154–55.

16. Clarke, *Anti-Slavery Days*, 155.

17. Edward J. Renehan Jr., *The Secret Six: The True Tale of the Men Who Conspired with John Brown* (New York: Crown, 1995), 144.

18. Reynolds, *John Brown, Abolitionist*, 162.

19. Clarke's text was Mark 6:20: "Herod feared John, because he was a just man." He said that if Brown were insane, he had the heroic insanity that transforms the world. *Autobiography*, 236.

20. Renehan, *The Secret Six*, 216.

21. Henry David Thoreau, "A Plea for Captain John Brown," October 30, 1859, http://avalon.law.yale.edu/19th_century/thoreau_001.asp.

22. Ralph Waldo Emerson, "Courage," November 8, 1859, https://www.bartleby.com/90/0710.html, see Note 1. Emerson omitted the reference to Brown in the published lecture.

23. John Brown to George L. and Mary Stearns, quoted in Charles E. Heller, *Portrait of an Abolitionist: A Biography of George Luther Stearns, 1809–1867* (Westport, CT: Greenwood Press, 1996), 109.

24. Renehan, *The Secret Six*, 233.

25. Heller, *Portrait of an Abolitionist*, 114.

CHAPTER XI: EMANCIPATION

1. J. F. Clarke to Parker, dated October 5, 1859, finished on the 18th; #591, Clarke Papers, Andover Harvard Theological Library.

2. Bellows's 1859 address at Harvard Divinity School, "The Suspense of Faith," challenged Protestant (and Transcendentalist) individualism, calling for the liberal church to be more "catholic" in its inclusiveness.

3. Governor Banks removed Loring not for his role in the Burns affair, but for holding two judicial offices at once: as probate judge and commissioner for the Fugitive Slave Law.

4. Speech at Tremont Temple, November 19, 1859; Henry G. Pearson, *The Life of John A. Andrew*, 2 vols. (Boston: Houghton, Mifflin, 1904), 1:100.

5. Pearson, *The Life of John A. Andrew*, 1:109.

6. Pearson, *The Life of John A. Andrew*, 1:112.

7. Pearson, *The Life of John A. Andrew*, 1:115.

8. Pearson, *The Life of John A. Andrew*, 1:116–17.

9. Pearson, *The Life of John A. Andrew*, 1:141–43.

10. *Brooklyn Daily Eagle*, April 13, 1861.

11. Pearson, *The Life of John A. Andrew*, 1:150.

12. Pearson, *The Life of John A. Andrew*, 1:152–53.

13. Pearson, *The Life of John A. Andrew*, 1:176.

14. T. W. Higginson, "My Outdoor Studies," *Atlantic Monthly* 8 (1861): 302–9; "Snow," *Atlantic Monthly* 9 (1862): 188–201; "Life of Birds," *Atlantic Monthly* 9 (1862):

10; "Procession of the Flowers," *Atlantic Monthly* 10 (1862): 649–57; Tilden G. Edelstein, *Strange Enthusiasm: A Life of Thomas Wentworth Higginson* (New Haven, CT: Yale University Press, 1968), 247n27.

15. T. W. Higginson, "Denmark Vesey," *Atlantic Monthly* 7 (1861): 742–43; "April Days," *Atlantic Monthly* 7 (1861): 385–94; "Nat Turner's Insurrection," *Atlantic Monthly* 8 (1861): 176, 179, 185, 187; Edelstein, *Strange Enthusiasm*, 243n15, 246n24.

16. Edelstein, *Strange Enthusiasm*, 247.

17. Higginson, "April Days."

18. Edelstein, *Strange Enthusiasm*, 249.

19. Higginson became engaged to Mary Channing at twenty. He warned her that "my ever being a minister is far from certain." Edelstein, *Strange Enthusiasm*, 52. They married only after he was ordained. Her disability must have required considerable "manly" self-restraint.

20. Doris Kearns Goodwin, *Team of Rivals: The Political Genius of Abraham Lincoln* (New York: Simon & Schuster, 2005).

21. Pearson, *The Life of John A. Andrew*, 1:250.

22. J. F. Clarke, *Memorial and Biographical Sketches* (Boston: Houghton, Osgood and Co., 1878), 48.

23. J. W. Howe, *Reminiscences, 1819–1899* (Boston: Houghton, Mifflin and Co., 1899), 274–75.

24. Howe, *Reminiscences, 1819–1899.*

25. Pearson, *The Life of John A. Andrew*, 2:12–13.

26. Pearson, *The Life of John A. Andrew*, 2:45–47.

27. Introduction by Howard N. Meyer, ed., *The Magnificent Activist: The Writings of Thomas Wentworth Higginson, 1823–1891* (Boston: Da Capo Press, 2000), 19.

28. Quoted by Meyer from Dudley T. Cornish, *The Sable Arm* (New York: Longmans, Green, 1956), 21. See also Thomas W. Higginson, *Army Life in a Black Regiment* (1869; New York: W. W. Norton, 1984).

29. John Andrew to Lewis Hayden, December 4, 1862, Andrews Papers, Massachusetts Historical Society; quoted in Pearson, *The Life of John A. Andrew*, 2:70.

30. *Blue-Eyed Child of Fortune: The Civil War Letters of Colonel Robert Gould Shaw*, ed. Russell Duncan (Athens: University of Georgia Press, 1999), 23–24. For Copeland as a Disciple, see Bolster, *James Freeman Clarke*, 260.

31. Heller, *Portrait of an Abolitionist*, 145.

32. *Blue-Eyed Child of Fortune*, 37.

33. R. W. Emerson, *The Complete Works*, Centenary Edition, 12 vols. (Boston: Houghton Mifflin, 1903–4) 11:259. Meant as second revolutionary hymn, parallel to his "Concord Hymn," written twenty-five years earlier to dedicate the monument at the Old North Bridge.

34. Clarke, *Autobiography, Diary, and Correspondence*, 284.

35. Reynolds, *John Brown: Abolitionist*, 4.

36. Heller, *Portrait of an Abolitionist*, 142.

37. Sarah Greenough and Nancy K. Anderson, with Lindsay Harris and Renee Ater, *Tell It with Pride: The 54th Massachusetts Regiment and Augustus Saint-Gaudens' Shaw Memorial* (Washington, DC: National Gallery of Art, 2014), 3.

38. Bolster, *James Freeman Clarke*, 275.

39. Saint-Gaudens began work on the Shaw monument in 1884 and completed it in 1898.

40. Luis F. Emilio, *A Brave Black Regiment: The History of the 54th Massachusetts, 1863–1865*, republished from the 2nd enlarged edition, Boston, 1894, new introduction by Gregory J. W. Urwin (Boston: Da Capo Press, 1995), vii–x.

41. *Blue-Eyed Child of Fortune*, 50–51.

42. Anonymous letter to the Shaw family, Harvard University, Houghton Library, MS Am 1910 (14); reproduced in Greenough and Anderson, *Tell It with Pride*, 63.

CHAPTER XII: ORGANIZATION

1. Carlos Baker, *Emerson Among the Eccentrics: A Group Portrait* (New York: Viking, 1996); Susan Cheever, *American Bloomsbury: Louisa May Alcott, Ralph Waldo Emerson, Margaret Fuller, Nathaniel Hawthorne, and Henry David Thoreau: Their Lives, Their Loves, Their Work* (New York: Simon & Schuster, 2006).

2. E. Digby Baltzell, *Puritan Boston and Quaker Philadelphia* (1979; New Brunswick, NJ: Transaction, 1996), with a new intro by the author.

3. Emerson was generous to many friends but famously asked, "Are they my poor?"

4. Baltzell, *Puritan Boston and Quaker Philadelphia*, xiii.

5. Earl K. Holt III, *William Greenleaf Eliot: Conservative Radical* (St. Louis: First Unitarian Church of St. Louis, 1984).

6. Tucker, *No Silent Witness*, 23–39.

7. Holt, *William Greenleaf Eliot*, 39.

8. Tucker, *No Silent Witness*, 15, 39.

9. For the Eliot family and Unitarian evangelism, see John Buehrens, *Universalists and Unitarians in America: A People's History* (Boston: Skinner House, 2011), ix, 109–12, 117–18, 150–52.

10. Francis A. Christie, *The Makers of the Meadville Theological School* (Boston: Beacon Press, 1927).

11. J. F. Clarke, *The Christian Doctrine of Prayer* (Boston: American Unitarian Association, 1854), https://babel.hathitrust.org.

12. *The Complete Sermons of Ralph Waldo Emerson*, vol. I, ed. Albert J. von Frank (Columbia: University of Missouri Press, 1989).

13. Clarke, *The Christian Doctrine of Prayer*.

14. Walter Donald Kring, *Henry Whitney Bellows* (Boston: Skinner House, 1979).

15. Kring, *Henry Whitney Bellows*, 70–72.

16. Kring, *Henry Whitney Bellows*, 217.

17. Henry Whitney Bellows, "The Suspense of Faith: A Discourse on the State of the Church," in *An American Reformation: A Documentary History of Unitarian Christianity*, ed. Sydney E. Ahlstrom and Jonathan S. Carey (Middletown, CT: Wesleyan University Press, 1985), 371–97.

18. Huntington was reordained as an Episcopalian in 1860 and later became bishop of Central New York.

19. These were collected as "A Journey in the Seaboard States" (1856), "A Journey Through Texas" (1857), and "A Journey in the Back Country" (1860), and then reissued in 1861 as a two-volume work, *The Cotton Kingdom: A Traveller's Observations on Cotton and Slavery in the American Slaves States* (New York: Mason Bros.). See Louis Masur, "Olmsted's Southern Landscapes," *New York Times*, July 9, 2011, https://opinionator.blogs.nytimes.com /2011/07/09/olmsteds-southern-landscapes.

20. Kring, *Henry Whitney Bellows*, 238–39.

21. William Day Simonds, *Starr King in California* (San Francisco: Paul Elder and Co., 1917), 9.

22. Displaced in 2009 by a statue of Ronald Reagan, the Starr King image is now on the grounds of the state capitol, in Sacramento.

23. Bolster, *James Freeman Clarke*, 278–79.

24. George M. Frederickson, *The Inner Civil War: Northern Intellectuals and the Crisis of the Union* (New York: Harper & Row, 1965), 98; quoted in Kring, *Henry Whitney Bellows*, 269.

25. Kring, *Henry Whitney Bellows*, 301.

26. Kring, *Henry Whitney Bellows*, 306

27. Kring, *Henry Whitney Bellows*, 309–10.

28. J. L. Adams (1901–94), "Faith for the Free," in *The Essential James Luther Adams: Selected Essays and Addresses*, ed. G. K. Beach (Boston: Skinner House, 1998), 38.

CHAPTER XIII: EVOLUTION AND DIFFERENTIATION

1. Randall Fuller, *The Book That Changed America: How Darwin's Theory of Evolution Ignited a Nation* (New York: Viking, 2017), 11.

2. For a modern assessment, see Stephen O'Connor, *Orphan Trains: The Story of Charles Loring Brace and the Children He Saved and Failed* (Boston: Houghton Mifflin, 2001).

3. Franklin B. Sanborn to Theodore Parker, January 2, 1860; Special Collections, Concord Free Public Library; cited in Fuller, *The Book That Changed America, xx.*

4. John B. Wilson, "Darwin and the Transcendentalists," *Journal of the History of Ideas* 26:2 (April–June 1965): 286–90.

5. Fuller, *The Book That Changed America*, 11.

6. Fuller, *The Book That Changed America*, 56–57.

7. T. W. Higginson, *Out-Door Papers* (Boston: Lee & Shephard, 1886), 129.

8. Asa Gray, *Darwiniana: Essays and Reviews Pertaining to Darwinism* (New York: D. Appleton & Co., 1876).

9. Fuller, *The Book That Changed America*, 108, citing Gray, *Darwiniana*, 54.

10. Moncure Daniel Conway, quoted by Fuller, *The Book That Changed America*, 186; citing Sidney H. Morse and Joseph B. Marvin, *The Radical* (Boston: A. Williams & Co., 1869), 23.

11. Moncure Daniel Conway, *Autobiography, Memories and Experiences of Moncure Daniel Conway* (London: Cassell, 1904), 1:360; cited in Fuller, *The Book That Changed America*, 189.

12. Fuller, *The Book That Changed America*, 189.

13. Richard Kellaway, *William James Potter: From Convinced Quaker to Prophet of Free Religion*, 2 vols. (Bloomington, IN: Xlibris, 2014–15).

14. Kellaway, *William James Potter*, 56–57.

15. Kellaway, *William James Potter*, 2:9–10.

16. Kellaway, *William James Potter*, 2:10.

17. Emilio, *A Brave Black Regiment*, 9–10; Kellaway, *William James Potter*, 2:29–30.

18. Faye E. Dudden, *Fighting Chance: The Struggle over Woman Suffrage and Black Suffrage in Reconstruction America* (New York: Oxford University Press, 2011).

19. J. F. Clarke and Francis Ellingwood Abbott, *The Battle of Syracuse: Two Essays* (Boston: Index Association, 1875).

20. William J. Potter, *Free Religious Association: Its Twenty-Five Years and Their Meaning* (Boston: Free Religious Association of America, 1892), 8–9.

21. Stow Persons, *Free Religion: An American Faith* (New Haven, CT: Yale University Press, 1947); David M. Robinson, "The Free Religion Movement," in *The Oxford Handbook of Transcendentalism*, ed. Joel Meyerson, Sandra Petrulionis, and Laura Walls (New York: Oxford University Press, 2010), 617–27.

22. Clarke and Abbot, *The Battle of Syracuse*, back inside cover.

23. Child had pointed to similarities between the story of Jesus and the myths of Krishna, Osiris, and other gods. Predictably, reviewers had accused her of being more sympathetic to "pagan" ideas than to the Christian scriptures. Yet along with her advocacy on "the woman question," she also influenced Elizabeth Cady Stanton's later work on a *Woman's Bible* [1895].

24. During the war, Conway moved to London to advocate for the Union. He transformed a Unitarian congregation there to an ethical society. He published his anthology in 1874.

25. Lydia Maria Child, "The Intermingling of Religions," *A Lydia Maria Child Reader*, ed. Carolyn L. Karcher (Durham, NC: Duke University Press, 1997), 419–34; T. W. Higginson, *The Sympathy of Religions: An Address, Delivered at Horticultural Hall, Boston, February 6, 1870* (Boston: Reprinted from *The Radical*, 1871), http://www.gutenberg.org/files/25792/25792-h/25792-h.html.

26. J. F. Clarke, *Ten Great Religions: An Essay in Comparative Theology* (Boston: Houghton Mifflin, 1913), https://archive.org/details/tengreatreligion1913clar.

27. Higginson, *The Sympathy of Religions*, 2.

28. Leigh Eric Schmidt, *Restless Souls: The Making of American Spirituality* (San Francisco: Harper, 2005), 117, sources at 304n23.

29. Lydia Maria Child, "The Intermingling of Religions," *Reader*, ed. Karcher, 434.

30. Caroline H. Dall, *Woman's Right to Labor, or, Low Wages and Hard Work* (Boston: Walker, Wise & Co., 1860).

31. Philip McFarland, *Hawthorne in Concord* (New York: Grove Press, 2004), 296.

32. Bolster, *James Freeman Clarke*, 285.

33. Booth claimed to have shouted words attributed to Brutus in killing Caesar, "*Sic semper tyrannis*," "Thus always to tyrants," after shooting Lincoln. No one reported hearing him.

34. Bolster, *James Freeman Clarke*, 284–86.

35. Bolster, *James Freeman Clarke*, 286–88.

36. Tetrault, *The Myth of Seneca Falls*.

37. *Daughter of Boston*, xxi, quoting a diary entry from 1870.

38. Elaine Showalter, *The Civil Wars of Julia Ward Howe: A Biography* (New York: Simon & Schuster, 2016), 167–68; citing her journal of May 13, 1863, held at Houghton Library, Harvard, MS Am 2119 (1107), www.juliawardhowe.org/genealogy/journals/index.htm.

39. His preference for men like Sumner? Use of prostitutes? His infidelities? The last seems likely.

40. Showalter, *The Civil Wars of Julia Ward Howe*, 170–71.

41. Showalter, *The Civil Wars of Julia Ward Howe*, 173.

42. Howe, *Reminiscences*, 258.

43. Showalter, *The Civil Wars of Julia Ward Howe*, 180–82.

44. Howe, *Reminiscences*, 374–75.

45. Laura E. Richards and Maud Howe Elliott, *Julia Ward Howe, 1819–1910*, 2 vols. (Boston: Houghton Mifflin, 1915–16), 1:389.

46. Julia Ward Howe, *Appeal to Womenhood Throughout the World*, broadside (Boston: September 1870).

47. Showalter, *The Civil Wars of Julia Ward Howe*, 191.

CHAPTER XIV: CIRCUMFERENCE AND EXPANSION

1. "Letter to a Young Contributor," *The Magnificent Activist*, 528–42.

2. Brenda Wineapple, "The Letter," in *White Heat: The Friendship of Emily Dickinson and Thomas Wentworth Higginson* (New York: Anchor, 2008), 3–5.

3. Lyndall Gordon, *Lives Like Loaded Guns: Emily Dickinson and Her Family's Feuds* (New York: Viking, 2010), esp. 116–42, showing both the stigma then associated with seizures, and prescriptions for Emily typical for treating them. Her nephew Ned also had a seizure disorder.

4. Wineapple, *White Heat*, 54–55.

5. Alfred Habegger, *My Wars Are Laid Away in Books: The Life of Emily Dickinson* (New York: Random House, 2001), 217.

6. This is as Higginson had it in his 1891 essay on his letters from her. *The Magnificent Activist*, 546. Cf. ED to TWH, April 25, 1862, in *The Letters of Emily Dickinson*, ed. Thomas H. Johnson and Theodora Ward, 3 vols. (Cambridge, MA: Harvard University Press, 1955), 2:404.

7. ED to TWH, June 7, 1862, in *Letters*, 2:408–9; Wineapple, *White Heat*, 10, 93, and note at 327; T. W. Higginson, "Gymnastics," *Atlantic Monthly* 7 (March 1861): 283–302.

8. ED to TWH, June 7, 1862, in *Letters*, 2:408–9.

9. T. W. Higginson, *Malbone: An Oldport Romance* (Boston: Lee & Shepard, 1882), online at https://books.google.com.

10. ED to TWH, January 1876; in *Letters*, 2:546.

11. Wineapple, *White Heat*, 192–93; ED to TWH, December 31, 1873; Higginson papers, Houghton Library, Harvard.

12. Wineapple, *White Heat*, 210–13; ED to TWH, September 1877, in *Letters*, 2:590.

13. Wineapple, *White Heat*, 215, ED to TWH, two letters, fall 1877, *Letters*, 2:592, 594.

14. Wineapple, *White Heat*, 218. The editor of the *Springfield Republican*, Samuel Bowles, died in early 1878.

15. Wineapple, *White Heat*, 224; TWH to Ellen Conway, Nov. 4, 1878; Special Collections, Nicholas Murray Butler Library, Columbia University, New York.

16. Wineapple, *White Heat*, 226; "'Go traveling with us'!" ED poem #1561 per R. W. Franklin.

17. Wineapple, *White Heat*, 265.

CHAPTER XV: SUCCESSION

1. Bolster, *James Freeman Clarke*, 298–300.

2. J. F. Clarke, *Orthodoxy: Its Truths and Errors* (Boston: American Unitarian Association, 1866), iii, preface.

3. J. F. Clarke, *Steps of Belief; or, Rational Christianity Maintained Against Atheism, Free Religion, and Romanism* (Boston: American Unitarian Association, 1870).

4. Bolster, *James Freeman Clarke*, 303.

5. Bolster, *James Freeman Clarke*, 290–91.

6. J. F. Clarke, *Common Sense in Religion* (Boston: James R. Osgood and Co., 1874).

7. J. F. Clarke, *Oration Delivered Before the City Government and City of Boston, in [the] Music Hall, July 5, 1875* (Boston: Rockwell and Churchill, City Printers, 1875).

8. Clarke, *Memorial and Biographical Sketches*, 211.

9. Elisabeth Gitter, *The Imprisoned Guest: Samuel Howe and Laura Bridgman, the Original Deaf-Blind Girl* (New York: Farrar, Straus, and Giroux, 2001).

10. Showalter, *The Civil Wars of Julia Ward Howe*, 200–204.

11. Showalter, *The Civil Wars of Julia Ward Howe*, 203.

12. Clarke, *Memorial and Biographical Sketches*, 142–43, from a sermon, January 16, 1876, https://babel.hathitrust.org.

13. Showalter, *The Civil Wars of Julia Ward Howe*, 204–8, 210.

14. *Seventieth Birthday of James Freeman Clarke: Memorial of the Celebration by the Church of the Disciples* (Boston: by the Committee, 1880), 11.

15. *Seventieth Birthday of James Freeman Clarke*, 16.

16. *Seventieth Birthday of James Freeman Clarke*, 19.

17. Julia Ward Howe, *Margaret Fuller, Marchesa Ossoli* (Boston: Roberts Brothers, 1883).

18. T. W. Higginson, *Margaret Fuller Ossoli* (Boston: Houghton Mifflin, 1899).

19. Clarke, *Self-Culture*, 6.

20. Clarke, *Self-Culture*, 7.

EPILOGUE: APPLICATION

1. Gay Wilson Allen, *Waldo Emerson: A Biography* (New York: Viking, 1981), 669; Clarke, *Memorial Address* (Concord), https://babel.hathitrust.org.

2. J. F. Clarke, *Anti-Slavery Days: A Sketch of the Struggle Which Ended in the Abolition of Slavery in the United States* (New York: John W. Lovell, 1883).

3. J. F. Clarke, *Manual of Unitarian Belief* (Boston: Unitarian Sunday School Society, 1884).

4. J. F. Clarke, "The Five Points of Calvinism and the Five Points of the New Theology," *Vexed Questions in Theology: A Series of Essays* (Boston: George Ellis, 1886).

5. Bolster, *James Freeman Clarke*, 361–62.

6. Clarke, *Autobiography, Diary and Correspondence*.

7. Bolster, *James Freeman Clarke*, 350.

8. James Bradley Thayer, *A Western Journey with Mr. Emerson* (Boston: Little, Brown, 1884), 49. Emerson gave a lecture, "Immortality," on Sunday evening, April 23, 1871. Before going to Yosemite, he gave two more lectures at the Unitarian church in San Francisco.

9. John Muir, *Our National Parks* (Boston: Houghton Mifflin, 1901), 135.

10. John Swett, in "Ralph Waldo Emerson," Sierra Club website, John Muir online exhibit, http://vault.sierraclub.org/john_muir_exhibit/people/emerson.aspx, accessed May 31, 2019.

11. John Tallmadge, *Meeting the Tree of Life: A Teacher's Path* (Salt Lake City: University of Utah, 1997).

12. Donald Worster, *A Passion for Nature: The Life of John Muir* (Oxford, UK: Oxford University Press, 2008).

13. The Harvard University Lectures, conceived by President Charles Eliot, were not a success. Emerson's lectures only later appeared in print as *The Natural History of the Intellect: The Last Lectures of Ralph Waldo Emerson*, ed. Maurice York and Rick Spaulding (Chicago: Wrightwood Press, 2008).

14. Cornel West, *The American Evasion of Philosophy: A Genealogy of Pragmatism* (Madison: University of Wisconsin, 1989); David M. Robinson, *Emerson and the Conduct of Life: Pragmatism and Ethical Purpose in the Later Work* (Cambridge, UK: Cambridge University Press, 1993).

15. Louis Menand, *The Metaphysical Club: A Story of Ideas in America* (New York: Farrar, Straus, and Giroux, 2001).

16. William James, *The Varieties of Religious Experience: A Study in Human Nature* (London: Longman Green, 1902).

17. An earlier group of this name tried to bring Boston and Concord Transcendentalists together.

18. Edelstein, *Strange Enthusiasm*, 321.

19. One white Unitarian NAACP founder was the Rev. John Haynes Holmes, grandson of one of Parker's lay supporters. Another, Mary White Ovington, worked for the NAACP until her death, in 1947.

20. Francis Jackson Garrison to Ellen Wright Garrison, May 11, 1911, Villard MSS, Houghton Library, Harvard; Edelstein, *Strange Enthusiasm*, 400.

21. Cathy Tauscher and Peter Hughes, "Jenkin Lloyd Jones," *Dictionary of Unitarian and Universalist Biography*, September 20, 2007, http://uudb.org/articles/jenkinlloydjones.html.

22. Cynthia Grant Tucker, *Prophetic Sisterhood: Liberal Women Ministers of the Frontier, 1880–1930* (Bloomington: Indiana University Press, 1990).

23. Quoted by Tauscher and Hughes, "Jenkin Lloyd Jones."

24. "Parliament of Religions, 1893," *The Pluralism Project*, Harvard University (website), http://pluralism.org/encounter/historical-perspectives/parliament-of-religions-1893.

25. Jone Lewis, "Julia Ward Howe: What Is Religion?," *Women's History Guide* (blog), http://womenshistory.info/julia-ward-howe-religion, accessed September 3, 2018.

26. *Charles Gordon Ames: A Spiritual Autobiography*, ed. Alice Ames Winter (Boston: Houghton Mifflin, 1913), 151–52.

IMAGE CREDITS

Page 260   Thomas Wentworth Higginson and his daughter Margaret on a tricycle: Todd-Bingham Picture Collection (MS 496E). Manuscripts and Archives, Yale University Library.

Page 268   James Freeman Clarke: Unitarian Universalist Association. Minister files, Andover-Harvard Theological Library, Harvard Divinity School.

Page 278   John Muir: John Muir Portrait, John Muir Papers, Holt-Atherton Special Collections, University of the Pacific Library. ©1984 Muir-Hanna Trust.

Page 288   Theodore Parker Monument by William Wetmore Story: Photograph by Julia Bolton Holloway.

INDEX